The Church in all its glory

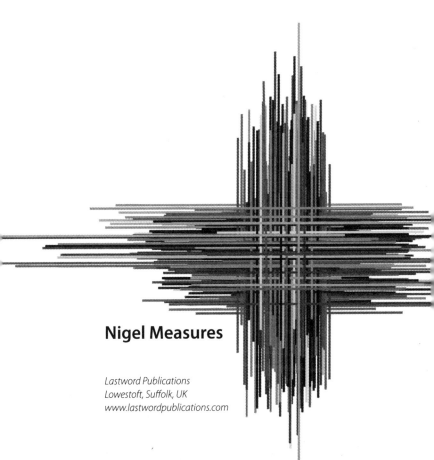

Nigel Measures

Lastword Publications
Lowestoft, Suffolk, UK
www.lastwordpublications.com

First published 2010, by Lastword Publications
www.lastwordpublications.com
Lastword Publications works with authors and musicians, businesses and charities to provide professional results with maximum impact.

ISBN 978 0 9559439 3 5

Useful website links:
www.khanyisa.org
www.sojo.net
www.newfrontierstogether.org

Design and production by The Upper Room (London, UK) +44 (0)20 8406 1010

To Lisa, Ben, Katey and my Khanyisa family

Acknowledgements

Thanks to my wife Lisa – for your love, your strength, your encouragement, your support, your fun and your faith. You have kept me going and believed in me all the way. Thanks also for your chapter on children and mission – it truly is outstanding. Thank you to my children Ben and Katey for your patience with daddy over the past few months and helping make this book possible. Thank you to my eldership team – John and Michelle Jacobs, Jonathan Reed and Tata Dom Mabikwe, for allowing me time to write as well as for your friendship all these years. Thanks to Lydia Mhlanga and Angela Kemm for all you taught me in my early days in South Africa. Thank you to Linda Martindale for editing the book, your many hours of reading and all your helpful insights. Thanks also to Siviwe Minyi for your proof reading, advice and comment. Thanks to Geoff Stevens for your amazing artwork and design of the book, as well as to Phil Stoddart for publishing 'God's Stump' and being a great guy to work with. Thank you to Tony and Sandy Farr for the use of your house in Betty's Bay – I think five of the chapters are a result of my time there. Lastly, thank you to my friends and family of Khanyisa church. This book is dedicated to you and all we have gone through together. We have walked a long walk and my life truly has been enriched by you all. May we continue to wrestle with God's heart for diversity and build church community together that will bring glory to Him.

Nigel *May 2010*

Endorsements

Some cross cultural missionary writers are content to simply share their own experiences and leave readers to connect the dots, but Nigel Measures goes the second mile by offering clear advice to those who would follow his example by offering true friendship - and not just handouts - to the poor. Here is a rare testimony of commitment that doesn't judge us as slackers, but invites us to come along for the ride.

Bart Campolo *Urban minister, speaker, and writer*

Nigel's book is a courageous and honest attempt to address the very real issue of how to build a multi-racial (-cultural) church. It is provocative and thought provoking and will motivate you into action. The world waits to see local expressions of a church that genuinely reflects what it means to be one new man in Christ.

David Holden *Team leader, pastor and author Newfrontiers UK*

This book presents you with provocation and challenge. It will provoke any reader to rethink whether their views on cross cultural issues are really well formed and mature. It challenges you to consider whether you have really practically engaged with the issues raised by relating with those of another culture. The book contains many stories that made me laugh and yet it conveys tremendous integrity. The author is not proposing vague theories but speaking out of many years of his own experience which has often been very painful as well as very rewarding. This book is important and deserves to be widely read and discussed. In a time when many speak of living in an increasingly multi cultural society the writer raises the right questions and suggests some good answers.

John Hosier *Bible teacher and author*

Endorsements

God's Stump is not just a well written book (which it is) but a book full of revelations and real life encounters. Nigel and Lisa Measures are a couple that have very faithfully obeyed and followed Christ for many years touching the lives of so many..

It has been a joy getting to know them and their lovely children and being able to spend quality time with them in Guguletu..

I know the pages of this book will not only bless you but change you and give you a great passion for the glorious church from the villages, urban centres and cities. It is worth reading this book prayerfully and be willing to take action!

Edward and Fridah Buria Team leaders, Newfrontiers Kenya

I met Nigel in 1988 when he made a trip to Cape Town, South Africa and, since then, watched him change and grow in his passion for crossing cultural divides and seeing him do it with joy, resilience and a deep sense of wanting to get to grips with what the Bible has to say about it. We worked together for a number of years and I was continually struck by the way he was unafraid to get involved in standing up for the oppressed in sometimes very volatile situations. He has lived what he has written in his book and has 'earned the right' to speak up on this subject which is on the forefront of people's thinking as the world changes and becomes more multi-cultural – and yet remains divided.

As I read chapter after chapter, I was amazed and enthralled by the way Nigel has taken very difficult concepts and put it in very readable form. I have a great passion to see the Church lead the way in being fully, intentionally multi-cultural and would highly recommend this book as a tool to help with understanding God's heart on this subject.

Angela Kemm Pioneer evangelist Newfrontiers

Foreword

When one seeks to deal with the question of multiculturalism, non-racialism and other 'isms' that accompany this, given the history of division and apartheid in South Africa and the world over, one is amazed at the resourcefulness of the Church. It is very easy for us as humans to look for quick solutions, whether political or otherwise, in the quest to live in communities where there are less divisions or where multiculturalism is alive and well. To put it bluntly, it is easy to turn a blind eye to human suffering or to pretend that different cultures are 'not wired' to live together and therefore 'lets carry on with our merry ways'. It is absolutely refreshing and invigorating to see how the Church is able to produce ordinary men and women who are instruments in the creation of the Kingdom of God. One such man is Nigel Measures.

Through this volume, Nigel Measures should be honoured and given recognition amongst many who have given of their lives in the crafting of the meaning of Church and its glory. He has appropriately given the title of the book God's stump: the Church in all its glory to invite us all to explore the vexed question of multiculturalism and the Church today. He, in his usual frank style, is throwing a ray of light to all whether they are believers or not, that the road to reconciliation, diversity, non-racialism and multiculturalism come as a result of obedience to God's calling. In his case which is well documented here, it meant being obedient by leaving England and coming to South Africa. As he puts it: 'South Africa was never on my agenda…South Africa was apartheid, racists… similarly 'cross-cultural' and 'diversity' were not in my thinking either…' Such is the journey. It would be fair to say that Nigel does not seek to provide a blueprint or answer questions you may have regarding these issues. He engages and leaves you thinking.

When I first met Nigel in the early 90s, in the middle of Gugulethu, a predominantly Xhosa speaking black township outside Cape Town, little did I know that our friendship would translate into him asking many deep questions about life in the kingdom. Each chapter in this book is more than just a narrative of how he and his family, located within the communities surrounding Khanyisa Community Church, were able to wrestle in an honest manner with issues of reconciliation, diversity and the Church. This book is a powerful and systematic appeal to the reader to share in the recognition of grace and selfless obedience in the creation of new communities free from any divisive 'isms'. I commend this book for intensive use by Christians whether in their groups or in their individual capacities. To me, after reading chapters in this book, I was welled up with tears of joy, as I realise every word speaks of hope. The book is the celebration of obedience, self giving and total commitment to see how that which was stumped grows and becomes a beacon to nations. I am amazed indeed at the resourcefulness of the Church.

Siviwe Minyi
Media producer, journalist and pastor
Gugulethu, Cape Town, South Africa
May 2010

God's stump

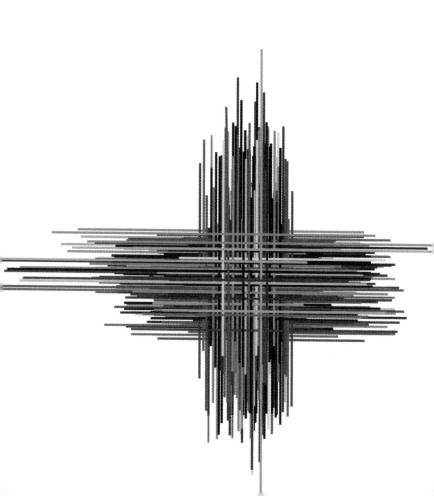

Contents

Introduction **One man's journey**

> '[Diversity]… forces us to change, disrupts our cozy patterns, engages us in a world where our deficiencies are exposed. Yet for all the less than appealing features of cultural and ethnic variety, important insights about God and his world go undiscovered if we avoid creative engagement with human diversity.' (Duane Elmer)

South Africa was never on my agenda – travelling was – but never to South Africa. The nation was apartheid, racists, politics, White [1] people and segregated beaches, and I wasn't interested. Similarly 'cross-cultural' and 'diversity' were not in my thinking either. I enjoyed meeting people from different cultures, trying new foods and experimenting with different languages but that was about it. I never dreamed that diversity was something on God's agenda.

I first came to South Africa by accident in the June of 1988 while studying Geography at the University of London. My attempts to arrange research for my final year dissertation in other parts of Africa had failed and I was left with only one option – Cape Town. As such, I found myself on a plane bound for a three-month stint in South Africa that was to change my life. My research, in conjunction with a lecturer from the University of Cape Town, was to be done in Khayelitsha the largest township of Cape Town.

Khayelitsha was a new town birthed and developed in 1983 under the old apartheid government and came as a surprise to many as since 1955 only a limited number of Black Africans had a legal right to remain in the Western Cape. From 1966 onwards most had suffered a deliberate policy of harassment and exclusion so the announcement of this new township seemed to indicate a change occurring in government policy. However, in reality it was, as Gillian Cook says, 'a desperate response by the government to gross overcrowding, unsuccessful forced removals and escalating violence in the Western Cape'.[2] The government vision was that all Black African residents in Cape Town, starting with 'squatters' from the Crossroads community, would live there without any rights to land. Their allocated 'core' houses, which were a mere 24-32 square meters in size for an average household of 8 people, were then to be upgraded in size as time went by and as income levels grew. Such was the philosophy of thinking behind this new town. However, within two years 99 year leaseholds were granted on the houses, several large controlled squatter 'site and service' areas had developed (Site B, C and Green-point) and any ideas of moving all Black Africans to Khayelitsha were dropped. My project was to assess the levels of upgrading that had occurred in the core houses – the result of which, in short, was that only 44% of all houses showed visible evidence of any alterations.

Tea and Coca Cola

My way into Khayelitsha to carry out this research was through a White lady called Angela Kemm who was part of what was then the Vineyard Church[3] in Cape Town. Angela was an amazing evangelist with a heart to preach the gospel and very quickly succeeded in 'distracting' me from my research. I soon found myself regularly visiting with her, making friends and being exposed to the vibrant Khayelitsha township life. She introduced me to her friend Elisabeth Kama who lived in one of the core houses in E-section Khayelitsha. Elisabeth graciously took me under her wings, invited me to stay with her in her house as well as educated me into the complexities and delights of Xhosa culture and chicken feet!

Wandering the streets as a White man was a time-consuming and eye-opening business. I lost count of how many times I had to explain what I was doing there (I'm sure some suspecting me of being police), as well as drank copious quantities of tea and coca cola at seemingly every house I walked by. Whatever I was offered I accepted and was overwhelmed by the hospitality and welcome that I received. I sat with 'Mamas' and 'Tatas' (Mothers and Fathers) hungry to learn more and hear their stories. Politically I was clueless towards any race tensions and genuinely oblivious to any possible dangers because of the political climate. Travelling on trains and taxis I felt secure and safe and never once feared for my life as I was told I would. What I hadn't realised at the time was that whenever I walked to carry out my surveys, Elisabeth always sent her son Madoda to follow me to ensure I was safe.

Sitting on the toilet

In the middle of my visit I went on a short two-week excursion to explore the delights of other parts of South Africa. On my seventh day I found myself sitting and praying in a Durban city centre public toilet with a strong feeling that I needed to return to Cape Town. This didn't make sense as I was fully enjoying my time away and I didn't think it was the curry I ate the night before. I phoned Angela to see what she thought and rather surprisingly she said, 'Come back, we've got work to do in Khayelitsha'. Within a few hours I was back on a bus embarked for Cape Town not quite knowing what I was doing or what God had in store. I was soon to find out.

Sangomas

Unknowingly to Angela and others in the church, a well-respected church leader had been having an extra-marital affair, as well as struggling with a personal drink problem. Consequently he was facing many problems and not surprisingly, things were not going his way. To make matters worse he decided to visit with a local sangoma (witchdoctor) to get things to improve. The sangoma told him that he had been cursed and if he paid more money he would 'be shown' who the offending parties were. In a mirror the faces of three church members were revealed and a fight in the church soon followed.

The three men were mere innocent victims of course and had not cursed anyone. The faces 'seen' were those of men with whom the leader was jealous and was threatened by within the church. Fortunately it was not long before the real truth was revealed and the pastor sadly had to step down from church leadership. Much grace and wisdom were needed in helping to heal broken relationships within the church.

I arrived in the middle of this and Angela asked me to go with her to visit the sangoma in question amongst the corrugated iron shacks of Green Point in Khayelitsha. Though he worked from a shack, his business was obviously doing well as he had a large BMW parked outside. Angela and I marched around his hut seven times (symbolic of Joshua) while praying and speaking in tongues. I then proceeded to give a gospel message to the many people queuing to see the sangoma. As I did so a man arrived, out of the blue, and proceeded to translate for me from English into Xhosa. I was very grateful for this – but Angela was even more so. While I was speaking someone had stood behind Angela and held a knife to the base of her back. Only with the arrival of my translator did he back off and we all left there safely. I had been oblivious to everything. As it turned out this witchdoctor's business closed down a few weeks later and I was excited that we had had the privilege of leading several people to the Lord.

This was my first experience of mission and my first real encounter with people from a different culture and background to my own. I was psyched – this cross-cultural thing was easy – no problems at all! Consequently I returned to the UK excited and feeling a strong sense of calling to return to South Africa in the future. This eventually came about only six years later in the May of 1994. My interim years were spent finishing my university course, as well as a four and a half year stint as a policeman within the Surrey constabulary. Throughout this time, however, my burden for South Africa would not leave and eventually David Dennington, the pastor of my church in

Chertsey said to me, 'You have been talking about South Africa so long now – why don't you just go?' So that is what I did. I handed in my notice, sold my car and arrived in Cape Town just after the elections of 1994.

Culture shock

Culture shock, culture shock, culture shock! I arrived in South Africa with a whole bunch of hidden motives and pre-conceived ideas that took me years to discover and deal with. Any expectations that I may have had resulting from my first trip to Cape Town were very quickly shattered. Where I had visions of preaching the gospel and leading thousands to the Lord I found myself singing 'I am a teapot' in a Tambo Square squatter community crèche. I was held up at gun-point, burgled on six occasions and attacked with a knife all within a year period. Where I thought crossing cultural boundaries was easy I found myself struggling with my own racism and prejudices, clash of world views and culture as well as differences of money, wealth, education and background. This cross cultural thing was not as easy as I thought!

Change

Things had changed. The country had changed. Angela had changed and I needed to change. South Africa now was not like South Africa of 1988. The first democratically elected government was in place under the inspiring leadership of Nelson Mandela and there was much excitement, hope and nervous anticipation all around. Angela was not the same lady I had known in 1998. Her passion for Jesus hadn't changed but her radical outworking of the gospel had. God had led her into politics and was now working in a new community – a very political community called Tambo Square.

Tambo Square – originated in the late 1980s where, in the midst of political turmoil, approximately 650 families from a shack area of Nyanga known as KTC (named after the local trading centre), up and moved to a vacant piece of land close to the Guguletu day hospital. The catalyst for this move was yet another attack of arson that the residents had experienced by politically motivated vigilantes within the KTC community. Enough was enough and these 650 families moved to form a new community that became known as Tambo Square – named after the famous political activist Oliver Tambo who led the banned ANC in exile through many of the turbulent struggle years.

This new land was not ideal – in fact it was a quagmire and quickly flooded during the Capes stormy winter months. There were no roads in the area and the shacks were densely packed together. The residents of Tambo Square differed from other residents of KTC due to their political activism. Tambo Square was an ANC stronghold and actively resistant to the apartheid policies of the National Party government at the time. Through the years, even before moving to Tambo Square, the residents had regularly gone to the authorities and pleaded for better living conditions, essentially a piece of land with houses – promises were made but never fulfilled.

Protest

Enough was enough and at the end of July 1990 various Tambo women and children stormed to the Cape Provincial Administration's Offices in Goodwood refusing to leave until their grievances had been addressed. The women remained in the building for five days! On the last day the authorities relented and gave residents assurance that one million Rand[4] would be set aside for their housing needs, as well as a piece of land for them to build on. By November the land was officially allocated on what turned out to be an excellent spot situated strategically between Guguletu and Manenberg (two historically hostile communities). This area, with its beautiful views of Table Mountain, is now called Tambo Village where Khanyisa, the church that I lead is located today.[5]

On arriving in Cape Town instead of returning to Khayelitsha, Angela now took me to Tambo Square. She had been involved there since 1992 and was now good friends with one of the community leaders, a Coloured lady called Lydia Mhlanga[6]. Together, they were part of a housing committee that had been working tirelessly in their efforts to secure housing for the Tambo residents. By default I too joined this committee and was suddenly exposed to politicians who had little or no time for white ex-policemen from the UK. These leaders showed me no mercy and I was put firmly in my place at the bottom of the food chain. With time I would earn my 'colours', their respect and develop genuine friendships that have lasted until today. To this group I am deeply indebted for the many lessons learned about the privileges of crossing cultural and socio-economic boundaries.

Isiganga

The 'isiganga' was an open piece of sandy land situated amidst the sprawling shacks of Tambo Square. Here the community would hold open-air residents meetings while the housing committee would give feedback on the latest developments and 'hiccups' in the housing process. It was here that we would also gather people to pray and seek God for the housing and his wisdom in overcoming the many obstacles that came the community's way. Without doubt a miracle was needed as the majority of the people came from very impoverished backgrounds who thought owning a house was an outright impossibility. We would lie in the sand and call upon God for his help. As we prayed 'skollies'[7] would walk around us bringing their stolen televisions and fridges to distribute to eagerly awaiting family members and friends. We would pray all the more and eventually had the privilege of leading several people to the Lord.

One old lady, Elisbeth Blou, affectionately known as 'Mam Khulu' (Grandmother), refused to attend our gatherings. She had seen Angela once before while selling drugs in a town called Noordhoek. She couldn't believe this same White lady was coming to pester her and went out of her way to avoid coming anywhere near the 'isiganga'. One day, however, while cooking sheep's feet outside her shack she heard us singing in the distance. She was reminded of the story of Noah and how some people did not take God's word seriously. Unsure as to why she was doing it, she found herself walking to the 'isiganga' and that day Mam Khulu became a Christian. When she eventually moved into her new home in Tambo Village her husband was 98 years old – the first time he had ever lived in a house. Today, now a lady in her nineties herself, and her husband long since passed away, she still gives testimony and thanks to God for his kind provision towards her.

Intestinal parasites

I have very fond memories of the 'isiganga', one – not the least – being because it was here that I met my wife Lisa. She had already been visiting in the townships with Lydia and Angela, before I even came to South Africa. Her roots are of English stock, like my own. Her parents emigrated from the UK to South Africa in the early 60s. She, however, was born in Pretoria, later schooled in Durban and eventually studied to be a hairdresser in Cape Town. One day while reading the book of Nehemiah, God challenged her to remember the poor. Thinking at first that she must go to India, her pastor Simon Pettit advised her to start closer to home and hence Lisa also found herself visiting and making friends in Tambo Square.

At the 'isiganga' one day I was struck to see this beautiful young girl pull up in a bright red VW Beetle. We were introduced and found ourselves talking to a frail and sickly man called Elijah. He was very excited as God had healed his daughter who had been suffering with diarrhea and intestinal worms coming out of multiple bodily orifices. She had been prayed for previously and now he was delighted to tell us that all the worms had gone. So delighted, in fact, that he had kept the worms in an old brandy bottle for us to see. As we gazed at these hideous snake-like parasites, trying to imagine how on earth these could have been inside a human being, our friendship was forged and romance soon blossomed. Our wedding in the April of 1996 was a vibrant affair bringing together friends like Elijah and Mam Khulu from the shacks of Tambo, with wealthy 'high-society' socialites – clients of Lisa's whose hair she had cut for many years. This was a clash of worlds that caused quite a stir.

Discomfort and more change

Through the housing, God opened up the door for the gospel to spread. Tambo residents became Christians and wanted to visit Jubilee, which was the church we were part of at the time. Jubilee was meeting at a school in the suburb of Wynberg and had been, up to that point, a predominantly White middle-class congregation. Thus it didn't go without a stir having poorer Black families visiting on a Sunday morning. White parents were irate when some Black child pulled their daughter's long blond hair. Black folk were irate when they encountered a racist attitude or someone refused to sit next to them. It was an uncomfortable business all around. White people wanted to know why we were now singing 'Black' songs while our Black folk wanted to know why everything was always done in English.

Teaching and envisioning were necessary and Jubilee, under the leadership of Simon Pettit, started a process of transformation. Thinking had to be challenged, theology wrestled with and we were forced to re-examine the practicalities of how we practiced church community and fellowship. Some, of course, embraced this change while others, put off by the uncomfortable wrestling process, ended up leaving the church.

This was also a key season of change for me where God used many people to envision and enlarge my thinking. Besides Angela, Lisa, Simon and Lydia, I would listen for hours to friends like Siviwe and Desmeline Minyi share their stories of pain and struggle to see genuine transformation occur both in the country and in the church. Tata Dom, an old man in his 70s who had been a Christian and church pastor for more than 50 years, became like a father to me. He would tell me of White church leaders not allowing him into their houses or to drink coffee out of one of their cups. He would laugh about his time as a chef – always having to train up the White or Coloured man to be 'over him' but how God always vindicated and honoured him.

I learned to listen and in so doing my life was transformed. It drove me to scripture and to seek and wrestle with God in a new way. I had come to South Africa with somewhat of a 'Black is beautiful' attitude and ideology. God however, started to broaden my vision beyond 'Black only' to that of a multi-cultural vision of all colours, tribes and nations reconciled in Christ.

Robust babies

Together God birthed in us a vision to plant a multi-cultural church in Tambo Village. Community leaders had already offered us land in order to 'build a church', so the thought was already in our heads. Furthermore, since Tambo was sandwiched temptingly between Guguletu and Manenberg the opportunities for reconciliation appeared endless. As a result many of us, Black and White together, sought the Lord more intently for his wisdom, leading and guidance. A church plant group was formed and met together. Eventually, in the May of 1999, we started a congregation of Jubilee that met in Guguletu. In the same month Lisa gave birth to our son Benjamin. Somehow we saw him as a prophetic sign of what the church was meant to be – robust and healthy. Nine months later Khanyisa church was finally birthed in the February of 2000.

Khanyisa

I woke up one morning with the word 'Khanyisa' in my head. I didn't have a clue what it meant, only a strong feeling this was to be the name of the church. In chatting to Siviwe I discovered that 'Khanyisa' is a Xhosa imperative meaning 'Be the Light'. Such has been our desire since to build a diverse church community of rich, poor, Black, Coloured, White, educated, uneducated, old, young, male and female: together acting as God's light to the world. It is light because such relationships stand out as startling in the midst of a world of division, hostility and separation.

I don't see Khanyisa as a typical township church and neither is it a White English church. We have sought to demonstrate community that communicates something of God's heart for the nations and peoples of the world. We are a local church building in a local city. Cape Town, even after 15 years since the demise of apartheid, is still very segregated. Apartheid intentionally separated and we are calling people together intentionally. Many suburbs' churches attract middle-class Black, Coloured and refugees into their congregations, yet very few attract and build 'with' the poor. Fewer still of the wealthy, White and middle-class will dare to venture the other way into the townships. At Khanyisa that is exactly what we are inviting people to do. As you may rightly imagine building church this way had not been without its misunderstandings struggles and discomforts all around.

Struggle

This journey has been a great adventure for all of us at Khanyisa, bringing immense joy, pleasure and delight. In it we have discovered more of God by working out our freedom in Christ through our relationships with one another. At the same time it has not been easy. As a church community our racism has been exposed, our prejudices revealed and our love of money challenged – an uncomfortable process at the best of times and one for which few of us at times have not wanted to run away from.

Uganda

Such a journey has caused me to grapple with many practical and theological questions around crossing cultural and socio-economic boundaries. One such occasion came at the end of 2007 when I had the privilege of visiting an amazing church located in Kampala, the capital city of Uganda. This was probably one of the best examples of a cell church that I had ever seen and I was very excited to be there. The church numbered about 18,000 people that gathered at various 'Celebration points' throughout the main city on any given Sunday morning. It was great to be in some of their meetings and I was struck by the lively and relaxed atmosphere and the evident sense of God's presence in their midst. The church leadership also impressed me and seemed to be very genuine, humble men and women of God who loved Jesus and the people they were leading. One pastor explained to me that of their 1500 cell groups that met during the week, 500 of them were rubbish and needed some attention! I had to laugh as he didn't seem to be particularly phased by the situation. The leadership very graciously asked me to speak at one of their mid-week Bible study groups – a mere gathering of only 1000 people! Who could fail to be impressed?

Homogony

I was also impressed by the many and varied ministries carried out by the church to the poor and destitute in the city. Abandoned HIV-positive babies were being gathered off the streets and cared for and thousands of orphaned children were being nurtured and schooled in childrens' villages. Without doubt I was encouraged and stirred by all I saw. However, on returning to my home in Cape Town I found myself wrestling and struggling over what I had just witnessed and the way I was seeing church built there compared to the way I felt God was leading me at my home church back in South Africa. The primary difference was one of homogeny. Of the 18,000 people I had just seen I would guess that about 75-80% of the church were students and young working people in their 20s and 30s from fairly middle-class backgrounds. There were very few old and very few poor. What is more, the church was deliberately building an English-speaking community in response to what they felt God had told them. This seemed to make sense in a country of more than 300 languages where English could act as a unifying point of contact between the peoples especially with its turbulent history of conflict and division.

Contrast with South Africa

The way they were building church in Uganda seemed to stand in contrast to the way we were building back home. Were we doing the right thing? I found myself questioning what we were doing and wrestling with a temptation to no longer have to struggle with diversity, but rather settle for building church in a more homogenous manner. Surely that would be easier? Surely we would see much faster and greater church growth? What have we got to show at Khanyisa? Certainly not the impressive numbers I had witnessed in Uganda. Does the end justify the means? Does it really matter how we are building community together as long as people are getting saved? Are we not better to go a more homogenous route if more people get saved that way? Surely God is happy the more people that get saved? Does it really matter if we do not engage with one another in any deep and meaningful way?

Questions

This book seeks to examine some of these questions. Questions that I have had to face; questions that I believe are relevant to all in God's church. It raises questions to do with the dynamics of making cross-cultural and cross-economic friendships, as well as building radical multi-cultural church communities. Questions such as:

- What does it mean to build radical church communities in a racially, culturally and socio-economically divided world?
- Is diversity on God's agenda? If so, what does that mean in practice? What does the Bible say about all of this?
- What is God's heart for the nations? What are the implications to us as individual Christians and local church communities?

- Are all called to cross racial and socio-economic barriers or just those who are 'gifted' to do so?

- What is the place for homogeny in God's church? Do homogenous churches grow faster than heterogeneous churches?

- Should all churches be cross cultural? Is that even possible? If so, how do you build them?

- Are some people called to certain people groups? What about Peter to the Jews and Paul to the Gentiles?

- What about the poor? Who are the poor anyway? What place do the poor have in our church communities? What does it mean for me to remember the poor? What does it mean for my local church?

- Does it matter how we go to the nations or the way we build community as long as people get saved? Does the end justify the means?

- Is it possible to have deep and meaningful relationships and fellowship across cultural boundaries, class boundaries or even education boundaries? How do you do it?

- What does unity in the church mean in practice?

The list can go on. Many of these questions are not easy to answer. But it is around these and other questions I invite you to wrestle with me.

Don't be fearful of wrestling

To mention wrestling can, for many of us, conjure up rather negative thoughts and connotations. It suggests things like conflict, confrontation and hard work, characteristics that few of us would willingly embrace and most, if we are honest, will go out of our way to avoid. This is no less true for me – I don't like wrestling, I don't like struggle and I don't like confrontation!

In wrestling one takes the risk of getting hurt, however, it's important to note that not all wrestling and struggle is bad. In fact wrestling can be healthy and beneficial. Harry Belafonte, the actor and political activist once said, 'Do not look on struggle as some harmful negative thing. Struggle has great power and great beauty. Do something and do it in struggle'.[8] Such also seems to be the biblical call as we are exhorted to 'overcome', 'struggle' and 'fight.' In a modern world prone to seeking the comforts and pleasures of life we must not make the mistake of avoiding something because it takes us out of our comfort zones.

As Duane Elmer says, many of us do not willingly embrace diversity because *'it forces us to change, disrupts our cozy patterns, engages us in a world where our deficiencies are exposed. Yet for all the less than appealing features of cultural and ethnic variety, important insights about God and his world go undiscovered if we avoid creative engagement with human diversity'.* (Elmer 1993:23)[9]

I hope that by sharing some of our struggles and wrestling with God, Christians and local churches elsewhere may be provoked to push the boundaries of cultural and economic diversity. This is not a model for others to copy, but rather the fruit of struggle to provoke God's church in all communities of the world. I guarantee that this path of diversity is one of great blessing, but the only thing I can't guarantee is that you won't take a few knocks along the way.

1 Life from a Stump

> *'We must avoid shallow but seemingly attractive and people-pleasing messages that merely reflect popular worldly opinion. Instead we must be open to hearing seemingly not so attractive, not so people-pleasing, rather 'stump-like' messages that are in fact from God – life-changing, church-changing and world-changing!' (Nigel Measures)*
>
> *'There shall come forth a shoot from the stump of Jesse, and a branch from his roots shall bear fruit' (Isaiah 11:1)*
>
> *'In that day the root of Jesse, who shall stand as a signal for the peoples – of him shall the nations enquire and his resting place shall be glorious' (Isaiah 11:10)*

'What have you done?' These were Lisa's words to me as she stood in horror gazing at the devastation I had just caused in the garden. What had once been towering trees and overgrown white and pink Oliander bushes, were now nothing other than stumps! Ugly, unattractive and unseemly abrasions of distorted tree stumps spoiling what had been up to that point a relatively attractive garden. I stood there sheepishly with my borrowed chainsaw in hand, still overcome with the adrenalin I'd experienced of attacking these trees with a vengeance. Boy, had it felt good! The experience had definitely cleared away the cobwebs and obliterated the effects of any unwanted stress and high blood pressure that I may have been feeling. As Lisa glared at me demanding a response I slowly found myself coming down to earth. 'They will grow again' I firmly reassured, subtly trying to assert my position as the 'head of the house' letting her know that I can do what I want in 'my' garden and she, as my wife, must lovingly trust my actions. 'Well, they'd better do so' she replied appropriately putting me in my place. Not to be outdone and to ensure I had the last word I humbly retorted, 'Yes dear!'

As it transpired I was right. Amazingly, these ugly, insignificant and hopeless stumps protruding out of the ground are now totally unrecognisable. Out of nothingness have emerged thousands of green and succulent shoots forming a dense hedge over laden with now even more abundant white and pink flowers.

Stumps

'What on earth is a stump?' A simple enough question perhaps, but one in which, in my particular context amidst the dynamics of different languages, had to be speedily answered. Some thought I was talking about a 'stamp' ie a postage stamp, while still others thought I was asking them to 'stamp' their feet. Clarification was necessary. To explain my point, while preaching one particular Sunday morning, I called a brave but nervous 14-year-old boy to the front of the meeting hall and asked him to pretend to be a tree. Then, amidst the cheers of his not so encouraging friends, I energetically pretended to chop him (the tree) to the ground leaving only a 'stump' protruding in the earth. It was an academy winning performance and at last I could see comprehension dawning on people's faces. I was talking about a stump! Why didn't I say so in the first place?

Having gotten over that particular hurdle, I then had to face the next one – 'What on earth has a stump got to do with anything?' What does a stump have to do with diversity and God's heart for the nations? What does a stump have to do with traversing cultural and economic divides? To answer these questions I led them to the prophet Isaiah who seemingly was faced with similar thoughts.

Isaiah's 'Stump'

In Isaiah chapter six, Isaiah received an incredible vision from the Lord as God called him and set him apart to preach a message of salvation to the people of Jerusalem and Judah.

The context of this vision was one of major un-holiness that had spread through the entire society and culture of Judah. Judah had been ruled by King Uzziah for 52 years in Jerusalem and had been a good king up until the point he decided to desecrate the temple of God. Chronicles tells us that, 'his fame spread far for he was marvelously helped until he became strong'. [10] Uzziah decided he was going to deal with God on his own terms – after all he was the king. He thought he could be in charge and went into God's holy temple and made sacrifices that only the priests were permitted to do. The outcome of this was that Uzziah turned leprous and spent the remainder of his life in isolation, separated from the rest of the people of God. Perhaps the lesson to be learned is that we serve a holy God who is not to be messed around with!

At some point following the death of Uzziah, God showed himself to the prophet Isaiah in a vision that was to change his life for ever. Isaiah saw the Lord seated upon a throne surrounded by heavenly beings each crying out 'Holy, Holy, Holy is the Lord of hosts'. [11] It was a fearful encounter for Isaiah, one in which he was acutely made aware of his own sin and unworthiness in comparison to the holiness of God. Almost immediately however, his lips were touched with purifying fire and God opened a door for him to receive mercy and forgiveness. The Lord then gave Isaiah an invitation and opportunity to be used by him – one to which Isaiah willingly responded and said, 'Yes Lord, here I am send me'. [12] I wonder, however, if Isaiah would have responded so quickly if he had known what he was letting himself in for?

Although Isaiah's vision started off with a dazzling encounter with heavenly beings and the holy God of Israel, the vision then changed and finished off with a surprising and perhaps even disappointing conclusion – yep you've guessed it – a picture of a stump. [13] Stump!? What do you mean stump? How can one go from strange heavenly beings to a stump in the ground? As Eugene Petersen says, this was not a word that was 'likely to inspire a newly ordained prophet to, as we say, 'do great things for God'.[14] What has a stump got to do with anything?

Metaphor of the 'Stump'

Like any picture or metaphor, the stump can be applied at various levels and can provoke and challenge our thinking in a multitude of ways. A metaphor takes a word that is commonly used to refer to a thing or action that we experience by means of our five senses. It then uses it to refer to something that is beyond the reach of our immediate senses. For example, we all know that a rock is a hard mass of minerals that can be seen, touched, carved and mined. Metaphorically, however, the Bible tells us 'the Lord is my rock' (Psalm 18:2). This doesn't mean that God is a mass of minerals, but rather that he is our fortress and deliverer, the one we can run to and find refuge, strength and safety. A powerful metaphor indeed that can greatly impact and change our lives as one ponders on the seemingly unending depths of such a simple thing. In fact, Christians today are still coming to grips with the full implications of this particular metaphor and its application in their lives.

Biblical writers loved to use metaphors to open our minds to the wonders of God and his ways. Let's explore some of the depths of this seemingly insignificant metaphor of the stump and see some of its relevance for us today.

Judgment on Judah

Firstly, the stump was a prophetic picture of what was going to happen to the people of Judah if they did not respond to the voice of God. Like a large tree that could be felled down leaving only a stump in the ground, so the same would happen to the people of God if they did not change their ways.[15] In fact, this prophecy was eventually fulfilled when the Assyrians invaded and ravaged the land of Judah leaving it desolate, ugly, defaced and barren. A hundred years or so after Isaiah's last sermon his country was a field of stumps,[16] both literally and figuratively.

Isaiah's ministry and message

In another sense the stump was to become a metaphor for both Isaiah's ministry and the message that he preached. At the outset, God commissioned Isaiah to do some great preaching, but he also warned him at the same time, that he would be a failure because the people would not take heed of his words! He was told that 'they will hear but not understand, see but not perceive'. [17] Eugene Petersen in his paraphrase version of the Bible 'The Message' puts it this way,

'Make these people blockheads, with fingers in their ears and blindfolds on their eyes, so they won't see a thing, won't hear a word, so the won't have a clue about what's going on, and, yes so they won't turn around and be made whole.' (Isaiah 6:9)

Unsurprisingly, Isaiah asked the Lord how long he might have to do this for. God told him to do so until all the cities were laid waste, the people had left their houses and the countryside looked like a field of stumps with every tree cut down! This, as we've seen above, is what happened – for forty years Isaiah preached amazing sermons, but the people did not repent and were eventually taken into exile. By modern standards of defining successful ministry, this was an outright failure. By modern standards of impressive ministry, Isaiah's ministry was not much too behold. It was about as eye catching as a tree stump – not worth looking at.

Just as people might so easily overlook a tree stump in the ground, so the people of Judah overlooked both Isaiah the messenger and the message that he preached.

The messenger – To the people of Judah, Isaiah was not a significant preacher. Perhaps he didn't come from the right place or perhaps his ministry was not packaged in a style that they liked? Perhaps they deemed him to be not of the right calibre for a preacher? Perhaps he was just a 'nobody', not worth the time of day? Whatever the case – Isaiah was overlooked and disregarded.

The message – To the people of Judah, Isaiah did not have
a message that they wanted to hear. Perhaps his message
did not tickle their ears? Perhaps his message was not the
comfortable or trendy enough in line with what they wanted to
hear? Perhaps his message did not tally with their theology or
understanding of how God wanted them to be. Whatever the
case – Isaiah's message was overlooked.

Today we must be careful not to do the same. We must avoid
despising a message from God because it is deemed too
insignificant, not packaged in the right way or perceived as an
insignificant stump in the ground. We must avoid shallow but
seemingly attractive and people-pleasing messages that merely
reflect popular worldly opinion. Instead, we must be open to
hearing seemingly 'not so attractive', 'not so people-pleasing,'
rather 'stump-like' messages that are in fact from God – life-
changing, church-changing and world-changing! Similarly, we
must be careful of not hearing God's voice because the messenger
is not quite what we expect of a messenger of God. Perhaps not
the right education level, perhaps not from the right culture or
background – the messenger despised and regarded as a stump
in the ground. Let's avoid missing out on Jesus because his
messenger was too 'stump-like' to even be given a second glance.

The 'stump' is Jesus

The last verse of Isaiah 6, 'The Holy seed is its stump' (v13), lets
us know that there is more to this stump than first meets the
eye. The stump is the holy seed from which salvation will grow.
This stump is a person, insignificant in appearance, but who will
be the salvation of the entire world. Isaiah chapter 11 reveals
more of this 'stump' saviour;

'There shall come forth a shoot from the stump of Jesse and a
branch from his roots shall bear fruit and the Spirit of the Lord
shall rest upon him, the Spirit of wisdom and understanding,
the Spirit of counsel and might, the Spirit of knowledge and the
fear of the Lord'(Isaiah 11:1-2)

The stump is Jesus! The Saviour of humankind who left heaven in its entire splendor and came as a 'stump' – deemed of no value by most, subjected to humiliation and death on a wooden cross – a stump. This is incredible – that the God of heaven and earth, the giver of salvation would choose to reveal himself to us and appear to us as a stump!

Overlooking Jesus – So incredible and 'stump-like' was the coming of the Lord Jesus Christ that many people overlooked him, despised him, rejected him and did not esteem him. He, as Isaiah chapter 53 tells us came like, '… a root out of dry ground; he had no form or majesty that we should look at him and no beauty that we should desire him. He was despised and rejected by men… And we esteemed him not'. [18] The coming messiah did not come as many expected – but rather in a manner that was insignificant and stump like. Jesus was born in a stable as a baby – not worth the time of day, not worth much attention and response. Some, however, were able to see beyond the stump – a few common and uneducated shepherd boys, as well as a few educated and wise men from different lands and nations. Yet in reality, only a few were open to see.

Such is still the case in the world today where many still despise 'Jesus in the manger' and pay no regard to the 'Saviour riding on a donkey'. Perhaps more frighteningly, however, is the possibility that we in God's church may overlook and disregard Jesus in our midst. Matthew 25 tells us a story about how at the judgment seat of God there will be a separation of the sheep from the goats. The story seems to give a warning of how it is possible to 'overlook' and 'miss' Jesus and even fail to 'minister' to him. Jesus will say to some people, 'For I was hungry and you gave me no food, I was thirsty and you gave me no drink, I was a stranger and you did not welcome me, naked and you did not clothe me, sick and in prison and you did not visit me?' [19] This is shocking and one can almost register the surprise on their faces as they respond, 'Lord, when did we see you hungry or thirsty or a stranger or naked or sick or in prison and did not minister to you'? (v44). How on earth could they have missed out on 'ministering to Jesus'?

It seems that such a tragedy is indeed possible. Jesus was found amongst the poor, yet the poor, like Jesus, can be so easily disregarded, deemed to be of no great value and too 'stump-like' to be given much attention. Let's not make the same mistake. Let's avoid overlooking Jesus by overlooking those with whom Jesus is found. Let's be careful of stepping over or onto Jesus when he doesn't appear in a bundle worthy of the attention of the modern sophisticated world.

A shoot from the 'stump'

Jesus came like a stump and died on a stump. He also became a stump. Like a mighty oak he was felled down, crucified, destroyed and seemingly chopped of all life, never to grow again. Yet death could not hold Jesus in the grave. Isaiah prophesied that out of the root of the stump new life would 'bud' forth and spread through all the recesses and corners of this world. The stump will bear fruit. Jesus will come endowed with the Spirit of God and his reign will be unlike anything anyone has ever witnessed before. He will rule his kingdom with Spirit led wisdom, understanding, counsel and strength and he will be one who has real knowledge and intimacy with the living God. [20]

The striking characteristic of his rule will be righteousness practically demonstrated in justice for the poor and needy of this world. Whereas worldly kings have no time for the poor of society regarding them to be of little value and worth – mere stumps, the coming Messiah who is dressed and ready for action will faithfully give himself to their cause. [21] God delights to take that which is deemed as nothing in the eyes of the world and make it into something. God delights to take that which the world so easily despises and looks down upon and use that to display and manifest his glory. The stump reminds us of God's heart for all the people's of the world – even those who, from a worldly point of view, are deemed insignificant and of little importance in the greater scheme of things. The stump reminds us that with God, 'the Lord does not see as man sees, man looks on the outward appearance, but the Lord looks at the heart'.[22] The stump provokes us to give ourselves to what God deems valuable and important and not that of the world.

The fruit of the 'stump' is radical community

Isaiah continues by highlighting some of the evidence or fruit that will emerge from the stump with the coming kingdom inaugurated by Jesus. From the stump new life will shoot forth that will have an impact on society like nothing ever seen before. Alec Motyer puts it this way saying,

'First the Messiah buds forth and then, through him, new life for people becomes possible on a world wide scale and the life of nature itself is transformed.'[23] (Motyer 1993:124)

The coming of Jesus ministry is so powerful it can transform nature itself. New life in Jesus will reveal itself through the radical transformation of relationships. Where relationships were once hostile and full of animosity they will be transformed to that of love and friendship. Relationships that were once inconceivable and totally impossible from a worldly point of view will now become reality. Incredibly, these relationships will act as a sign or a banner to the peoples of this world demonstrating that God is at work.[24] Such relationships will astound the world.

New relationships – Isaiah prophesied that the wolf and the lamb will dwell together, the leopard and the goat will lie down together and the calf and the lion will eat together![25] Surely that is impossible – that sort of thing just doesn't happen? I've lived in Africa long enough to know that lions don't eat alongside young succulent juicy bucks – they eat them! The first time

I ever went to the Kruger National Park bordering between South Africa and Mozambique, I was privileged to witness three young male cheetahs chase and kill an Impala in front of my eyes. It was a bloody and gory business!

On another occasion, while trekking within the wilds of the Okavango Delta in Botswana, our party stumbled upon a pride of eating lions. Our guide was a cheerful man called 'Happy' who did not carry a gun and consequently insisted that we obey his slightest commands. As we gazed at these hairy beasts gorging themselves on the flesh of an unfortunate Wildebeest, 'Happy' fervently whispered to us, 'do not run – back away slowly.' We dutifully complied! It's not uncommon to witness lions eating buck – that's what happens in the world. However, when God's kingdom invades – everything changes and we start to witness the unusual and even the impossible.

This is what Isaiah said would happen. He prophesied that the fruit of Jesus' ministry would be the formation of new and unusual relationships that stand in sharp contrast to what is generally witnessed in the world around us. To some such relationships are merely bewildering, while to others they are deemed outright impossible. In the world today and throughout history, factors like race, class, education and economics have kept people apart. They act like invisible barriers preventing the formation of genuine relationships, friendships and community. Few have attempted to cross such divides; some because of the effort involved, and others deeming them too impossible to traverse. It's interesting to note that in South Africa for a long time it was taught that certain species do not mix. Just as a lion cannot mix socially with a buck so it is the same for Black and White. It was taught that Black and White are different species and are not meant to go together. Many believed this to be true. This, of course, is a terrible lie that has infiltrated worldly and cultural thinking not just in South Africa – but all over the globe.

The prophet Isaiah had different ideas in mind. To him Jesus coming kingdom would be demonstrated by the pulling down of dividing walls that keep people apart. Race, culture and economics are such dividing walls that the church should actively be crossing to visibly display the new humanity found in Christ. Can deep and meaningful relationships occur across racial, cultural and economic divides? Can Black and White, old and young, male and female, rich and poor, educated and uneducated build in genuine 'koinonia' together in a meaningful way? Yes – they not only can, but should. The stump gives us a picture of reconciled, unusual and surprising relationships found in Jesus Christ and his coming kingdom – the lion and the lamb!

New activities – Isaiah expounds further and lets us know that not only will seemingly impossible relationships (from a worldly thinking point of view) occur, but togetherness and community will also be manifest. A bear for example, will 'graze' along side a cow, a lion will 'eat' straw like an ox and the wolf will 'dwell' with the lamb.[26] These strange and new founded relationships are doing things together. Since when do bears, lions and goats eat straw together? Surely these things don't happen?

In 2007 my home church Khanyisa sent a small mission team to Angola. This was a grueling trip that entailed a non-stop three-day drive from Cape Town up through the Western side of South Africa, across the Orange River into Namibia. Then up through the 'Desert Kingdom' over another border post into Angola and eventually arriving at the small village of Menonge. The team was a diverse bunch of men and women, young and old (age range of 21 up to 56), Black and White, English and South African. Some in the group were unemployed, one lady was an occupational therapist and another was a 'domestic-cleaner' working in her house. Others worked with children and those who were HIV positive, while to the other extreme one man was an experienced actuary working in one of the top financial institutions in South Africa. It was a diverse bunch of people whom, if it hadn't been for loving Jesus and being part of the same church community, probably would not have associated with one another.

The team served in the village helping to build a small orphanage, as well as serving local churches with training and teaching material. The team were themselves having lots of fun, joking and laughing together, as well of course having the occasional fight! Afterwards we heard that the biggest impact of the team was not so much the 'good works' done but rather the relationships displayed. This was the first time that the villagers had ever seen a mixed team come into Angola (all previous teams had been White only) and people couldn't get over the obvious relationship, friendships and activities that were occurring together. Cooking, repairing the vehicles, carrying equipment, hammering nails and doing drama were all done by team members together. The younger members were teaching and sharing the gospel, as well as both men and women. This was not normal – perhaps the 'lions were eating straw' and the 'children were playing amongst vipers?' The stump, therefore, not only gives us a picture of unusual relationships, but also of togetherness, activity, unity and community displayed in those relationships.

New roles – Isaiah further tells us that the commonly accepted roles that people play within society will also be turned upside down. Isaiah says a little child will be the one 'leading' the calf and the lion.[27] In most cultures of the world this is not normal – since when do children do the leading? They may in rural Africa lead sheep and goats, but never lions. Surely that role is designated to that of an adult?

Many would perceive that certain jobs, ministries or types of work can and should only be done by certain types of people. Lisa and I once watched a British costume drama and

TV series called 'Sharpe'. The series, based on the Napoleonic wars in 19th Century Spain, looks at the life of a British soldier who is promoted through the ranks to officer status by Lord Wellington. Unfortunately, he is not readily received by the other officers who consider Sharpe to be of common birth and education and therefore not qualified for true officer status. Officers have to be gentlemen and those of 'good breeding' born into the upper-class and wealthy families of society. Sharpe was considered an outcast for not being a 'true officer and a gentleman'. He may have had the rank of an officer, but he could never truly enter in and mix with the other officers as 'common' and 'privilege' just don't go together.

Sharpe was not accepted and received in his role as an officer. He was judged not capable and acceptable for that job because of his particular background. Such is how we can treat and judge one another in our different cultures today. We can think that only the most highly qualified, educated and business people will make the best leaders in God's church. Those who are not so educated can be deliberately or subconsciously, excluded from certain roles and deemed 'not quite up to the job'. Alternatively – if they are in those roles, their ministry may not be received or accepted in the same way as those 'more suitably' qualified.

Many years ago I was part of a Newfrontiers workshop on racism held in Cape Town. It was an open and honest time in which one person commented, 'Why does it seem that there is more enthusiasm when a White person plants a church, than when a Black person does the same'? His perception was that certain White people were not so ready, willing or excited about Black leadership – seeing it not quite as significant or important as White leadership. Rightly or wrongly, that was how he felt. Perhaps some of us must be careful of missing out on what God is doing when he delights to take the least-likely and anoints him or her to do the leading?

God's ways are not our ways. The ways and wrong thinking of the world are not manifest in God's Kingdom. God seems to delight to use the so called 'weak and foolish' in the eyes of our respective cultures to shame the wise. Can an ex-prostitute or street dweller be caught up together with rich business men in apostolic mission? Can a White farmer in South Africa come under the leadership of a young Black man from the townships? Yes, I believe they not only can, but should. We should expect to see the unusual and uncommon in God's kingdom.

The fruit of the stump will act as a signal to the nations

The stump then points to radical, strange and new community found in Jesus and his coming Kingdom. The question to be asked perhaps, is whether this new radical community is meant to be experienced here on earth now or is it something we will only see in heaven? Does Isaiah's vision of the stump and the fruits thereof have implications for God's church today?

The answer is in this passage. The radical community that Isaiah prophesied is not a far distant dream-like hope that we will one day experience in heaven. Something of heaven can be tasted now on earth. Diverse, united and reconciled relationships are meant to be experienced and demonstrated now. The reason being is that that the rule and reign of our coming King Jesus, demonstrated by unusual and reconciled relationships, will act as a sign or signal revealing the knowledge of God to the nations. Isaiah says,

'In that day the root of Jesse, who shall stand as a signal for the peoples – of him shall the nations enquire and his resting place shall be glorious.' (Isaiah 11:10)

In other words reconciled relationships across worldly divides, made possible by the Spirit of God, will give a vivid demonstration that God is alive. They are a demonstration of heaven on earth, God's Kingdom come now that will cause people to seek and enquire of the Lord. Nations of the world will come to knowledge of the Lord by witnessing unusual, diverse, radical and reconciled church community.

Don't overlook the 'stump'

The stump then is a simple metaphor not to be missed.

- It is a call not to overlook Jesus and his ways and a reminder that God's ways are not our ways and his thoughts are not our thoughts.

- It is a call not to miss God's message if it does not come with words that are pleasing to our ears or through a messenger of our choice.

- It is a reminder to us not to evaluate successful ministry by the standards set by the world around us – by size, by numbers, by 'bigness' and impressiveness.

- It is a reminder that Jesus can be found in places we would least expect and through people we would least choose.

- It is a reminder of the great lengths Jesus took to reconcile us to him and to one another – his death on a stump!

- It is a vision to provoke the church to build radical diverse and united community that will glorify God in the nations

- It is a vision to pursue, embrace and wrestle with diversity and all that it means to be an awe-inspiring community of believers where, 'there is neither Jew nor Greek, there is neither slave nor free, there is neither male nor female, for you are all one in Christ Jesus.' [28]

The stump is an unusual picture that can in one simple word sum up much of what we will be talking about in this book. It is a picture that reminds us of fallen sinful hateful humanity, a 'chopped down' remnant of our Creator's original intentions. Yet it is also evidence of the grace of God, of new life sprouting forth and what God can do with those who embrace his kingdom. May this picture provoke us;

- To love Jesus more, be open to his ways, discover him in new places and find him through people we would least expect.

- To cross the cultural and economic boundaries of our societies and love people who are different to ourselves.

- To intentionally be part of building and demonstrating diverse cross-cultural and cross-economic church communities that sound out something of God's heart to the nations.

May we be a church where we not only love one another as well as the world, but better than the world; a church that will astound the world and cause the world to ask questions; a church that will magnify God and can in no way be missed or overlooked.

2 Glorious diversity

> 'Scripture celebrates the colourful mosaic of human cultures.
> It even declares that the New Jerusalem will be enriched by
> them since, 'the kings of the earth will bring their splendour
> into it' and, 'the glory and honour of the nations will be
> brought into it' (Revelation 21:24,26). If they will enrich human
> life and community in the end, they can begin to do so now.'[29]
> (John Stott)
>
> 'After this I looked and behold a great multitude that no one
> could number, from every nation, from all tribes and peoples
> and languages standing before the throne and before the Lamb
> clothed in white robes with palm branches in their hands crying
> out with a loud voice, Salvation belongs to our God who sits on
> the throne and to the Lamb.' (Revelation 7:9-10)

There is something beautiful in diversity that can't be found to
the same extent in homogeny. I am privileged to live in one of
the most beautiful cities in the world – Cape Town. Every day
I wake up to see the craggy mass of Table Mountain towering
protectively over the city, somehow reminding me that God
is in control. One of my favourite walks up the mountain is a
pass called Skeleton Gorge – a perfect climb on a hot day as
it is almost entirely in the shade at all times. Not just any old
shade, but the kind provided by majestic Milkwood, Red Alder,
Wild Peach, Yellowwood, Assegaaibos and other indigenous
trees. The forest is alive with the sound of chirping insects,
melodious bird songs, scavenging porcupines and running ice
cold mountain water. The view along the way is breathtaking,
offering panoramic glimpses of Kirstenbosch botanical gardens
across to the majestic Hottentot mountains of Somerset West.
Skeleton Gorge is indeed beautiful and is probably one of the
two most popular routes up Table Mountain.

Other equally popular spots for the many less energetic Capetonians are the tranquil hiking trails scattered amidst the towering pine trees of Tokai forest. The forest has its own beauty and is a pleasurable place to visit for an afternoon 'braai' (barbeque) on a hot summer's afternoon. However, in my opinion it seems to fall very short of the beauty, excitement and splendour offered by Skeleton Gorge only a few kilometers away – the main difference being one of diversity. Tokai forest consists only of pine trees – attracting the life of picnicking locals and dog walkers, but not much else. Homogeny has a certain beauty – but diversity offers so much more.

A Messy path

Diversity, however, is messy. Where the forests of Tokai are orderly, neat and easy to navigate, the trails of Skeleton Gorge are uneven, at times absent and on occasions outright treacherous. Below the indigenous forest lie sprawling vines, fallen branches, rotting trees and wild overgrown shrubs. Where there is life there is also death. It is not neat, orderly and tidy. To walk the path of diversity means going along a much more adventurous and dangerous trail – not easy or comfortable, but offering panoramic views and perspectives that otherwise would not have been seen along the easier roads.

Diversity in God's church

Perhaps the same can be said of diversity in God's church? Most would probably agree that there is something beautiful in diversity that glorifies God. John Piper says *'As different peoples of the world unite in worship to God the beauty of their praise will echo the depth and greatness of God's beauty far more exceedingly than if the redeemed were from only a few different people groups' (Piper: 1993:212).* [30]

On several occasions visitors to Khanyisa have commented, 'This is what heaven is going to be like,' being stirred by the variety of different people amongst us worshipping God.

I would agree! I am often amazed by God when one witnesses a White English speaking businessman worshipping alongside an unemployed Xhosa speaking Mama. I sometimes wonder, 'How did these two worlds ever meet?' I can also think, however, in response to such 'Khanyisa being like heaven' comments, with 'Oh, I hope not – if heaven has this many problems I'm not sure I want to be there.' Diversity is indeed beautiful, but it can be a messy and difficult business.

Old and young

Besides cultural and socio-economic diversity at Khanyisa we face the interesting dynamic of young and old. Our church attracts large numbers of children and young teenagers from the surrounding areas during the week and on Sunday mornings. Many of these kids come from abject poverty and difficult home situations, often made worse by addictions and substance abuse. Most come without parents or other family members, which makes for interesting dynamics in attempting to build church community. The children can be wild and the teenagers rude. Our older Black folk then blame the 'Whities' and grumble about 'this cross-cultural church' who give the youth too much liberty. Our White folk pull their hair out and try to tell themselves that, 'this is a township thing'. Our visitors, on the other hand comment once again, 'Oh, this is what heaven is going to be like!' and I feel a growing urge to smack them in the face!

A boy called Malusi

How does one handle this? Tell the kids to, 'get lost' and the teenagers to, 'shut up'? A few months ago following a Sunday morning meeting I found myself the last to leave and lock the building. I was not in a good mood – the service had gone well, but I was tired and angry having discovered the disgusting state of the toilets. Several of the cubicles had been locked on the inside, some of the toilet seats were covered in faeces and most of the floor was flooded with water! My language was not good and I wanted to screech at any child that crossed my path!

Having cleaned up the mess I was bordering on furious by the time I came to lock the doors and leave. Outside I discovered several children messing around in some builders' sand that was lying in the yard. Enough was enough and I unceremoniously shouted at them to 'suka' (go home) and kicked them out of the gate. I secretly hoped nobody was watching me. When I eventually came to lock the outer gates I found a little boy who appeared to be about five years old sitting in a pile of broken glass just outside the church yard. He was only wearing one shoe and was sobbing! I recognised him as one of the children I'd just told to go away. On speaking to him I discovered that some of the older boys had bullied him and that his other shoe had been buried in the pile of sand where I'd seen him playing. I felt terrible and even more so when I discovered his name was Malusi (meaning shepherd) and he was in fact eight years old! I hadn't been much of a 'shepherd' to him!

Hunt for the shoe

We went back inside and hunted around in the sand to see if we could find the missing shoe, but had no success. The next step was to take him home to explain how his shoe had been lost and promise that we would buy him a new pair of shoes. On getting to his shack I was shocked when his mother said to me, 'Don't you want to adopt him – I don't want him'? I couldn't believe what I was hearing. She said that she had a boyfriend whom she, loved and 'didn't want to lose' – so consequently Malusi was not staying with her, but with someone else in the community. Back into the car again and we drove to Malusi's 'other home' only to discover the house was full of adults smoking 'dagga' (cannabis)!

I left that day with a heavy heart for Malusi and his family, as well as being convicted about my own attitude and the rottenness of my heart. I was frustrated over the messy dynamics of what it means to build church with old and young and especially with poorer children without their families. However, it was a turning point for me in my attitude. I now understood why Malusi was often the first to arrive on Sunday morning and the last to leave in the afternoon. We, of course, did buy Malusi a new pair of shoes and have been 'best friends' since. I was also surprised to find out that he was, in fact, friends with my son Benjamin. Malusi has since come to our house to play with Ben and we have witnessed his mother coming to the Lord. He is now living back home with his mother once again and we are slowly witnessing God's kingdom advance in his family.

Not an easy path

It has not been an easy path. We have had to make decisions as a church not to turn away children without their parents. We have had to explain and help our people from different backgrounds to understand the values upon which we are building church. We have had to make changes in the way we do things, including the purchase of a 400-seater tent (where our Sunday children's work is run) as well as revamping our entire 'Kool-Kidz' programme to accommodate more children. Through it all, however, we have seen doors open into many families and are slowly seeing the gospel spread.

For many of the Khanyisa leaders going this route was never an issue. Monwabisi Ngwadla is a trainee elder at Khanyisa who first came to us ten years ago as a young teenager. He says, 'If you hadn't accepted me like that, I would not be here today, so of course we have to open the doors to the children and youth – you never know what God will do.' His mother Thembeka would also agree. She has since become a member of the church and in turn is now an outstanding leader in our children's ministry. She too has seen the benefits of what happens when one braves the path of diversity and is taken out of one's comfort zones.

Blessings of diversity

Building diverse church community is, without doubt, a
strenuous and messy business. It demands transformation of
thinking as well as openness to change and new ways of doing
things. For those brave enough to walk the path it leads to new
panoramic views of God, of oneself and of others that would
never be discovered on the less strenuous paths of homogeny.
Rob Bell and Don Golden put it this way;

*'You hear perspectives you wouldn't normally hear, you walk in
someone elses shoes, you find out that the judgements you had
previously made about that group of people or that kind of men or
that kind of women or all those kids simply don't hold up because
now you're getting to know one of 'those' and it's changing
everything. You learn that your labels for different people groups are
insufficient because people are far more complex and unpredictable
and intelligent and creative. You used to have a rigid stance on
a particular issue but now you've heard the other side and it's
impossible anymore to categorize them all as stupid and uninformed
and heartless, because you realise that they have thought about
their position and they have weighed the consequences and they
have some good points that you must consider. In the new humanity
our world gets bigger, our perspective goes from black and white to
colour, our sensitivities are heightened, we're rescued from sameness
and uniformity, because the wall has come down and peace has
been made' (Bell & Golden: 2008:154 -155).* [31]

God loves diversity

From the first few verses of Genesis to the end of Revelation,
God's heart and passion for diversity seems to ooze through
the pores of the Bible. The diversity so wonderfully displayed
through God in creation – the vast numbers of stars in the sky all
named by him, the plant life, the animal life, light and darkness,
land and sea, mountains and plains, vegetable and mineral and,
of course, man and woman. Why did God display such variety
in all aspects of his creation and look on it with such pleasure

declaring it as 'very good'?[32] It's almost as If God couldn't help himself because such diversity reflects the very nature and being of who God is. This diversity displayed at the very onset of creation gives us a glimpse of the character, grace and glory of God that could never have been adequately seen if God had made a creation of similarities. As Duane Elmer says, 'God… in authoring diversity was trying to tell us about himself'.[33] There is no getting around it – God in his very nature and being is diverse. He is God the Father, Son and Holy Spirit!

Diversity of peoples

God's love for diversity is further displayed in his deliberate creation of a vast array of different nations and people groups throughout the earth. It is shocking to know that all nations of the earth, even the ones we don't like, are all made in the image of God[34]. It's also important for us to note that every nation on the face of the earth has had its origins and will from the mind of God. Not one was an accident, a mistake or something that God never quite intentioned. Paul highlights this when he was talking to the proud citizens of the city of Athens when he said, '(God) made from one every nation of men to live on the face of the earth, having determined allotted periods and the boundaries of their habitation'[35]. This is such a humbling thought as not one of us, not one culture, tribe or nation, can dare to think that somehow we are slightly more special or slightly more of worth and value to God than other peoples. No – God has made everyone of us in his image to display his glory – equal in the eyes of God.

Glorify God

David Devenish reminds us in his excellent book on mission that God's purpose in making so many different nations was,

'to fill the earth with people who would reflect him in every way, bring praise to his name, live for his glory and establish his rule and kingdom throughout the earth'.[36] *(Devenish 2005: 22)*

This was rather short lived as it was not long before Adam and Eve sinned and God's original plan to fill the earth with his glory came to an abrupt halt. Even after the flood and having experienced God's grace in their lives, the people of the earth decided they didn't want to be scattered and fill the earth with the knowledge of God. Rather they wanted to stick together, make a name for themselves and build a city with a tower that reached to heaven as opposed to seeking God's will and his glory.[37]

Consequently, God brought seeming judgment and confusion at Babel and left the nations to their own devices. No longer could the different peoples communicate through one language and instead differing languages and dialects came into being that separated the various nations of the earth. The result of this intervention by God was the origin of the multitude of different nations, clans, families, races and nations that cover the world today.[38] In one sense, the city of Babel became a symbolic picture of the division and antagonism that still exists amongst the peoples of the earth today.

This judgment at the city of Babel may have seemed harsh, but actually as Dewi Hughes reminds us this was, ultimately, the means God employed to bring about his original intention that human beings should fill the earth and bring praise to his name.[39] God immediately set into place a plan of action that would do this, resulting in the eventual redemption of all the people of the earth. This plan involved choosing a sinful undeserving man called Abram through whose 'seed' God would eventually send his Son Jesus. In Christ God planned for the formation of a new city – the people of God who, in contrast to the city of Babel would be a people united in perfect community and eternal love. Also, in contrast to Babel they would be a people united in their intention to please and honour God rather than making a name for themselves or their tribes. This city was to consist of people from all tribes and nations.

God gave Abram an incredible promise;

'Now the Lord said to Abram, 'Go from your country and your kindred and your father's house to the land that I will show you'. And I will make of you a great nation and I will bless you and make your name great so that you will be a blessing… And in you all the families of the earth will be blessed.' (Genesis 12:1-3)

God chose to form and bless through Abraham, one particular nation Israel, in order that other nations of the world would also be blessed. The crazy thing is – Abraham believed God. He dared to believe that God in his grace could choose a man like him and make him into a father of nations – even though he was old and his wife was way beyond child-bearing age. He dared to believe that from him and from his 'seed' God would raise up a Saviour in whom all other peoples and of the world would be blessed.

Today God's promise to Abraham still stands for the church. God still wants to bless a people who will in turn be a blessing to all the ethnic peoples of the world around us. Abraham is one of the few men in the Bible referred to as a 'friend of God' and he is renowned in the Hebrews 'hall of fame' as a man of faith because he dared to believe God.[40] Will we too dare to believe God to use us and reach out and bless the peoples of the world in our own countries and in the nations?

God's heart for the nations

One book of the Bible that communicates something of God's passion for the nations around us is the book of Jonah. I find Jonah to be one of the most invigorating, heart-felt and exciting books of the Old Testament. It is, however, a book that can be easily dismissed and deemed perhaps as a great story to be told to children in Sunday school, but not quite worthy of the attention of 'mature adults'. If one did a survey of popular opinion, looking to establish who we thought were the greatest prophets in the Old Testament I'm not sure that many of us would put Jonah high up on the list – perhaps Isaiah or Jeremiah but somehow Jonah doesn't quite make the mark.

It's interesting though, that Jonah is the only prophet that Jesus compares himself to by name whereby he willingly and intentionally associates himself with and links himself to Jonah. In talking to the scribes and Pharisees Jesus said;

'Just as Jonah was three days and three nights in the belly of the great fish so will the Son of man be three days and three nights in the heart of the earth' (Matthew 12:40)

Hot or cold

Jonah is a book of great contrasts and extremes, attacking the senses on all sides with its sounds, smells, feelings and emotions. Jonah the man, is a 'what you see is what you get' kind of guy, being either hot or cold with no room for any form of luke-warmness in-between. He reminds me of Nathaniel in the New Testament of whom Jesus said – 'Behold an Israelite indeed in whom there is no deceit'.[41] In one breath we see Jonah boldly declaring his faith as a Hebrew and follower of the Lord, then in contrast we hear news that he has quite confidently told other people that he has been disobeying God and running away from his presence. Whatever he does he seems to do in extreme measures – whether it is snoring while he sleeps on a boat (as the Greek Septuagint version of the Bible declares) or being swallowed and then later 'vomited' out of a fish.[42]

Great extremes

Similarly, the non-Jewish mariners that Jonah meets on the ship bound for Tarshish also seem to have an extremity about their nature. They start off as fearful and superstitious people casting lots as a means of direction but rapidly become, 'men who feared the Lord exceedingly'.[43] The same can be said of the Assyrian citizens in the city of Nineveh. Before our eyes they turn from a people who have passionately given themselves to wickedness to a people passionately giving themselves to repentance. Not only do they call every man, woman and child to fast and pray with sackcloth and ashes, but they also make the animals do it as well.[44] If you are going to do it – you may as well do it well! Even the weather can't but help be dramatic, ranging from strong winds and mighty tempestuous seas[45] to scorching east winds and blazing sunshine.[46]

Ruined my life

Emotions and feelings also run deep. A few years ago my daughter Katey came running into our kitchen, closely followed by her older brother Ben. She had tears streaming down her face and both were attempting to speak, or should I say shout, at the same time. Ben was saying, 'It's her, I didn't do anything,' while Katey more dramatically declared, 'No it's not – It's Benjamin, he's ruined my life!' What Ben had done that had so terribly ruined her life I'm not quite sure, but Lisa and I had to stop ourselves from laughing. Such intensity of emotions experienced by my daughter seems to be very similar to that experienced by Jonah.

In chapter four Jonah is ecstatically happy and joyful because God has provided him with some cool shade from a very fast growing plant, to protect his head from the sun.[47] Almost immediately though, his joy turns into anger and despair as he blames God for allowing a worm to come and eat up his shade.[48] So much so that he asks God to take his life and declares, 'It is better for me to die than to live.[49] His strong emotional reaction was rooted in a deeper grudge that he was holding against God for having the audacity to forgive and show mercy to a bunch of (in Jonah's opinion) undeserving no-good Assyrians who should have been destroyed.[50]

Jesus and Jonah

Jonah is a fascinating character, which makes me wonder about Jesus willingness and intentionality about being associated with this man. There are certainly similarities between Jonah and Jesus.

- Jonah was from Gath Hepher an area three miles from Nazareth where Jesus was raised as a child.

- Both Jesus and Jonah seemed to have no problem with sea travel being equally renowned for sleeping peacefully and calmly in the midst of raging storms – much to the anger and irritation of their fellow passengers. [51]

- Perhaps more significantly though was Jonah's experience of three days inside the fish – a dramatic and prophetic sign pointing to Christ dying on the cross and being raised from the dead on the third day!

There are, however, two things about Jonah that stand in sharp contrast to that of Jesus.

- Jonah was grumpy, emotionally immature and at times outright childish when things didn't quite work out in line with his selfish desires and when he couldn't get his own way. This is such a stark contrast to Jesus who is gracious and compassionate, slow to anger and rich in love. [52]

- Secondly, Jonah went reluctantly to the nations while Jesus went willingly. This perhaps is the biggest contrast that reveals Jesus to be one who is 'greater than Jonah'. [53] Both Jesus and Jonah were sent to the nations. Jonah in fact, was the only Old Testament prophet sent directly to preach to the Gentiles, yet he went reluctantly full of racism and superiority, miserly in his desire to extend God's grace to a fallen people. Jesus, on the other hand, is passionate to extend his love and mercy to every people on the face of the earth.

Selective racism

Interestingly, Jonah only seemed to have a problem towards some of the peoples around him and was selective in his attitudes towards others. He was happy, for example, to associate with 'foreigners' on a boat bound for Tarshish in Spain, but to go to the Assyrian people closest to him he had major race issues. It's funny how even in world mission today many of us are willing to cross the seas to go to specific nations of the world, but we are a lot more reluctant to go to those right in our midst. This is true in my home country of South Africa with many crossing borders to preach the gospel in other parts of Africa, but reluctant to cross railway lines or motorways to the numerous nations on our own doorsteps down the road.

Jesus in contrast was sent by God to the world. He, unlike Jonah, went willingly and eagerly – passionate to please his father in heaven and passionate to extend God's love and mercy to the thousands of peoples of this earth who like Ninevah, 'do not know their right hand from their left'. [54] The book of Jonah illustrates to us something of God's overwhelming love for even the wickedest nations and peoples of this world. What surprises me is Jesus' willingness to associate himself with a prophet like Jonah who really didn't carry this same passion. Just as Jesus was so willing to be misunderstood, associating with little children and those deemed of little value in the eyes of the world, so he is willing to be associated with an overlooked racist prophet, just as he is so willing to be associated with us.

Thomas Carlise's poem 'You Jonah' closes with these lines;

'and Jonah stalked to his shaded seat and waited for God to come around to his way of thinking. And God is still waiting for a host of Jonahs in their comfortable houses to come around to his way of loving.' (Thomas Carlise) [55]

We need to catch something of God's heart for the diverse nations and people around us and come round to 'His way of loving'. His love extends beyond the borders of our comfort zones reaching out from our Jerusalems, Judeas then into our Samarias and to the ends of the earth.

Who are the nations?

I wonder who or what you imagine when you think of different nations of the world? There can be a tendency to think of political states or countries defined by their geographical borders such as the United States of America, China, England or South Africa.

Nations in the Bible, however, are more than this – referring rather to different people and ethnic groupings (more like clans) with cultural and language differences that cause separation and distinction between these various groups of people.[56] When God gave his promise to Abraham he spoke about nations in terms of 'families of the earth',[57] indicating smaller groups of people than we might at first imagine who could so easily be overlooked. The reality is there are more nations than we can begin to realise – even in our own communities. Invariably without being aware, we can be almost blind to the existence of different peoples within our own countries and communities. This is something that Ralph Winter calls 'people blindness'.[58] Let me use my home church and the community of Nyanga and Guguletu as an example.

Everyone is the same?

When I first went to Guguletu my assumption was that everyone was basically the same – after all they were all Black people! I soon learned that among the predominant Xhosa tribe there are distinctions between 'proper' Xhosa and Xhosa-speaking people. Proper Xhosa such as amaGcaleka and amaRharhabe claim descent from an ancestor named Xhosa. Other Xhosa-speaking peoples such as Thembu, Mpondo, Mpondomise, Bhele, Zizi, Hlubi and Bhaca, have long histories of their own and are proud of their distinct tribal identities.[59] Then within each of these tribal groupings there are numerous clan distinctions covering many families or sub groups of people such as Magaba, Dlamini or Madiba (the clan name by which Nelson Mandela is affectionately referred to), each with their variations in culture, language and traditions.

Then there are different 'housing' type areas each with their own distinct sense of community feeling and identity. This has resulted from a combination of economics, as well as South Africa's torrid and turbulent past. Nyanga, for example, was established in the late 1940s in response to overcrowding in

Langa, which was at the time the only 'African' township of Cape Town. This original development consisted of free-standing and semi-detached houses with outside toilets. Then in the mid 1950s the National party government introduced a policy declaring Cape Town as a Coloured Labour Preference Area. This terrible policy made it difficult for Black Africans to be employed in the Western Cape and made it illegal for 'Blacks' without employment to live in the region. To implement their policy an emergency camp now known as KTC was created with the purpose of relocating all Black African squatters in the Cape peninsula to KTC while deciding whether individuals could stay or should be 'removed' to distant homelands. In the 1960s the government then opened single-sex hostels for migrant labour for government and private employers. These hostels, however, soon became overcrowded providing accommodation for entire families and not just single individuals. On top of this, despite large scale intimidation and harassment by the police, many illegal squatters (mainly woman from the Eastern Cape) continued to move into Cape Town resulting in the formation of other communities such as New Crossroads.[60]

With such differences in origin, housing and varying access to services (like sewage, water and electricity) it should come as no surprise that there are often tensions and hostilities between these sub-communities. This is not to mention further differences that exist on the basis of class, status, education and socio-economic levels, as well as the presence of Zulu and Basotho people living in the area and refugees from Congo, Angola and Zimbabwe.

Nations within nations

All in all it can be said that Guguletu does indeed consist of nations within nations. Some of these groupings could be considered to be nations in the biblical sense while others are more sociological groupings defined by status, political backgrounds, education, economics and other variable factors.

Together, however, they demonstrate that there are more nations and people groups than any of us can even begin to imagine, as well as revealing the magnitude of diversity that can exist amongst even similar peoples. Suffice it to say, one doesn't necessarily have to encounter a person from a different nation to have a cross-cultural experience. Many of the peoples I have mentioned in Guguletu speak the same language, but vary greatly in their world-views, thinking and outlook on life. Such differences can all lead to cross-cultural conflict.

People within peoples

This of course, is not just a phenomenon unique to South Africa – all over the world, even in seemingly homogenous communities, we encounter 'people within peoples'. At the end of 1986 I moved from my home town of Sunderland where I'd grown up, to study at the University of London. I was a 'northerner' moving into deepest darkest southern England. I joined Runnymede Community Church under the leadership of David and Shirley Dennington and it was here I experienced my first taste of culture shock. I think the shock was mutual. Various people struggled to understand my Geordie accent and others seemed to find me quite forward. For example, I would go and visit people without being invited! Not only that, I would arrive at the house, give a quick knock at the door and then walk inside! This was the norm where I grew up – but 'down south' that was not the case. We may have all been English but our cultures were quite different.

North-South divide

I remember at University studying the 'North-South' divide where one author drew a satirical map of England based not on reality but peoples perceptions of England from a Londoners' point of view. In this map the city of London was portrayed as being nearly larger than the whole of England itself – after all London is where everything happens – anywhere else was a mere insignificant 'blot' on the landscape. Civilization was portrayed as stopping just north of the Watford gap and modern transport only went as far as Manchester. After that you hit the Arctic Circle where any northern savages living there were all backward, uneducated and still used dogs and sleighs to get around.

I was the dog and sleigh man arriving in the most civilized county in England – Surrey (where there are less speed cameras per head of population than any other county in England!). My time in 'homogenous' Chertsey became one of cross-cultural diversity – one to which I was initially blind. There were 'working-class' people and 'middle-class' people. There were those from council estates and caravan parks, as well as those with large family homes. There were unschooled people together with university lecturers, northerners and southerners, Asians, New Zealanders, Indians and travelling gypsies. What I had thought was a fairly homogenous community was a lot more diverse than I'd first anticipated. I had to go through a process of having my eyes opened to the different 'nations' that existed in my midst.

People blindness

Each of us need to be aware of any 'people blindness' that we may have and in turn have our eyes opened to the wonderful diversity of peoples within our own countries and communities, as well as those throughout the world. Duane Elmer says that as we engage *'in the process of learning about other cultures, affirming our various ethnic heritages and honouring (if not celebrating) diversity we enlarge our appreciation of God… Perhaps we are most like God when we also look around and affirm as good, peoples of traditions different to our own and diligently seek to appreciate the beauty God has chosen to express in others'*.[61]

Diversity in heaven

It's exciting to know that when we get to John's amazing prophetic revelation in the last book of the Bible, there is a fantastic confirmation that God's redemptive plan will succeed. There is no 'perhaps' about this – it is going to happen and what God planned before the foundation of the world will succeed. John writes;

'After this I looked and behold a great multitude that no one could number, from every nation, from all tribes and peoples and languages standing before the throne and before the Lamb clothed in white robes with palm branches in their hands and crying out with a loud voice, Salvation belongs to our God who sits on the throne and to the Lamb!' (Revelation 7:9-10)

What an amazing hope and promise to know as John Hosier says that, 'At the end of history, there will be some from every nation or people group who will for eternity be worshippers of God…' [62] What is also astonishing is that John (the prophet – not John Hosier) seems to make it clear that the final goal of God in redemption will not be to obliterate the various distinctions between the peoples of the earth, but rather that they will be gathered together as a glorious unified assembly of the people of God. There will still be recognition of different tribes, different nations, different peoples and different languages. We won't all have been congealed into a single homogenous people group who all look the same. The glory and honour of the nations will be brought into heaven. [63]

Bruce Milne says *'…Nothing of ultimate worth from the long history of the nations will be omitted from the heavenly community. Everything which authentically reflects the God of truth, all that is of abiding worth from within the national stories and the cultural inheritance of the world's peoples, will find its place in the New Jerusalem. This will hardly surprise us if we have drunk at the wells of human culture and have experienced the deepening of sensitivity, broadening of understanding and enlargement of heart and mind which such engagement can promote.'* [64] *(Milne 2002:32)*

Implications

This is a great hope, but I wonder what implications this has for us in the church today? Is this just a hope that we will only witness once we get to heaven or should the church communities that we are part of be demonstrating something of 'heaven' here on earth now? Are the glory and honour of the nations to be discovered and tasted now or are they only the 'dessert' to be tasted after the 'main course' has been eaten on earth? If God is glorified in diversity and passionate for the all nations of this earth, is this same passion to be shared by all of God's church or merely a 'certain type of person'. Should all local churches be 'cross-cultural' or just some who are 'called' to do that?

I'd like to suggest three implications to the church in response to this knowledge of God's heart for diversity and his passion for the nations of the world:

1 Every Christian and every local church is called to cross racial and cultural boundaries

2 Every Christian and every local church is called to cross socio-economic boundaries.

3 We are called to build diverse church communities that glorify God

If embraced, diversity is a beautiful path leading us to new heights and depths in our exploration of God and one another. As Duane Elmer says it was, *'God who authored human diversity. This fact calls all of us to deal with cultural diversity, see it as good and honour it as the handiwork of the wise and sovereign Creator'* .[65]

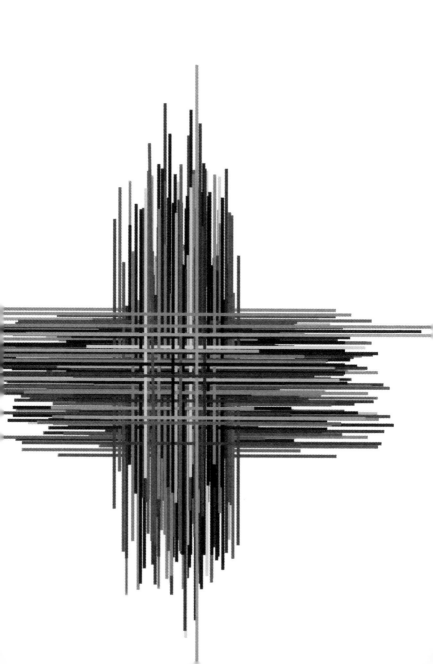

3 Lift up your eyes

'There are many excuses that the world would use to avoid crossing racial and cultural boundaries, but there is no place for such excuses in the church. All Christians of all countries of all ages and all sexes are called to cross the dividing walls that separate the many fields in front of our eyes that are ripe unto harvest.' (Nigel Measures)

'As long as there is time, and as long as there are nations to reach, Jesus' demand to go and make disciples is valid.' (John Piper)

'Any burden we may have for specific nations, sociological groups or peoples of this earth that does not spread and reach out to other nations as well, is no true prophetic burden from the Lord. We serve the individual 'peoples' of this world by helping them to understand God's heart for the nations around us. We serve the nations of this world by bringing them into contact and fellowship not only with God, but one another. Failure to do so is a compromise on the very heart of the gospel.' (Nigel Measures)

Simon Pettit was a giant of a man; both in stature and nature, and had an amazing ability to cross both racial and socio-economic boundaries. Until his sudden and tragic death in the January of 2005, Simon used to give apostolic oversight to the various Newfrontiers churches throughout the continent of Africa. He and his wife Lindsey were good friends to Lisa and I and helped us very much in our early days of church planting.

Besides Simon's infectious laughter and his passion for life, perhaps one of the things that impressed me most about him was his ability to connect with different types of people.

Whoever he was talking to would receive his undivided attention and were made to feel special. Similarly, whether he was preaching at an international conference addressing thousands of people, or sharing the gospel under a tree in rural Malawi, he just seemed to 'get through' to all he came into contact with. Dominic Mabikwe is now 82 years old and one of the elders at Khanyisa. He was first drawn to us as a church in response to his friend telling him how well Simon had preached at a township funeral. Tata Dom was intrigued and came along for a visit – and has stayed with us ever since. Simon was just gifted that way.

Going but not knowing where

Simon, in his genuine love for people was naturally passionate for mission, for church planting and making disciples of all nations of the world. He once preached on Jesus parting words to his disciples in Matthew 28;

'All authority in heaven and on earth has been given to me. Go therefore and make disciples of all nations baptising them in the name of the Father and of the Son and of the Holy Spirit, teaching them to observe all that I have commanded you. And behold I am with you always, to the end of the age' (Matthew 28:18-20)

As he approached the end of his sermon he shouted in an enthusiastic manner for people to 'Go!' One man was so stirred by what he had heard he immediately got up out of his seat and ran out of the meeting hall as fast as he could. About half an hour later he 'sheepishly' returned and came to the front to talk to Simon. He explained,

'I was so excited about going, I just had to go. I started running down the streets and then suddenly realised I didn't know where I was supposed to go to. I thought I'd come back and ask'.

It's wonderful to see such enthusiastic, if not somewhat untamed passion to follow Jesus' command to go. The question to be asked is 'who is to go?' Does it apply to all Christians today or just the twelve disciples that Jesus spoke to?

All are to go?

Few would disagree that Jesus' command to make disciples of all nations was not just a requirement for the first century Christians, but one that is still applicable for all in the church today. Jesus said, '…go therefore and make disciples of all nations… And behold I am with you always until the end of the age.[66]' The words 'to the end of the age' give an indication that this commission is relevant through all history until Jesus returns. Only once the end has come will we be released from the task.

Also, since Jesus had earlier warned his disciples that the end would not come until his kingdom had been proclaimed throughout the whole world,[67] it is a pretty safe bet to assume, as John Piper says, 'As long as there is time, and as long as there are nations to reach, Jesus' command to go and make disciples is valid'[68] We have work to do! This is perhaps a daunting task for many of us, but the encouraging news is that the one who has been given all authority in heaven and on earth will be with us in the achievement of this commission.

This also means that the church will and should always be on the forefront of communicating the gospel with different racial and cultural groups. It is impossible to go to the nations and not have to cross racial, cultural, language, class, worldview, education and economic barriers between various people and ethnic groups. Mission motivates us to cross these boundaries.

Lift up our eyes

The Great Commission was not the first time that Jesus had exhorted his disciples to cross racial boundaries. On one occasion his disciples returned from a food hunting mission, only to discover Jesus in deep conversation with a Samaritan woman.[69] They were shocked – they couldn't believe that Jesus would do this 'cross cultural thing,' let alone comprehend that they might have to do it as well. Jesus, however, had other plans for them and used the opportunity to broaden and challenge their thinking. He said to them, 'Look I tell you lift up your eyes and see that the fields are white for harvest.'[70]

Their eyes were blinkered and pointed down. There was a harvest in front of their faces that they could not see. People were 'ripe for the picking', but the disciples couldn't comprehend that they might be the ones who were to go to them. Jesus challenged them to lift up their eyes and see, throw off their 'people blindness' and realise 'going cross cultural' was for them. A whole number of excuses or reasons could have been given why this was NOT applicable to them, but Jesus gave them no room to manoeuvre. The same is true for us today. There are many excuses that the world would use to avoid crossing racial and cultural boundaries, but there is no place for such excuses in the church. All Christians of all countries of all ages and all sexes are called to cross the dividing walls that separate the many fields in front of our eyes that are ripe unto harvest. This cross cultural thing is for all of us!

Crossing cultural boundaries

Jesus further emphasised this point to his disciples following his resurrection when he said to them;

'You will receive power when the Holy Spirit has come upon you and you will be my witnesses in Jerusalem, in all Judea and Samaria and to the end of the earth.' (Acts 1:8)

They were to be Christ's witnesses crossing racial and cultural boundaries to reach the various nations of the world – whether close to home in their 'Jerusalems' or as far afield as the ends of the earth. The same is true for us!

Jerusalems – This logically would be the peoples and cultures we are most familiar with and therefore the most comfortable with. However, as we saw in the previous chapter, we need to recognise that the nations are amongst us even in our 'Jerusalems'. We know, for example, from the book of Acts that Jerusalem was a diverse and multi-cultural city. The coming of God's Holy Spirit at Pentecost was witnessed and heard by people from North Africa to Italy, as well as by Jews and Arabs.[71] Even being at 'home' in our 'Jerusalems' doesn't exempt us from coming into contact with other cultures. In the age of global travel it is not uncommon to find the nations coming to us.

Judeas and Samarias – We are also called to be witnesses slightly further afield in our Judeas and Samarias. This is of course, representative of people we are less familiar with and even people we hate and dislike. Historically, the relationship between Jews and Samaritans was one of pure hatred and distrust. For the early church disciples to engage with people they previously hated, could not have been an easy or a comfortable business. The same is true today.

Ends of the earth – Lastly, we are called to be witnesses far afield to the ends of the earth! For some this will mean uprooting and travelling to different geographical nations of the world. For others of us it will mean reaching out to the nations who have come to us. One thing is for sure, whether at home or abroad, if we are to be witnesses to all nations we can't escape the inevitability of cross-cultural interaction.

Reasons going cross-cultural may not be for everyone

Going to the nations will involve crossing cultural and racial boundaries. Having said this we may be tempted to disqualify ourselves from the task – leaving it to others who are 'better at it' than us. It is after all a daunting and intimidating commission. Four seemingly genuine arguments are commonly used as reasons why crossing cultural boundaries may not be applicable to all:

1 It takes a certain type of person to do the cross-cultural thing.

2 Cross-cultural is for those who are good with languages.

3 Cross-cultural is a gifting from God that not everyone has.

4 God calls some people to one homogenous grouping.

1 Is 'cross-cultural' just for the adventurous?

Question: Isn't it just for certain 'types of Christians', the adventurous travelling types and those who are 'inclined that way', who are called to go to the nations and do the cross-cultural thing?

To answer this question, one only has to look at the early disciples to see the 'types of Christians' Jesus seemed to delight to call to go to all the earth. Naturally speaking not many were the adventurous or travelling sorts. They were uneducated fisherman, who had spent the vast part of their lives on a small lake called the Sea of Galilee. They were local boys and not well travelled. Until their involvement with Jesus most hadn't interacted with or even met many 'foreigners' so when they did so, their prejudices, attitudes and racism quickly became apparent. In Luke chapter 9, for example, Jesus and his disciples were about to enter a Samaritan village, but the Samaritans wanted nothing to do with Jesus because they had heard he was heading towards Jerusalem. James and John were not happy with this news and were under no qualms about calling fire down from heaven in order to consume them. [72]

None of these disciples were ideal 'first choice' candidates with a 'natural inclination' for crossing racial boundaries. Yet it was to such disciples, with all their 'nonsense' that Jesus asked to go and make disciples of all nations. We might not think we are the natural types who can go to the nations – but whether we feel inclined or not the same calling is upon us.

2 Is cross cultural just for those good with languages?

Question: What about language? Aren't we taught that when working cross culturally we must learn the language of the people we are working with?

Language is a natural barrier that can understandably hinder friendship and relationships across cultural divides. Studying other languages therefore, is an excellent means of learning to enter the worlds of those different to ourselves. It is a good thing that all should be encouraged to do. The temptation, however, may be to disqualify ourselves from certain cross-cultural relationships on the basis that we are 'useless with languages'. We may argue, 'I can't even speak my own language well, let alone someone else's. How then can I go to the nations?'

Though language may prove to be a hindrance, it is not, however, an insurmountable obstacle. I love the testimony of Angela Kemm who discipled me cross culturally when I first came to South Africa. As a White South African woman she has been involved in the townships of Cape Town since 1986, but even today she still struggles to speak Xhosa. She told me one day,

'I tried, I begged God for help, I felt utterly useless. I'm not particularly 'dof' (Afrikaans' word meaning stupid) so I couldn't understand why I was taking so long to learn until God showed me that he was not going to allow me to speak the language easily. This would make sure that I would always need a Xhosa person with me to interpret what I said. Once I knew the language, I would act in my own independent way and he was not having this. Instead of the people being dependent on me, I was the one who was dependent on them!'

Language is no reason not to engage with people of a different culture!

3 Is cross cultural for those who are gifted that way?

Question: What about gifting? Are some people gifted to 'cross-cultural ministry' and others not?

This perhaps is one of the biggest 'excuses' that many of us could use for not reaching out and relating with different cultures to ourselves – 'I'm just not gifted that way'. To answer this question a few comments on gifting are worth mentioning:

We're not all gifted the same way – It is true that there are a great variety of gifts within the Body of Christ. Just as a body is made up of many different parts, so in God's church we have many members with different gifting to do various things. Some are gifted with leadership, others with gifts of healing etc. To see a healthy body each part must be doing what it is gifted and called to do. [73] The Bible is also quite clear that not everyone is gifted in the same way – not everyone is an apostle, not everyone is a prophet and not everyone is an evangelist. We each have gifts that differ according to the grace given us. [74]

Some are clearly gifted – Few would deny that certain people are gifted in certain contexts. I mentioned Simon earlier who had an ability to relate to many different types of people. The apostle Paul, perhaps more than other early church leaders, had an amazing passion and ability to connect with both Jews and Gentiles. Mother Theresa had amazing compassion and ability to reach out to poor and 'marginalised' on the streets of Calcutta, and so the list can go on. It is a mistake, however, to look at such people and disqualify ourselves from any form of cross-cultural interaction because we do not have the same gifting. We could say things like, 'I could never do what they do' or 'I'm just not gifted that way'. We should not allow such heroes to intimidate us, but rather inspire and provoke us in our cross-cultural exploits.

Kingdom life for all to partake –The Bible makes it clear that though we may not all have certain gifting we are all, none the less, to partake in the ministry of that gifting. For example, we are all called to evangelise and be witnesses, though not all of us are gifted as evangelists. [75] We all can and are especially encouraged to prophesy, though not all of us are gifted prophets. [76] We are all to teach and admonish one another, even though not all of us are called as teachers. [77] Similarly, we are all called to be apostolic though not all of us will be apostles.

The church is an apostolic community. Jesus said, 'in the same way the Father sent me, I am sending you'. [78] We are a sent people, a commissioned people – a people on a mission. There is no such thing as an apostolic church and non-apostolic church or an apostolic person and non-apostolic person. Every local church is to be apostolic by nature, just as every individual Christian is to be apostolic – we are all sent! Not all will be called to be missionaries in the far corners of the globe but all of us are to be caught up in going to the nations. Not all have the gifting of the apostle Paul or Mother Theresa, but all of us are to lift up our eyes and reach out across cultural boundaries to the many nations in our midst.

Judging gifting by levels of Joy – Christians in the church today frequently evaluate their gifting, and what they do or don't do, on the basis of what makes them 'feel nice'. I once heard a pastor exhort his congregation to reflect upon, 'what are you wired towards?' or 'where do your passions lie'? He was endeavoring to help his people find their gifting and place in the body of Christ. He emphasised that serving God is a joyful business and if we operate within our gifted spheres we should be energised by what we do.

This is a common teaching in which there is, of course, some truth. Serving God is meant to be a joyful and life-giving relationship. It is not always helpful, however, to evaluate our gifting and what we participate in within church life, purely on the basis of our 'joy levels' and our 'energised levels.' Feelings can come and go as do our levels of joy in ministry. I know, for example, that I'm gifted to be a church leader and preacher, but there are times when I feel like 'killing' my sheep. If I went by feelings my congregation would be dead by now! Sometimes the people I lead do not energise me, they frustrate me and I want to tell them exactly which river they can go and jump into! If I fully judged what I was called and gifted to do by my energy and joy levels I would have given up a long time ago!

The same is true cross-culturally. Many disqualify themselves from daring to enter the worlds of others on the basis that it does not 'energise them'. Alternatively, they deem cross-cultural ministry not to be 'their thing' as they don't feel particularly 'wired that way' or because there is too much potential for misunderstandings and conflict. Feelings of 'inclination' should not hinder us from entering the worlds of others. Just as we ought not to dismiss gifting and participating in church ministry purely on the basis of subjective emotion, neither should we dismiss the call to cross racial and cultural boundaries on the basis of 'nice feelings and 'energy levels'.

4 Are some called to homogeny?

Question: What about homogeny? Does God call some people just to one particular culture, nation or sociological grouping?

Some of the teaching around homogeny, homogenous evangelism and homogenous church will be examined in more detail in chapter six. Suffice it to say at this stage, it is not uncommon to hear individuals and churches talk of targeting specific people groups or types of people such as; students, businessmen, refugees, Iranians or Polish immigrants, to name but a few. If that is the case how does such an apparent call to homogeny fit into a broader vision of reaching out across racial boundaries? Some could be tempted to see cross-cultural diversity as an issue irrelevant to them because they are called to go only to the rich and wealthy or only to the middle-class families or just the Chinese speaking people of their particular town or city.

One example that springs to mind that exemplifies and justifies this thinking is that of Paul's' call to the Gentiles and Peter's call to the Jews. Before examining that, however, I'd like to make a couple of observations on discerning the will of God;

God has told me – Firstly, when a person says, 'God has told me' it doesn't leave one with much room to manoeuvre. After all, if God has said, who are we to question his will? Discerning the will of God, however, is not always easy and we do at times get it wrong. This is why any prophecy, for example, needs to be weighed and tested [79] as sometimes what we feel is a word from God is actually too much cheese from the night before.

I remember one church service we held a few years ago where our friends Gary and Nicky Welsh were guest speakers. Being the 'humble' church pastor that I am, I was secretly hoping for a good meeting to suitably impress them. I realised things might not be going to plan when a lady in the church, who had brought six disabled teenagers along, came to me and asked if we could stop the meeting to pray for their 'masturbation problems'. Having a moment of panic imagining where I might have to 'lay hands' I gently suggested that I pray for them at the end of the meeting.

A few minutes later, with Gary and Nicky blissfully unaware of that little incident, I noticed several of our young teenage girls bringing boxes of bananas and cartons of 'Liqui-fruit' cold drink to the front of the hall. This time Gary looked at me with questioning eyes to see if I knew what was going on. I didn't have a clue so went off to investigate. A young lady who had recently joined the church came to me and asked me to trust her! She said 'God had told her' to bring these bananas and cold drink to give out at the meeting and would I give her a few minutes to explain. I didn't have much of an option as by this stage the front of the hall was now piled high with bananas and drink cartons surrounded by several kneeling teenage girls all crying their eyes out. I stopped the meeting and gave the young lady an opportunity to speak. She then commenced to speak about 'Mother Earth'.

Oh my goodness – how I wanted the world to crack open and swallow her up – with me included. I can't recall exactly what I did next as the following few minutes were a bit of a blur, but somehow I returned the meeting to some level of 'decency and order'. As it so happened, what this young lady had thought was 'God has told me' turned out to be a 'psychotic episode' for which she later received appropriate medical attention. The reality is that any sense of prophetic direction both to us as individuals and as church communities always needs to be weighed, discerned and tested.

Motives – Secondly, we must dare to honestly evaluate the motives and intentions of our hearts, especially when it comes to discerning which people we will go to and which people we won't. The heart, as Jeremiah appropriately reminds us, 'is deceitful above all things'.[80] A young man who feels 'led' to attend the Thursday morning prayer meeting may actually be motivated by the 'hots' he has for a young girl. The one who feels led not to attend a Wednesday night meeting may in fact be motivated by his desire to watch Manchester United playing Chelsea on the television. The person led to just students or just the English may be motivated by a genuine desire to follow God, but may also be motivated by laziness, racism, prejudice and may even, like Jonah, be running away from the will of God.

When I first came to South Africa I felt 'led' to move into the townships. What on the surface appeared to be a genuine love to serve some of the most historically oppressed communities of South Africa, was actually a desire by a young Englishman to show these 'White South Africans' a thing or two. My motive was not love but insecurity and a desire for 'one-upmanship' to show people how radical I was. The heart truly is deceitful. In evaluating what we feel God has called us to, we need to dare to take an honest look at the motives and intentions of our hearts. We need to pray like David, 'Create in me a clean heart O God and renew a right spirit within me.'[81]

The example of Peter and Paul

Let's now return to the example of Peter and Paul. The apostles Peter and Paul seemed to have been allocated different spheres of ministry – Paul to the Gentiles (uncircumcised) and Peter to the Jews (circumcised). The book of Galatians tells us that Paul,

'…had been entrusted with the gospel to the uncircumcised, just as Peter had been entrusted with the gospel to the circumcised (for he who worked through Peter for his apostolic ministry to the circumcised worked through also through me for mine to the Gentiles), and when James and Cephas and John, who seemed to be pillars, perceived the grace that was given to me, they gave the right hand of fellowship to Barnabas and me, that we should go to the Gentiles and they to the circumcised. Only they asked us to remember the poor, the very thing I was eager to do' (Galatians 2: 7-10).

The context of Galatians was one of Paul contending for the purity of the gospel. Paul had preached a message of salvation in Christ alone but others had since crept into the church saying it wasn't good enough, and one had to be circumcised as well. Some even thought Paul had 'short-changed' them in his gospel message by missing out some of the essential ingredients of salvation. Paul very unsubtly called them fools if they believed such a thing and reminded them of the pure unadulterated gospel that he had preached to them.[82] He also reminded them of the time he had met with Peter, James and John in Jerusalem and advised them exactly what he had been preaching to the Gentiles. They had been very happy with his gospel message and didn't make him add anything extra into the pot. If they were happy then so the Galatians should be as well.

Grace for particular people – He also told them how the apostles recognised that he had been given grace from God to preach to the Gentiles just as Peter had been given special grace from God to preach to the Jews. Not only were they happy with this but had given them the 'right hand of fellowship' as well. Both had been entrusted with the same gospel – the only differences being the different spheres allocated to them within which to preach.

It seems very clear from the context of Paul's dialogue, that God does call and 'give grace' to certain people for specific peoples and groupings. Peter was especially burdened for Jewish people while Paul and Barnabas were especially burdened to preach to the Gentiles. In Corinthians Paul touches on this when he emphasises that God has given different gifts and ministries to his body as well as different levels of effect of those gifts and ministries. [83] Thus it is not unreasonable to conclude that God does call and burden people with specific people groups – like the 'Zulu nation' or the 'Afrikaner nation'. It would also be reasonable to conclude that God could give some a special burden for students, for example, or even business men.

Heart for other nations as well – It's important, however, to note that despite any primary burdens they may have had for specific people groups, both Peter and Paul still had a heart and passion for other nations as well. Throughout their ministries they never solely ministered to a homogenous grouping – they each ministered to both Jews and Gentiles. They both engaged in cross-cultural ministry. In fact, God in his dealings with them (especially with Peter), went out of his way to ensure that this was the case. Any resistance to relating with other nations or any reluctance to crossing racial barriers was dealt with ever so severely.

Drastic measures – We see a good example of this in Acts chapter 10. Peter was in the coastal town of Joppa and was wavering in his commitment to reach out to other nations besides the Jews. Interestingly Joppa was the town that Jonah fled to when running away from God and didn't want to go to the people of Ninevah. Perhaps Peter too had been resisting God's promptings to go to the nations? Whatever the case, God took some drastic measures to ensure that Peter acted appropriately and didn't forget the other nations.

Peter fell into a trance while he was praying (a very polite way of saying he fell asleep) and received a vision three times telling him to kill and eat animals that according to his Jewish heritage were considered unclean. Three times Peter resisted this call to which God told him, 'What God has made clean do not call common (or unholy)'. [84] It has been said if God speaks to you once he is talking, but if he has to say something three times he is shouting! God was definitely shouting here though Peter was slow to catch on to the meaning and woke up 'inwardly perplexed'. [85]

Peter didn't have too long to think about it when the Holy Spirit told him to go along with three Gentiles who unexpectedly arrived at his door. This probably added to Peters' perplexity as according to his Jewish tradition it was not lawful for him to associate with Gentiles. [86] Peter and his six companions were taken to Caesarea to the household of a Gentile man called Cornelius who told Peter of his own vision in which he'd been told to go to Joppa, find Simon called Peter and to bring him back here to tell him some news.

Understanding dawns – Peter now understood. He suddenly realised that he had regarded other nations of the world to be unholy and unclean. He further recognised his own prejudices and racism along with his own resistance to God's new kingdom. In Christ any nation who fears the Lord is acceptable and clean to God. [87] His eyes were now 'lifted up' and he was free to preach the gospel and lead Cornelius and his household to the Lord. Peter may have had special grace from God to preach to the Jews, but God would not allow him to get away with just going to the Jews – he had to go the Gentiles as well.

Peter to Rome – It's also interesting to note that although Peter started off in Jerusalem he was forced, following conflict with the authorities, to leave for 'another place'. [88] Many seem to think that this 'other place' was Rome, which Peter then made his headquarters for the next 25 years until he died in the days of the Emperor Nero. [89] Peter with his passion for the Jews ended up living and ministering in a Gentile-dominated city in a foreign land.

Paul's passion for cross-cultural diversity – Similarly, Paul may have had special grace to preach to the Gentiles, but he was always generous and eager to share the gospel with Jews as well. [90] In fact, rarely do we see Paul ministering solely to a homogenous grouping of 'Gentiles alone'. Even in Acts 18 when Paul frustratingly exclaimed, 'From now on I will go to the Gentiles'[91] (following a failed effort to witness to some Jews), only a few verses later he was once again reasoning with Jews in the synagogue at Ephesus. Diversity was passionately on his heart. It was even something he was willing to publically confront Peter over when he sensed Peter was compromising in this area.

In Galatians chapter 2 we witness a head-to-head confrontation between the two great apostles. Peter had been to visit Paul in Antioch where he happily fitted into the diverse church lifestyle fellowshipping with both Jewish and Gentile Christians, sharing meals together and breaking bread with one another. One day, however, an intimidating group of Jewish believers arrived in Antioch from Jerusalem. Peter, fearing what these Christians might think, withdrew and separated himself from eating with the Gentile converts. And then, to make matters worse, key leaders such as Barnabas along with other Jewish Christians also withdrew and followed Peters' example.[92] Paul was furious for a number of reasons.

- Firstly, by Peter not eating with the Gentiles he was communicating a message that their salvation was not complete – that he believed they needed to be circumcised to be fully saved. Paul could not allow this and publicly rebuked him for his play acting and hypocrisy. The centrality of the truth of the gospel was at stake – that all sinners, both Jew and Gentile are justified by Christ's work on the cross and not by any 'works' that we may do.

- Secondly, the church's witness to the nations was at stake. Salvation in Christ alone is visibly demonstrated by 'one new man' in Christ – Jew and Gentile together in God's church. Not to eat and fellowship with the Gentiles communicated a false testimony to the world of who God is and what Christ achieved by dying on the cross. There was no way Paul would allow Peter to compromise on the gospel and to settle for just mixing with the Jews – deeper purposes of God were at stake.

Racial diversity is a prophetic burden from God. Grace to minister to specific people groups must slot into the larger vision of reaching all the nations of the world. Any burden we have for specific nations, sociological groups or peoples of this earth that does not spread and reach out to other nations as well, is no true prophetic burden from the Lord. We serve the individual 'peoples' of this world by helping them to understand God's heart for the nations around us. We serve the nations of this world by bringing them into contact and fellowship not only with God, but one another. Failure to do so is a compromise on the very heart of the gospel!

Last words

This 'cross-cultural thing' is for all of us! Crossing cultural boundaries is a God issue, relevant to all Christians of all countries and all nations. Just as all are called to go and make disciples of all the nations, so all are called to cross the racial, cultural and economic barriers that separate those nations. Not all will go to the ends of the earth but all can 'lift up their eyes' and stretch out their arms to the nations in their midst. Let's not exclude ourselves from such a call or be intimidated by those especially gifted to cross such boundaries. Rather let them provoke and stir us to greater love and exploits. And, let those of us who feel especially burdened and called to reach out to specific people do so with wide arms, stretched out like Jesus to embrace and connect all who would come to the cross.

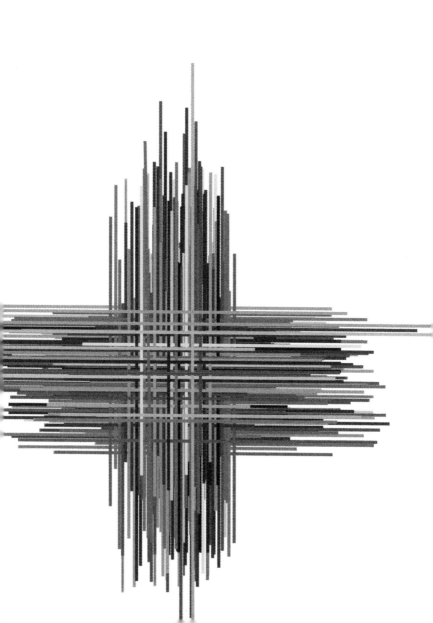

4 Freedom together

> 'If you have come to help me you are wasting your time, but if you have come to work out your liberation together with mine, then let us work together.' (Aboriginal woman)
>
> 'Church community adds a new dimension to the expression of the gospel. It is here that the lonely are added into families and the orphans find mothers and fathers. It's where the rejected find acceptance, the voiceless find an ear who will listen to them, the sick find healing, the HIV positive find support and sinners find deliverance.' (Nigel Measures)
>
> 'Jesus obviously wasn't gathering followers from the moral and spiritual upper-class of society. Jesus wasn't recruiting tried and tested and proven fighters, highly disciplined troops for the eschatological warfare that was imminent. He was openly inviting the hurt, the diseased, the rejects, the sick and the sinners… Any time we target our invitations to the people we assume are especially useful to the kingdom – the prominent, the wealthy, men and women with proven leadership abilities and skills that can benefit the kingdom – we are ignoring the way Jesus went about it… He said 'follow me' and ended up with a lot of losers. And these losers ended up, through no virtue or talent of their own, becoming saints. Jesus wasn't after the best but the worst. He came to seek and to save the lost.' (Eugene Petersen)

Several years ago on an especially cold and wet winter's morning I was visiting folk in a small shack area of Cape Town known as 'Palm Tree Community', [93] where approximately 22 so-called Coloured families lived in very impoverished conditions. There was no running water on site, no electricity and, of course, no sewerage system. One elderly couple called

Jann and Katrina, lived inside what had been at one stage an old farm well. Jann was affectionately known as 'Jann in die dam'[94] because of where he lived. To enter the 'dam' (the well) one had to crawl through a small door and then sit precariously upon wooden slats situated about twenty feet above water.

That particular morning I was not in a good place. Lisa and I had been married for nearly two years and had been trying for a family, but struggling to succeed. Lisa had already suffered one miscarriage when she was five months pregnant, losing a beautiful baby girl whom we named Jessica. The same had recently happened again, though this time when Lisa was three months pregnant. That day people were approaching me from all sides asking for 'sail' (black plastic sheeting) that could be used to cover the wooden and corrugated iron shacks to prevent rain coming inside. I was choked with emotion over the loss of my second child and wanted to scream and tell people that I didn't give a '*#@^!%*' about their sail and why wouldn't they just leave me alone?

Somehow, I found myself at the home of a lady called Margaret, who invited me inside her small shack for some tea. Margaret was Jann's neighbour and had been introduced to me the previous year following the death of her one-year-old son. As we drank tea together, Margaret shared with me again about the loss of her son, her pain and all that she had been through, and as she spoke God used her to bring healing to my heart. As she prayed for me in a language I hardly understood, I felt the 'dam walls' of my heart come crumbling down and my tears streamed that up till that point had refused to flow.

I went away that day humbled and amazed by God's grace. Margaret was not someone that I knew well and naturally speaking we had little in common together. From a worldly point of view, she was 'poor and uneducated', while I was a middle-class Englishman with a Geography degree. I had gone into Palm Tree to help her (and others), yet that day the tables had turned and she helped me. How could this happen? She was not a person close to me or someone I could say was a friend. Our lives had only interacted very briefly and today she is not even part of the church community I lead. Yet God used her to impact and change my life. If he could use someone like Margaret through such a fleeting encounter, imagine what he can do if such diverse lives are built into community together breaking down the dividing walls of economics, education and culture!

Crossing economic boundaries

It's only logical that if we are to go the nations of the world, not only will we encounter people who are different to us in culture, language and traditions, but also in class, education, wealth and socio-economic status. In other words, we will cross socio-economic boundaries as well as cultural or racial boundaries. In South Africa the two are intrinsically linked. The vast majority of poverty in South Africa is still seen amongst the Black and Coloured communities. Since 1994 and the abolition of apartheid South Africa has witnessed the emergence of a wealthier Black middle-class, as well as increasing evidence of 'poor Whites,' but there is no escaping it – the vast majority of the nations poor are Black. Hence, to engage cross-culturally in South Africa is almost impossible to do without also encountering poverty and socio-economic differences.

This is also true elsewhere in the world, where many of us may be open to handling cultural differences but somehow get caught short when encountering differences in wealth and class, poor and rich. A businessman friend of mine in The UK commented to me one day on his frustrations trying to make friends with someone from the local caravan-park. He said, 'We're just so different. I don't know what to talk to him about and I feel uncomfortable inviting him to my house. I've got so much money and he has nothing so I'm never quite sure what he is thinking.' This raises questions like, what does it mean for the church to cross the economic boundaries of our respective societies and remember the poor? Must all Christians 'help the poor' or just those who are gifted to do so? If remembering the poor and crossing economic boundaries is on God's heart – what does that mean for the church in practice?

To answer these questions it is helpful first to establish who we mean by the poor, as well as catching something of God's heart in this area. Knowledge of this will then help us establish our response and any practical implications for God's church.

Images of poverty

To mention 'the poor' will, for most of us, conjure up a variety of images in our minds. For some it could be dirty, poorly clothed, street sleepers queuing in long lines for hand-outs of soup, food and clothing. For others it could be starving Aids-stricken African refugees at the mercy of child-soldiers. To others it could be those from the slums of India scratching through the rubbish dumps frantically looking for anything that can be salvaged. Elsewhere, it could be a 15-year-old teenage girl from the council estate in Essex, England who is now on government benefits and child support, or those from the ghettos of inner city New York, Washington and Chicago. Images are varied and many.

Using this generic term, 'the poor', however, can give a rather nebulous idea of some strange grouping of people out there (wherever out there is) who are poor'. There can be a sense of us and them – us who are not poor and them who are poor, they who have nothing and us who need to help them. Are the poor such a clearly defined grouping for all to see?

Who are the poor?

Biblically many types of people could fall into the category of those who are addressed and referred to as the poor, for example, the widows and orphans, the aliens, the hungry, the thirsty, the stranger, the naked, the sick, the fatherless, those in prison, the oppressed, the exploited, the mistreated, the lonely, the poor in spirit, the defenseless, the slaves, the uneducated and those without shelter. [95] This is by no means a comprehensive list, but it doesn't take much to realise that the poor are more than just people begging by the side of the road. As Floyd McClung says, 'Poverty is more than just having no money, it is not having the freedom to make choices about one's own destiny.' [96] In fact, there are many complex challenges, issues and difficulties that the poor in our societies today are likely to face. For example; hunger, lack of housing, family beak down, rejection, drunkenness, awareness of sin, prison, lack of education/ schooling, hurts, abuse, sickness, working class/middle class divide, western/third world divide, lack of support, overlooked/ forgotten, despised, hard life, exploitation, lack of care/love, fear, lack of power/authority, frustration, despair/despondency, lack of access to education, lack of purpose/vision, inferiority, injustice, patronisation, lack of access to basic needs, feeling like they are a problem, acceptance, voiceless, lack of dignity etc. [97]

The poor, therefore, are numerous, covering a vast expanse of people from the aliens and refugees to the parentless, defenseless, exploited, rejected and sick, along with the destitute and those in need of the basic necessities of life. Generally speaking, they are also those who are overlooked and deemed of little value in the eyes of the world. They are the 'stumps' of society who are commonly forgotten, despised and rejected, but it is to such poor that the church is called to remember!

Remembering the poor is a 're-building the wall' issue

Crossing economic boundaries and remembering the poor is a crucial issue for the church today and is central to all of God's purposes for the nations. The entire Bible, of course, talks much about the poor. One book that gives us a glimpse of God's heart in this area is the book of Nehemiah. Not only does Nehemiah give a historical account documenting the events around the rebuilding of the walls of Jerusalem, it also stands as an amazing prophetic provocation to see restoration in God's church – the church restored and re-built to be all she is meant to be.

As one reads the book one is faced with chapter 5, a seemingly misfit chapter where sandwiched between various accounts of construction work, leadership challenges, battles and opposition; Nehemiah stops everything to remember the poor. Why would he stop such important kingdom-advancing work in order to remember the poor? What did the poor have to do with rebuilding the walls? Well, seemingly for Nehemiah, remembering the poor was not a peripheral issue to be taken or left as one pleased – it was a re-building the wall issue that was entirely central to God's purposes for that generation.

Famine, debt and slavery

In the midst of all the activity being carried out by the people of God; men, women, children and families were suffering. Indeed, they were suffering for a number of different reasons. Some had been so busy 'serving the Lord' and rebuilding the walls that they hadn't had time to grow food, and therefore were going hungry. Others had been affected by natural disaster and famine in the land, while still others had gotten into severe debt beyond what they could repay. [98] Furthermore, heavy taxation by the Persian government had added to their burdens, and was made worse by 'loan-sharks' in their midst who exploited their own people and charged astronomical interest rates. [99] Some families had gotten so desperate that they had even sold family members into slavery to the foreign nations around them. Ironically, Nehemiah had been buying people out of slavery only to discover his own people had sold them into slavery in the first place. [100]

Nehemiah's example

The situation was not good and Nehemiah too was not without blame. He, also, had been charging interest to his own people. His response, however, was to deal with this head on and he told the people that what was happening was not good. [101] They had to stop what they were doing, release people from their debts and stop charging high interest rates. Nehemiah also did the same, repented of his ways and further shared of his possessions by killing his own cows and sheep to feed the people around him on a daily basis. Remembering the poor was not something that could be separated from rebuilding the walls of Jerusalem – it was a re-building the wall issue.

The one could not happen without the other. It was essential that the poor were helped and wrongs put right, not only because it demonstrated the mercy and grace of God, but because the poor were valued children of God with an important role and part to play in God's kingdom. Men and women, common and educated, goldsmiths and perfume makers, rich and poor were all needed in rebuilding the walls. When it came to the purposes and plans of God none were excluded on the basis of wealth, privilege and education – all had a part to play.

The same is true today – if the church is to be restored to be who she is meant to be, we must not forget the poor. Failure to do so leaves the walls of the church down, vulnerable and open to attack as well as impotent in her witness to the nations. To remember the poor is not a peripheral issue for the church to take or leave if she pleases – it is crucial for every Christian, every local church and every church movement throughout the world. Remembering the poor is a 're-building the wall' issue.

Why are the poor on God's heart?

Why then are the poor so important to God? Is it that they are more righteous and worthy than the rich? No, the poor are sinners just as the rich. When we at Khanyisa first responded to the HIV epidemic in our midst, we witnessed a number of terrible things happenings among our poorer church members. Some had tried to evict lodgers from their shacks because they were HIV-positive. Others had refused to attend cell groups because they were fearful of being contaminated by an 'AIDS person'. We even saw HIV-positive people selling their food parcels in order to buy alcohol and get drunk. These were 'my' people within 'my' church that I had to shepherd and disciple. By the end of it I was under no illusions that there was anything inherently good or righteous about being poor!

Character of God – The poor, however, are definitely on God's heart. Though God is not against the rich [102] and certainly is not a God who romanticises poverty, everything in his very character and nature seems to cause him to move in their direction.

- God is gracious and compassionate and hears the cries of the afflicted. [103] He is moved and will respond to those who call upon him.

- He is a God of justice described as, 'the terrible God who is not partial and takes no bribe. God executes justice for the fatherless and the widow and loves the sojourner, giving them food and clothing.' [104]

- He consistently reveals himself to be on the side of the needy and against those who oppress them. [105] Freeing the oppressed is an expression of his kingdom and rule in the earth.

- He is also a God of mercy and delights to show mercy to undeserving people. Just as Nehemiah bought people out of slavery, so Christ has done for us. We serve a merciful God who paid the price to redeem from every tribe, tongue and nation, those who were slaves to sin.

Glory of God – God's glory is also at stake, as the poor are central to his purposes in the nations. God delights to use,

'What is foolish in the world to shame the wise; God chose what is weak in the world to shame the strong; God chose what is low and despised in the world, even things that are not, to bring to nothingness the things that are, so that no human being might boast in the presence of God.' (I Corinthians 1:27-29)

He loves to show mercy to those who most need it since it magnifies his name the most!

The Old Testament prophets spoke of a time when the Kingdom of God (rule of God) would be manifested through His people (the church). They prophesied of an age of justice instead of injustice, of 'good news to the poor' in which the poor would not only be reached by the gospel, but the poor themselves would become 'oaks of righteousness' and a 'planting of the Lord for the display of his splendor'.[106]

In other words, the work of God in the lives of the poor was to reveal something of the splendor of God to the nations of the world. When Jesus came, he declared that he was inaugurating what the prophets had spoken about and that the Spirit of the Lord was upon him to preach 'good news to the poor'.[107] Peter and John were poor, unschooled, uneducated and common fishermen. They were not 'high' people in the eyes of society, yet people marveled when they heard and saw them, realising that they had 'been with Jesus.'[108] Such was the work of Jesus in the lives of the poor that the glory of God was visibly evident to on-lookers around.

Kingdom of God – To remember the poor is a kingdom issue – Jesus came into this world preaching the kingdom of God – delivering people out of darkness into the kingdom of his Son. He not only preached salvation, but led people into a new way of living and loving – a whole new outlook on life under the rule, lordship and values of the King of Kings. As the sick were healed, the oppressed delivered, sinners received grace and mercy, injustice and exploitation stopped – this was the kingdom of God breaking like light into darkness and demonstrating God's rule on the earth.

Just as Jesus was commissioned to bring in the kingdom of God, so we as God's church have been entrusted to do the same. Jesus prayed, 'As the Father has sent me, I am sending you'.[109] Thus, as David Devenish says, we are to have a kingdom perspective that should affect 'how we help the poor, how we conduct ourselves in the world of work and business, how we work for justice, how we show compassion for street children and drug addicts, how we see the oppressed set free.'[110] It should also affect our attitudes and behaviour in the way we view people from other races, communities and socio-economic backgrounds, the way we view our money and possessions, the way we get married and the way we settle our differences. It's hard to escape it – the church is called to remember the poor.

What does this mean in practice?

Nehemiah and his people despite many obstacles and much opposition had a 'mind to work'[111] when it came to the vision that was set before them. Nothing was to deter them, bring them off the walls or hinder them from fulfilling what God had told them to do.[112] The poor were not an inconvenient distraction hindering the people of God from doing what they were meant to be doing – they were passionately on God's heart and central to his purposes in the restoration of Jerusalem. Nehemiah caught something of this heart and hence became mindful of the poor within all that he was doing. We too need to be mindful of the poor if the church is going to see the many nations of this world reached for the gospel.

The apostle Paul also became mindful of the poor within God's church. This was an apostolic burden that gripped his heart as well as the hearts of other apostles such as James and Peter.[113] Paul, however, was not only passionate about remembering the poor, but Galatians tells us he was eager to do so as well.[114] Such should be the case for Christians and local churches today – not only mindful of remembering the poor, but eager to do so.

The remainder of this chapter, therefore, will explore four ways we are to be mindful of the poor and eager to cross the socio-economic boundaries of our societies:

- Preach the gospel to the poor
- Help the poor
- Pursue relationship and fellowship with the poor
- Build together with the poor

1 **Preach the gospel to the poor**

The poor, like anyone else, need to hear the message of salvation found in Jesus Christ alone. Jesus said, 'The Spirit of the sovereign Lord is upon me to preach good news to the poor'.[115] Jesus is good news to the poor; therefore, any response that does not include sharing the gospel of Jesus Christ is falling short of what it means to remember the poor. As Gordon Macdonald says, 'The world can do anything as well as or better than the church. You need not be a Christian to build houses, feed the hungry or heal the sick. There is only one thing the world cannot do – it cannot offer grace.'[116] The church should be at the forefront of crossing the socio-economic boundaries in our societies to communicate the message of God's grace to the poor.

2 **Help the poor**

A second area of action, and one that probably most readily springs to mind when considering the church's response, is that of reaching out to the material and physical needs of the poor. As individual Christians, local churches and church movements, we have an apostolic mandate to reach out and minister with hands of hope to the practical, physical and material needs of the poor around us. Pure and undefiled religion, as the apostle James says, is 'to visit orphans and widows in their afflictions'.[117] It's no good, he expounds, to share of the good news of Jesus and not demonstrate it by helping with practical needs as well.[118] The two are meant to go together.

In 1988, Newfrontiers, my own family of churches were especially provoked to action in this area following a sermon preached by Simon Pettit, in which he challenged us to remember the poor. In the months that followed, many individuals and local churches made intentional efforts to reach out across the socio-economic boundaries (some for the first time), with hands of hope to the poor in their midst. Here is a list of some of the areas of response;

'Addiction – drug and alcohol abuse; Advocacy and legal – being a voice for the voiceless; Agriculture and Horticulture; Asylum seekers and refugees; Children and Young people; Clothes and food distribution; Counseling; Disability, Mental health and Special needs; Education; Elderly; Emergency relief; Ethnic Minorities; Family and Community Support; Health; HIV/AIDS; Financial advice (including debt advice); Housing and homeless; Human trafficking; Marriage and relationship advice; Micro enterprise and business; Pregnancy crisis; Prison and ex offenders; Sex workers; Employment and skills training; Water and sanitation.' [119] *(Newfrontiers magazine 2009)*

Many churches, of course, have been active in their response to this apostolic mandate for a very long time, while others of us are more recently waking up to its importance. It is crucial, however, that churches do 'wake-up' in this regard. As Ronald Sider says, 'There is no greater menace in the church than a born-again Christian without a social conscience.' [120] None the less, though there is always room for improvement and growth in this area, there is great evidence of God's church not only crossing economic boundaries to preach the gospel, but also demonstrating it by caring for the needy as well.

3 Pursue relationship and fellowship with the poor

A third area of response, however, is not so readily demonstrated in the church's efforts to remember the poor – that of seeing the poor added into genuine church community and fellowship and relationship with others who are not poor. The fullness of the good news of Jesus Christ to the poor is not only sharing the salvation message and caring for their material needs, it is seeing the poor added into relationship within the church body. Remembering the poor involves proximity, relationship, interaction and fellowship that can only be found in real church community.

Church community adds a new dimension to the expression of the gospel that cannot be experienced through ministry alone. It is in community that the lonely are added into families, the orphans find mothers and fathers, and the widows find husbands, sons and daughters. It's where the rejected find acceptance, the voiceless find an ear who will listen to them, the sick find healing, the HIV positive find support and sinners find deliverance.

The Poor are more than a ministry – Many local churches have fantastic ministries reaching out to the poor and marginalised of societies but struggle when it comes to seeing them added into church family. The temptation is to regard the poor as a mere ministry at the side of the church (people the church helps) but not necessarily as integral members making up the life and health of the body. Even the language that we use can reinforce this attitude and practice. We talk of ministry 'to the poor' rather than ministry 'with the poor'. This may sound pedantic but such language can reflect deeper rooted attitudes and behaviour. There can be an 'us and them' mentality that, at best, is rooted in ignorance and, at worst, is rooted in superiority – they need me but I don't need them.

We need to get beyond seeing the poor as a ministry to be helped but as fellow brothers and sisters in the church with whom we work out our freedom together in Christ. An aboriginal woman once said;

'If you have come to help me you are wasting your time, but if you have come because your liberation is bound up with mine, then let's work together.'[121]

This is a helpful comment to take note of when discerning what it means to remember the poor. It is more than doing something for these people, giving them the gospel or giving money to help them – they also help us! The poor are valuable and important to God and are not only those we must help but those God would use to help us and set us free if we will allow him to do so.

Fellowship with the poor – Jesus never saw the poor as a ministry of people to be helped. Yes – he ministered to their spiritual and physical needs, but he also became friends with the poor and had his needs met by them. It was a two-way relationship in which Jesus fellowshipped and shared in the lives of uneducated and common fishermen, despised lepers and overlooked women. Jesus had his physical, emotional and, at times, spiritual needs met by such people. He ate with the poor, was in proximity with the poor, prayed for the poor and encouraged the poor to pray for him. [122] Jesus' response to our poverty was never merely to give us the gospel or minister to our needs – it was to bring us into loving fellowship and two-way relationship with him. The church should do the same as she seeks to remember the poor.

Relationship changes everything – The fullness of the gospel of Jesus Christ takes on a whole new meaning when in community. It is one thing giving food to someone begging at the side of the road or donating money into a fund to help street sleepers or HIV orphans. It's another thing, however, when responding to one's friend who is struggling and in need. The book of James says,

'If a brother or sister is poorly clothed and lacking in daily food and one of you says, 'go in peace, be warmed and filled', without giving them the things needed for the body, what good is that?' (James 2:15-16)

The words brother and sister imply closeness and relationship, something more deep and intimate than a casual acquaintance or a one-off encounter. How can we fail to respond in compassion when it's our friend who has no food on the table or our brother who is struggling to raise money for his studies? This was the case in Acts chapter 2 where;

'All who believed were together and had all things in common. And they were selling their possessions and belongings and distributing the proceeds to all, as any had need.' (Acts 2:44-45)

Who wouldn't do such a thing for a fellow brother or sister?

Relationship further challenges the presumptions, stereotypes and assumptions that the wealthy and educated can make about the poor and vice versa. Paul exhorted Philemon to undergo a change of thinking with how he viewed Omnesimus, his once runaway slave. Paul had sent Omnesimus back to Philemon so they could be in fellowship and community together. Philemon, however, had to stop judging Omnesimus and relating to him as just a slave (and a disobedient one at that), but had to cherish him as a beloved brother in Christ. [123] Real fellowship across socio-economic boundaries will change the worldly order of things and affect how we treat and perceive one another. Such is the power of community.

Proximity, friendship, relationship and fellowship, therefore, are all part of what it means to remember the poor. This, of course, is not an easy path as building real relationships across the socio-economic divides will inevitably bring a multitude of uncomfortable challenges that need to be overcome. [124] Yet this path of fellowship is not one that should be avoided because it's not comfortable, but rather eagerly desired and sought after if the church is to truly remember the poor.

4 Build together with the poor

The fourth area of response to truly remember the poor, and one that is largely neglected by the church today, is seeing the poor like everyone else, caught up in God's purposes and finding their place in the body of Christ.

Ministry, mission, gifting and purpose are not privileges confined to the middle-class, the educated or the rich and wealthy of this world. It is a New Testament expectation that all who are children of God will be 'living members' of the church building up the body of Christ. The poor are no exception to the rule. God, in fact, especially delights to use the 'weak' and 'foolish' in the eyes of this world to shame the wise and strong.

Oaks of righteousness – The prophet Isaiah gave insight into this when he prophesied about the coming Messiah inaugurating a new age of justice instead of injustice. He said that good news would be preached to the poor, and that the poor would not only be helped and released from captivity, but also caught up in the purposes of God. They would be called;

'… oaks of righteousness, the planting of the Lord, that he may be glorified. They shall build up the ancient ruins; they shall repair the ruined cities, the devastations of many generations' (Isaiah 61:3-4)

Purpose and mission – The poor have an integral part to play in seeing the 'ancient ruins' repaired and rebuilt. The gospel is not only an invitation to freedom and new life worked out in relationship, it is also an invitation to purpose, action and mission. It's a call to 'rebuild the ancient ruins' and repair devastated cities!

Jesus didn't just preach good news to the poor, bind up their broken hearts and set the captives free. He also equipped, released, anointed and empowered them for ministry. The poor were caught up in the purposes of God. He gave authority to the poor to go and cast out demons. He gave gifting to the poor and invited the poor to join his leadership team alongside himself. He commissioned the poor with responsibility to preach the gospel and make disciples of all nations. Jesus respected, valued, listened to and appreciated the poor, so much so that he commissioned them to go and make disciples of all nations.

Ministry together – The gospel brings dignity, value, freedom and release. The poor must be raised up and find their place as apostles, prophets, pastors, teachers and evangelists in God's church. The poor, along with everyone else, are to discover their gifting and place in the body of Christ, serving and being involved in every area of ministry; with the youth, with the children, in leadership, in discipleship, in counselling, in deliverance, in worship, in Sunday morning meetings, in cell groups, in the prophetic, in eldership, in HIV/AIDS ministries, in evangelism, in mission, in giving the notices, in service, in ministry of helps, in church planting, in taking the gospel to the ends of the earth.

Poor in action – In the early church the poor, like anyone else, were used by God and found their place in the body of Christ. The unschooled and uneducated disciples became apostles sent to the nations. The Christians from among the churches in Macedonia, [125] many of whom were obviously materially poor, wanted to help the church in Jerusalem. Why should they be excluded from the privilege of giving just because they were poor? They had dignity and purpose and eagerly gave out of the little they had to help others elsewhere.

The poor also helped the poor. In 1 Timothy chapter 5 the widows in the church were actively involved in helping serve other widows. The gospel released them from dependency and clothed them with dignity. All were of value and had a part to play building up the body of Christ. Ministry and gifting was not confined to men only, Jews only, educated only or rich only. The body of Christ consists of many members of all types and backgrounds (slave and free) who all partake of the Spirit of God and contribute into the life of the church. [126]

Targeting the rich above the poor – Are some people of greater worth and value and use in the kingdom of God than others? Our theology, of course, will tell us no – all are equal in the eyes of God, but our practice, however, can be something entirely different. Few of us fail to be impressed by the educated 'Saul's' of the world and readily dismiss the 'David's' and 'shepherd boys' around us. Invariably churches all around the world are overlooking the poor.

It is currently very popular among churches, for example, to speak of 'targeting' the major cities of the world. Numerous church movements with a passion for church planting and mission are excitedly strategising about how the gospel can be taken to all our major cities and centres of commerce around us. Cities are the places where the greatest numbers of people live and therefore potentially the places where we can see the greatest number of people added into the kingdom. Cities are the places of influence, trade, money and power. The influential and those with the ability to make a significant difference in society all live in cities.

It is important to clarify, however, who we mean when we say we are targeting the cities of the world. Do we mean the politicians; bankers; lawyers; doctors; industrialists; computer genius's, TV personalities, students and leaders of the future? Churches seem especially eager to target so-called influential people of our cities as if somehow they are of more value and worth than others. Is there a 'cream of the crop' type of person worth targeting above others? Are some people of higher calibre and thus of more value in the church than lower calibre people? What about the poor, the so-called losers (from a worldly perspective), the uneducated, the sick and the orphans? What about those who naturally-speaking aren't quite so influential and whose pedigrees are not so impressive? Are they also worth targeting? Are they the ones we are 'eager' to remember or are the ones we'll think about as a last resort?

Samaritan woman – Jesus' conversation with the Samaritan women at the well in John chapter 4 is a shocking reminder as to who Jesus considered worth targeting. This was a lady who from a worldly point of view, was not of high social standing or in a position of influence in society. For starters, she was only a woman, and a Samaritan woman at that, whose opinions and voice counted for little. To the Jews she was a dog. To make matters worse, she was known for being somewhat of a loose woman whose credibility and standing in society was as about as low as it could get. Yet despite her lack of status she managed to influence the entire town where she lived.

If in any way we subconsciously (very few have the honesty to confess out loud) deem certain people of greater value to the kingdom of God, then we are in great danger of compromising on the very heart of the gospel. I once attended a church planting and mission's conference, where it was taught when planting a new church, 'you shouldn't have too many poor people involved as they will drain the resources and demand too much attention.' An outcry and long debate ensued! Perhaps the reasoning behind such a comment was to consider how best to minister to the needs of the poor? This, of course, demands careful consideration, but should in no way result in the poor being overlooked on the basis of the perceived problems that they might bring. Such thinking may seem logical through worldly eyes but through spiritual eyes can seem foolish and ungodly. Paul viewed Omnesimus, the runaway slave spoken about in the book of Philemon, not as an irritation to be avoided, but rather as a partner in the gospel with a genuine contribution to make. David the shepherd boy was anointed as king above his seemingly more impressive brothers. We must remember that, 'man looks on the outward appearance but the Lord looks on the heart'. [127]

Cream of the crop – It is a dangerous and slippery path to go down when church leaders target certain peoples, sociological groupings or education types in preference to others. Language like the 'cream of the crop' should not enter our vocabulary. Whether we mean it or not it communicates a false message that some people are of more value than others in God's church. Do we honestly believe that students and educated are 'the cream of the crop' and will be of more influence and effect for the gospel than the uneducated? Have you seen some students? Do we honestly believe that the rich and those of high status of society can achieve more in God's kingdom than builders, construction site workers and waiters in a restaurant? Let's be humbly reminded again of Peter and John;

'Now when they saw the boldness of Peter and John and perceived that they were uneducated, common men, they were astonished. And they recognised that they had been with Jesus.' (Acts 4:13)

Eugene Petersen in his outstanding book on the ways of Jesus, highlights this point;

'Jesus obviously wasn't gathering followers from the moral and spiritual upper-class of society. Jesus wasn't recruiting tried and tested and proven fighters, highly disciplined troops for the eschatological warfare that was imminent. He was openly inviting the hurt, the diseased, the rejects, the sick and the sinners…
Any time we target our invitations to the people we assume are especially useful to the kingdom – the prominent, the wealthy, men and women with proven leadership abilities and skills that can benefit the kingdom – we are ignoring the way Jesus went about it… He said 'follow me' and ended up with a lot of losers. And these losers ended up, through no virtue or talent of their own, becoming saints. Jesus wasn't after the best but the worst. He came to seek and to save the lost' (Petersen 2007:239). [128]

In our desire to reach the many people of the cities of this world I urge us all to remember the poor. In our endeavors to reach students, please remember the poor. In our efforts to disciple and train up leaders for the future, please remember the poor. Don't just put the time and effort into discipling those we think will give us a better end result, but be willing to walk the long road of discipling the poor and allowing to the poor to disciple us. In our church leadership remember the poor. In our church structures and staff appointments remember the poor. In our worship teams, in our preaching, and in our Sunday morning meetings remember the poor. In every area of church life and ministry remember the poor – and be eager to do so! If there is going to be any 'erring' or biasness in God's church – then let it be in the direction of the poor.

Last words

In our commission to make disciples of all nations of the world we must remember the poor. To fail to do so is a compromise on the very heart of the gospel. Remembering the poor is not a choice to be taken or left according to whim or fancy, but a necessity for every individual Christian, local church and church movement worldwide. This includes preaching the gospel and sharing the salvation message, as well as practically reaching out to the physical and material needs of the poor around us. It also includes seeing the poor added into genuine relationship and fellowship within the church as well as the poor finding their place in the body of Christ and being caught up in God's purposes. Not only must we learn to worship together we must learn to live together.

As the church seeks to do this, the socio-economic boundaries of our societies that separate rich and poor, educated and uneducated, working-class and middle-class, will have to be crossed. Crossing such divides will invariably bring with it numerous uncomfortable challenges, frustrations, misunderstandings and conflict that many would naturally shy away from. Yet, such difficulties should not be avoided but rather eagerly embraced. As the poor are truly remembered God's kingdom is advanced, the nations are reached, the world is astonished, Christ is discovered and our heavenly Father is glorified. That indeed is a vision to be eager about!

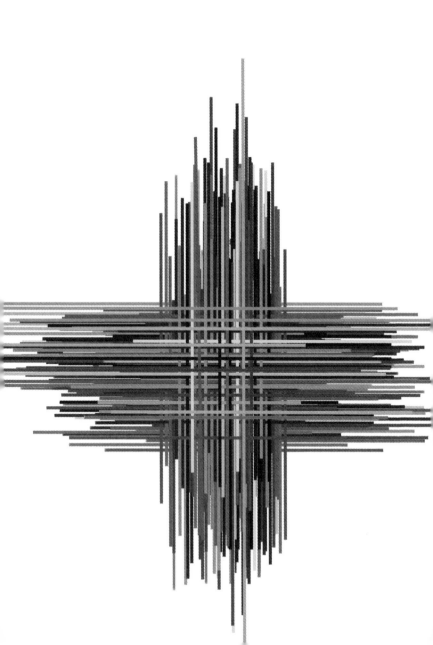

5 The church in all it's glory

> *'A church is the new humanity on display.' (Rob Bell and Donald Golden)*
>
> *'Factors of race, class, sex and national identity shape and define the lives of Christians just like everybody else. No one expects anything different from Christians. The predictability of the Christian lifestyle, or, more to the point, the loss of a distinctively Christian lifestyle, has severely damaged our proclamation of the gospel. We have lost that visible style of life that was evident in the early Christian communities and that gave their evangelism its compelling power and authority.' (Jim Wallis)*
>
> *'We cannot be Christ followers alone. This becomes clear from the moment we decide to follow Jesus along the conversion road. When we open our lives to him, he enters with arms around his brothers and sisters. Uncurling our clenched fists to receive the kingdom's gifts, they are touched by the hands of others. Without option we discover ourselves situated amongst a new family – the family of God.' (Trevor Hudson)*

I love the writings of the English author Adrian Plass. Several years ago he wrote a series of satirical 'diaries', with himself as the main character, highlighting the various amusing antics that we as Christians can get up to in daily church life. On one occasion he memoirs about his son Gerald who is part of a Christian rock band that call themselves, 'Bad News for the Devil!' He decides to go and hear them play and this is what he writes,

'Went to Unity Hall tonight to hear 'Bad News for the Devil' practicing. When I got there, stood outside for a moment listening to a noise that sounded like a piano falling down a lift-shaft with someone trapped under the lid. Turned out to be a number called

'Peace Will Come.' Privately thought a better name for the group would be, 'Rather Encouraging News for the Devil.' (Plass 1987:14) [129]

I wonder how many of us have had similar thoughts about God's church. We know it's supposed to be bad news for the devil but sometimes, if we are really honest, we can feel that some of what we are doing probably makes the devil feel quite satisfied.

Disillusionment with church

Increasingly, there are disillusioned or even hurt Christians who no longer want to be part of church community. It is not uncommon to hear Christians say things like, 'I love Jesus but not the church, I can worship Jesus in my own home – he knows my heart'. Is it really possible to love Jesus and not love his church as well? Is it possible to sing songs like, 'My heart burns for you Jesus' but then we don't love our neighbours around us? The reality is that the more we love Jesus and get to know him, the more we discover what is on his heart and there is no getting round it – the church is on his heart! So much so, the Bible tells us, that Christ loved the church and gave himself up for her! [130]

Though it is healthy to question and examine how we are building church and what is being offered to the world as genuine church community, we must however, be under no illusions – God is passionate about the church!

Jesus is passionate for his church

Church community is top of the 'to do' list for Jesus. He is currently active in building his church, against which we are firmly assured that the gates of hell will not prevail. [131] We are also promised that one day he will return for his beautiful and glorious bride – his church. Thinking of this reminds me of when Lisa and I got married on 13th April 1996. It was a fantastic day with nearly 300 people gathered at the wedding from a whole variety of different cultures, colours and backgrounds. Lisa had planned quite a dramatic musical piece to make her bridal entrance. The song was called 'Sing your praise to the Lord' written by Amy Grant, and the music was to play in the background as she made her entrance into the church building. The song started and I waited nervously as the long classical type musical introduction built up into an eventual crescendo. The doors opened dramatically and Lisa made her grand appearance.

At the appropriate point I turned to see her but I couldn't see a thing. Half the congregation had stood to their feet and had started to clap and 'ululate' [132]. There were cheers and shouting as Lisa, surrounded by numerous mamas circling her and waving scarves, walked down the aisle towards me. I was overwhelmed! It was and exciting and memorable day for both of us, but one that perhaps pales in comparison to the excitement, joy and anticipation that Jesus has waiting for his bride to come and be with him for ever in eternity. We may question God's church at times but one thing we must not doubt, God loves his church and one day he is excitedly returning to get her!

Church is community

Church is community. This, as Jim Wallis says, 'Is the underlying great assumption of the New Testament.' [133] From the book of Acts, right through the epistles, church is presented as community. Pictorially the church is presented as a body made up of many members or a holy temple built out of living stones. It is never just one member or just one stone. Only in the context of real community – a shared life together with other believers, can the new ways of God's Kingdom be worked out and put into practice. Christianity cannot be walked alone. Only in community can we love one another, [134] build up one another, [135] care for one another, [136] bear one another's burdens, [137] be kind and compassionate to one another, forgive one another and go and make disciples of all nations. [138] God has never been about just saving a bunch of individuals and preparing them for heaven. He has, as Biblical scholars like Gordon Fee suggest, always been about creating a people among whom he can live and who in their life together will reproduce God's life and character. [139]

This means it is impossible to have Jesus without church community. In the same way it is impossible to have a head without a body, so we cannot have Christ without his church – the two are inseparable. As Hudson says,

'We cannot be Christ followers alone. This becomes clear from the moment we decide to follow Jesus along the conversion road. When we open our lives to him, he enters with arms around his brothers and sisters. Uncurling our clenched fists to receive the kingdom's gifts, they are touched by the hands of others. Without option we discover ourselves situated amongst a new family – the family of God.' (Hudson 1995) [140]

This also means that the preaching of the gospel must always result in community. Mission and going to the nations cannot be separated from building local church. The two go hand in hand together as church community is needed to both go and make disciples, as well as disciple disciples! Disciples need to be made by community and added into community as true discipleship only occurs in community.

What does community look like?

The question perhaps is what does this community look like? This is something that Christians all over the world have wrestled with for centuries and we continue to do so today. From small 'house churches' to large 'cell churches' Christians in different ways are grappling with what it means to build church community. What makes church community different from any other community in the world? Opinions are varied and many but I'd like to suggest four aspects of local New Testament church community that are relevant to all local church communities today. Church community is to:

1 Be radical, loving and question raising
2 Visibly display Christ's 'New humanity' – 'one new man' in Christ.
3 Be intentionally seeking unity in the church where there is freedom from divisions amongst true believers.
4 Be a diversity of gifting and people.

1 **Radical, loving and question-raising**

There seems to be no escaping it – church is meant to be radical. How can it not be with Jesus as the head of it? Jesus is God breaking into history and he is still breaking into history today through his body – the church! Every metaphor we come across in the Bible regarding the church is radical and world changing. We are to be salt bringing healing to a rotting and decaying world. [141] We are to be light that shines out in the midst of darkness. [142] We are the aroma of Christ, both to God in heaven but also to those in this world who are perishing. [143] We are the body of Christ – his hands and his feet reaching out with God's love and grace to a lost a fallen world. [144] We are Ambassadors of Christ acting as his representatives while here on earth, reconciling people to God and with one another. [145] We are a chosen race, a royal priesthood, a holy nation, a people for God's own possession, aliens in a foreign world living for another King. [146] We are the army of God, clothed for battle serving a commander and chief who is Jesus. [147] And so the descriptions can go on.

Question-raising Christianity

No matter how we look at it there is an underlying expectation and call that God's church will be different and stand out amongst our respective cultures, families and communities. There is an expectation that in the way we live our lives as Christians, both individually and corporately as God's church, there will be something so different about us that the world will stand up and ask questions!

The apostle Peter had this expectation when he wrote to the Jewish and Gentile Christians in the five provinces of Asia Minor. He exhorted the believers to always be 'prepared to make a defense to anyone who asks you for a reason for the hope that is in you'. [148] Peter knew his people and had confidence in them with the way they were living their lives and acting out their faith in Jesus. He anticipated that their faith and actions together as Christians would cause a stir in the communities around them and that questions would be asked of them. Hence he wanted them to be ready to give an answer to any questions that may come their way.

When I was at school, I was fascinated by my grade 10 English teacher. She was a lady called Miss Gilliland and she was a professing Christian. Miss Gilliland was the sort of person who would stand out in a crowd – long bottle blonde hair, glamorous clothing, high heels and her face plastered in make up. Then of course there were her nails – long, bright red, plastic, false nails! Invariably, in-between her passionate expositions of Wordsworth poems and her 'nail-flicking' to which she was totally oblivious, someone in the class would raise the subject of Christianity. Delighted for a distraction, she would then equally as passionately tell of her faith in Jesus. Time would then run away with us and the class would be over. On leaving the classroom she would then proceed with her now familiar passionate gusto to light up and devour a well-earned cigarette.

Miss Gilliland intrigued me as she was not like any Christian I had ever come across before and was influential in making me think about my own walk with God. It wasn't many months later that I did become a Christian – responding to a gospel message by the renowned Dr Billy Graham, within the hallowed grounds of 'Roker Park', the then Sunderland Football Stadium! In hindsight, however, I'm not sure her 'smoking passion' was exactly what Peter had in mind for being a 'question-raising Christian'.

Diverse loving community

What does the church in action look like that will astound the world and reveal the knowledge of God throughout the earth? Will it be the size of our buildings, or the number of auditoriums and football stadiums that we mange to fill? Will it be our theological knowledge and excellent preaching of the word of God? Will it be the experience and evidence of the charismatic gifts of the Holy Spirit in our midst or signs and wonders with the sick being healed? Will it be the number of social ministries we are doing on behalf of the poor and oppressed in our societies? Will it be our prophetic challenge to kings and governments on issues of abortion and ethics?

These are all excellent and we must give ourselves to these things, yet I want to suggest the greatest need of our time is to build and demonstrate loving diverse local church communities of faith across racial, cultural, class, economic, educational and sociological divides that will astound the world. The church simply being the church that Isaiah prophesied about. The church loving and demonstrating community better than the world around us!

These are all excellent and we must give ourselves to these things, yet I would like to echo the sentiments of Jim Wallis who suggests, 'The greatest need of our time is for 'koinonia', the call simply to be the church, to love one another, and to offer our lives for the sake of the world.' [149] We need to build and demonstrate loving diverse local church communities of faith across racial, cultural, class, economic, educational and sociological divides that will astound the world. The church simply being the church that Isaiah prophesied about that will act as a signal to the nations of the knowledge of God. [150] The church loving and demonstrating community better than the world around us!

Loving better than the world

In the latter part of Jesus' Sermon on the Mount, he addressed some issues regarding our relationships with one another. He first challenged his disciples on how they were to relate to people who naturally speaking were close to them – their brothers and those from similar upbringings and backgrounds, [151] but then he went on to raise the topic of loving people who are very different to us;

'You have heard that it was said, you shall love your neighbor and hate your enemy, but I say to you love your enemies and pray for those who persecute you… For if you love those who love you what reward have you? Do not even the tax collectors do the same? And if you greet your brothers only what do you do more than others? Do not even the Gentiles do the same?' (Matthew 5:43-47)

It's wonderful when we see church communities loving one another, practicing hospitality and caring for one another in a beautiful way. I know many people who have been attracted to churches and in turn into a relationship with Jesus because of the amazing family feel and spirit demonstrated by church communities. I can think of many dynamic church families who are doing this very well, especially when it comes to those we can relate to easily, young married couples supporting young married couples or middle-class business people engaging in authentic ways with other middle-class business people, English with English, Afrikaans with Afrikaans, poor with poor, rich with rich. The list can go on.

Do such relationships and church families glorify God – yes, I have no doubt about it. But let's be honest, even the tax collectors can love those who love them. Even the Gentiles can greet and love those they are familiar with. Lisa and I used to stay in an area called Kenwyn, which is basically a Coloured and Muslim community in Cape Town. We had amazing relationships with those in our street and invariably witnessed fantastic community spirit, especially amongst the Muslim families. Plates of biscuits, cakes and my favourite samoosas were commonly being passed down the road and exchanged from house to house. Muslims also love one another in ways that bring glory to God.

Imagine a church, however, that not only loves those who are like us, but goes one step further and loves those who are very different to us. A church where we not only love as the world around us loves, but we love as Jesus has asked us to love. When we love our enemies and those who previously hated us then the world will wake up and ask questions like, 'How is such a thing possible?' Sadly, this is not always the case and often there is little difference between church communities and any other community. As Jim Wallis says,

'Factors of race, class, sex and national identity shape and define the lives of Christians just like everybody else. No one expects anything different from Christians. The predictability of the Christian lifestyle, or, more to the point, the loss of a distinctively Christian lifestyle, has severely damaged our proclamation of the gospel. We have lost that visible style of life that was evident in the early Christian communities and that gave their evangelism its compelling power and authority.' (Wallis 2006:21-22) [152]

Early church

Why did the early church make such a radical impact on the nations around them? One reason Michael Greene suggests in his classic study of evangelism in the early church was that,

'They made the grace of God credible by a society of love and mutual care which astonished the pagans and was recognized as something entirely new. It lent persuasiveness to their claim that the New Age had dawned in Christ.' (Greene 1970: 120) [153]

Even more astonishing was not just the way they loved one another, but the diverse nature of the relationships that occurred as well. Frequently, early believers were hauled before emperors to give an account for the way they were practicing church community. In the writings of one early church prosecutor who later became a believer, Minucius Felix reports Christians were charged with having,

'No appreciation of social status – because the Christians welcomed all as equals. Tatian spelled out the radical equality so despised by the class conscious snobs of the empire…'we do not make any distinctions in rank and outward appearance, or wealth and education, or age and sex." (Warner 1998: 86) [154]

Imagine that accusation coming to the church today?

The way

It's interesting to note that the early Christian believers were known primarily for the way they lived their lives, rather than what they believed. Before being called Christians, believers were first referred to as people of 'The Way!' The book of Acts records that Saul;

'…still breathing threats and murder against the disciples of the Lord, went to the high priest and asked for letters to the synagogues at Damascus, so that if he found any belonging to the Way, men or women he might bring them bound to Jerusalem.' (Acts 9:1-2)

In other words, the early Christians were known more for the lifestyle that they lived and the way they carried out their lives rather than for what they preached or believed. They were not known as the 'people of the experience' or 'people of right doctrine' rather they were people of 'the Way'. Their faith in Jesus produced a kingdom lifestyle that was visible for all to see. In the context of the early Graeco-Roman world where religious pluralism was the norm, such single-minded devotion to Christ would have stood out like a 'sore thumb'.

Sermon on the mount

Indeed the early church did stand out like a sore thumb as much of their behavior seemed to revolve very much around the teaching of Jesus on the Sermon on the Mount. They were known as a caring, sharing and open community that was sensitive to the poor and outcasts, as well as crossed all socio-economic and racial divides. Their love for God, for one another and for the oppressed was as Wallis says, 'central to their reputation. Their refusal to kill, to recognise racial distinctions, or to bow down before the imperial deities was a matter of public knowledge'. [155]

Wallis further quotes Aristides' description of early Christians to the Roman emperor Hadrian in this way,

'They love one another. They never fail to help widows; they save orphans from those who hurt them. If they have something they give freely to the man who has nothing; if they see a stranger, they take him home and are happy as though he were a real brother. They don't consider themselves brothers in the usual sense, but brothers instead through the Spirit in God.' (Wallis 1986:15-16) [156]

This is what we need today – a radical sense of Christian community where Jesus' message of the kingdom is more than an idea. A community open to all, where people are no longer divided into Jew and Gentile, slave and free, male and female, but where rich and poor, black and white, educated and uneducated, young and old, are reconciled together in Christ working out their freedom as one new person in Christ. Is that possible? Well, Isaiah prophesied that it would be – the lion would lie down with the calf! [157]

2 New humanity – one new man in Christ

A second remarkable aspect of the newly formed church communities witnessed in the New Testament was the unity displayed between once hostile, fragmented, bitter and rival peoples (especially the Jews and Gentiles). [158] The wonder of this especially shines through the book of Ephesians where Paul lets us know that God's purpose in sending Christ was to bring back and unite together all things in heaven and on earth – in him. [159] Whether it was men and women hateful to one another, man and God separated from one another or tribes and nations racist to one another – God's plan was to bring his entire world back together again in unity and see it under Christ as head of the church. [160]

Jew/Gentile division

There are many kinds of division among people in the world today; such as colour of skin, nationality, wealth, class, temperament, gender, education, area of country or language, but historically the Jew/Gentile division cannot be understated.

There was a gaping difference between Jew and Gentile. The
Jews had received grace from God that the other nations
(Gentiles) had yet to receive. Where the Jews should have
humbly shared of what they had and been a light to the
nations, they instead exploited their differences and turned
it into a barrier between them. The Jews looked down on
the Gentile nations as the uncircumcised, as aliens and those
without covenants of promise. They were those who had no
hope, they were those who were without God, they were those
who were of the world – in short they were inferior! The feeling
of animosity, however, was pretty mutual as the Gentile nations
also hated the Jews considering them proud and arrogant.
There was no love lost between the two! [161]

Separating wall

Pictorially the temple of Jerusalem communicated a message of
difference and separation. The centre of the temple contained
the 'Holy of Holies' where it was believed that God was present in
a unique way. Outside the temple building was the court where
the priests performed their sacrificial duties. Beyond here was
the court of the Jews where your average Jew could gather to
worship. Outside was the outer court for the Gentiles to worship
if they desired. If you were in the court of the Gentiles and you
wanted to go into the court of the Jews you were confronted by
a wall separating the two courts. On the wall was an inscription
that informed you that if you were a Gentile and went into the
court of the Jews, you would be killed! [162]

Christ brought down the wall

With Christ's death, however, God did a miracle that triumphed
over the former prejudices of both Jews and Gentiles. Peace
was made! Paul puts it this way when he excitedly informed
his hearers, a mixed group of Jews and Gentiles, slaves and
masters, men and women, Greeks and Romans that Jesus;

*'…himself is our peace who has made us both one and has broken
down in his flesh the dividing wall of hostility by abolishing the law of*

commandments and ordinances that he might create in himself one new man in place of the two so making peace.'[163] *(Ephesians 2:14-15)*

With his death on the cross Christ pulled down the dividing wall. The Gentiles who had been far off had now been brought near by the blood of Christ and they too, along with Jews were included in Christ as God's inheritance. The proof of this was that they also had been given God's Holy Spirit as a seal and down payment of their inheritance to come.[164] Paul likened what God did to the Jews and Gentiles to them becoming 'one new man' in Christ formed by God's Spirit into a single body.[165]

This new body is what Paul calls 'the mystery of Christ… hidden for ages'. The Mystery revealed is that the Jews and Gentiles are now united in one body in Christ. The dividing wall has been broken, the former hostility has come to an end and a new humanity has been created in Jesus. Christ through his body has made peace and reconciled them both to God through the cross by which he put death to their hostility.

Church is the new humanity on display

Furthermore, this new body – God's reconciled and diverse church – is to provide a visible demonstration for all in the world to see of what Christ achieved on the cross. Ephesians tells us this 'new man' is to astound the world. It is to,

'…bring to light for everyone what is the plan of the mystery hidden for ages in God, who created all things, so that through the church the manifold [multi-coloured] wisdom of God might now be made known to the rulers and authorities in the heavenly places.' *(Ephesians 3:9-10)*[166]

The church then is God's new humanity on display for all to see. It is to open people's eyes and even the eyes of angels by providing a visible demonstration of God's 'multi-coloured' and multi-faceted wisdom! It is to provide as Wallis says, 'Living proof that the oppressive and divisive facts of the world system need no longer hold sway and determine the course of men and women… Through it's ministry of reconciliation the Christian community becomes an instrument and foretaste of God's purposes for the world' [167] Community in God's church is to unite diverse peoples together who previously had nothing in common. Now in Christ such people discover that the only thing they have in common is the one thing that matters. People who had previously found themselves on opposite sides of a wall find out that the wall has been destroyed. People who had fought over an endless array of issues realise that peace has been made and there is nothing left to fight about.' [168] Such a church glorifies God and it is to such diverse church communities that we are commissioned and called to build and be part of, to glorify God in the nations.

3 Unity in the church

A third characteristic widely spoken about throughout the New Testament regarding church community is that of unity in God's church. John 17 gives us some interesting insights as we overhear Jesus praying for his disciples and the church on this particular topic.

Unity is crucial because the glory of God is at stake – The chapter starts with Jesus first praying for himself revealing his overwhelming desire to glorify his Father in heaven. Jesus prayed, 'Glorify your Son, that the Son may glorify you. [169] 'Jesus, however, was not only passionate that he would glorify God but that his disciples would as well, and soon directed his prayers towards them and for the glory that they also would bring to God. He especially prayed for God to protect them so that, 'they may be one as we are one.' [170]

Jesus was especially burdened for unity amongst his disciples. This could have come from an honest awareness of their propensity towards arguing with one another. However, the reason he prays is that they may be one 'as we are one'. In other words, unity among the disciples reflects something of the very nature of God – it reflects the Godhead! God in his very being is united – he is the trinity – God the Father, Son and Holy Spirit. Unity displayed by the disciples reveals something of who God is and brings glory to his name. As Duane Elmer says,

'The ultimate goal of our existence is to glorify God and we are most like God when we are in union with one another just as the members of the trinity are in union.' (Elmer 1993:26) [171]

Church unity then is essential to God being glorified in the nations.

Unity affects our witness to the nations – As the chapter develops, Jesus then turns his prayers away from his disciples towards us in the church today – those who would later believe in his name and follow him. He prays,

'I do not ask for these only but also for those who will believe in me through their word that they may all be one just as you father are in me and I in you that they also may be in us so that the world may believe that you have sent me.' (John 17:20-21)

Unity is also an important issue for us today. To Jesus our ability to be united with one another is directly linked to people in the world believing in him. When its members live together in unity, the body of Christ becomes the visible manifestation of the triune God.

Unity needs to be intentionally maintained – This passion for unity displayed by Jesus was a passion that gripped the writings of the New Testament apostles as well. In Ephesians Paul uses the imagery of the body to argue for unity in the church. He appeals to the believers to be,

'…eager to maintain the unity of the Spirit in the bond of peace. There is one body and one Spirit just as you were called to the one hope that belongs to your call, one Lord, one faith, one baptism, one God and father of all who is over all and through all and in all' (Ephesians 4:3-6)

It is interesting to note that Paul addresses unity in the body here, having just shown his listeners that the body is this 'one new man' made up of both Jews and Gentiles. [172] This new unity that has come about by God's Spirit and which is now visibly demonstrated is something we are exhorted to be 'eager to maintain'.

In other words such unity in diversity is something we are exhorted to intentionally lay hold of and maintain. We are to spare no effort in maintaining this unity. We are to apply our whole selves to this – our will, our sentiment, reason, physical strength and total attitude. This is not something we are meant to be passive about but something in which we must be intentional, deliberate and show great initiative. [173] Unity in diversity is not a nebulous thing that just happens amongst Christians omitting any action on our part. No – there is a sense that we should aggressively desire to visibly manifest this unity – this 'one new man' – as a glorious display to the world of who God is.

Unity visibly seen in every local church – Paul's concern for unity in the Ephesians' situation was not just a concern for general unity amongst believers in the church worldwide (though this is an important issue). He wasn't saying it is okay for Jewish Christians to meet in one corner and Gentile Christians to meet in another corner and then for the two to tell the world how much they like each other now. Real unity in diversity cannot be maintained and observed from a respectable distance. Only in close proximity and active community can unity in God's church be worked out in such a way to truly reflect the unity of the Godhead and glorify our Father.

The local church in Ephesus was a diverse community of believers consisting of Greeks and Jews, male and female, old and young, rich and poor. [174] As such Paul had to speak into specific situations of disunity that had come about because of diversity within the Ephesians' congregation. In chapters 4 and 5 he challenged believers about various sins that were happening in their midst that had caused discord and disunity in the body such as lying, anger, stealing from one another, bitterness, drunkenness, slander, sexual immorality and covetness. [175] He appealed to them not to give into this because such division grieves the Holy Spirit. The Holy Spirit is present with them to bring the body to full maturity. They must therefore keep being filled with the Spirit to ensure proper worship and proper relationships. [176] Unity in the body to Paul was something that had to be maintained at all costs.

To the many church communities that Paul wrote addressing unity, most of the divisions were problems that had arisen due to diverse types of peoples all being together within one local church. To the Corinthians he encouraged them to 'agree' and have 'no divisions' and 'be united in the same mind'. [177] To the Galatians he exhorted them to 'walk by the Spirit' so as not to 'eat and devour one another'. [178] To the Philippians he told them to, 'stand firm in one spirit'. [179]. To the Romans he appealed to them to, 'stop passing judgment on one another', nor put any stumbling block in 'your brothers way' and to make every effort to do what leads to 'peace and mutual edification'. [180] In fact, throughout the New Testament one does not get a sense of homogenous neatness with like and like meeting together. Rather the overwhelming sense is one of beautiful, but slightly messy diversity. One does not get an impression of Jews in one place, Greeks and Romans in another; slaves in one church, free in another, rich together but poor on their own. In Acts 6, or example, we see evidence of cultural tensions between Hebrew Jews and Greek Jews. Seemingly the Hebrew Jews were overlooking the Greek widows in the daily distribution of food. This more than likely was not a mere oversight but rather blatant discrimination.

Where there is human diversity there will always be opportunities for prejudice, division and injustice. This, however, does not mean we should avoid such human diversity but rather work all the harder to maintain unity in the midst of diversity. Such unity is crucial to God's multi-coloured church and such unity glorifies God.

4 Diversity in the church

The last characteristic of local church community that I'd like to examine is that of diversity. As we've seen in previous chapters God in his very nature is diverse, which is reflected in the diversity of creation, as well as the diversity of many nations throughout the world. The Bible tells us that heaven will be a diverse community of all tribes and nations bowing before the throne of God. What place is there for diversity in God's church now – both for the church universal and for every local expression of church community?

To answer this I'd like to take us to 1 Corinthians chapter 12 where Paul once again uses the image of the church as a body – this time not to appeal for unity in the church but rather diversity instead. Corinth was a fairly large church[181] and like Ephesus was a diverse and multi-cultural community crossing racial and economic boundaries. The majority of the congregation consisted of fairly poor and uneducated Gentile converts – though there were also Jewish believers in their midst, as well as rich and educated people.[182] It had a number of problems associated with such diversity. There were numerous cliques and factions with various members following different leadership personalities; and some of the wealthier Christians, suggests David Prior, were rather snobbish, wanted to keep to themselves and not eat or share food together with the poor.[183] Furthermore, there were problems with idolatry, sexual immorality, lawsuits against other believers, improper use of Spiritual gifts and many more. This was not an easy situation but throughout the letter Paul graciously and firmly addresses these many issues.

Diversity of gifts – In chapter 12 Paul picks up his picture of the body and fervently argues the need for diversity in the church as a necessary prerequisite for a mature healthy body. His basic concern was over the Corinthians obsession and imbalanced emphasis on speaking in tongues when they gathered for worship. To correct them he emphasised how in the same way a 'body' is made up of many different members so it is in God's church. Within the church there are a variety of differing gifts, ways of serving and different ministries that have all been given by God's Holy Spirit for the common good.[184] For the church to be a healthy 'body' such diversity of gifts and ministries all need to be operating effectively. Imagine what a body would look like if it only had one part – it wouldn't be much of a body – more of a blob and no use to anyone. A body has diverse 'members' such as the hands, eyes and feet all of which need to be functioning properly for this body to be healthy. It's exactly the same in God's church.

Diversity of people – Interestingly, as Paul emphasises the variety of spiritual gifts in the church, he also deems it necessary to emphasise the variety of types of people and their backgrounds that God uses to make up the body of Christ. He says,

'For just as the body is one and has many members, and all the members of the body though many are one body, so it is with Christ. For in one Spirit we were all baptized into one body – Jews or Greeks, salves or free – and all were made to drink of one Spirit.'
(1 Corinthians 12:12-13)

Why would Paul say this? Evidently such diversity of people were all together in the one Corinthian congregation. Paul's belief was that all such people make up the body of Christ and his expectation was that all types of people would use their gifting to build up the body of Christ. They were each living members of God's temple consisting of; Jews, Gentiles, slaves and free, all united and inhabited by God's Spirit and using their respective spiritual gifts to build up one another as they met together. In Corinth, however, the gifting and spiritual contribution of certain types of people was being neglected in favour of more 'spiritual' members.

Certain members of the body, on the basis of their cultural background, education and socio-economic status, were seen as being of less importance and value in the body compared to other types of people. Hence their contributions were not so readily received. They in turn could have also perceived themselves as inferior and as such held back on using their respective gifts. Such can be the case when people of poorer backgrounds come together with the more wealthy and educated of society. Paul, however, deemed it necessary to stress that regardless of one's nationality or culture (Jew or Gentile), and regardless of one's language or social status (slave and free), all who have faith in Jesus Christ are equally placed by the Spirit into the body of Christ.[185] Though they are different, each is equally part of the body as they have been placed there by the Spirit of God. Therefore, they need to be appropriately recognised and valued. One part of the body cannot think they are of less value than the other. Similarly we can't say we don't need various parts of the body.

Last words

Diversity, therefore, is an essential ingredient for local church communities to be healthy and effective 'bodies,' acting as Jesus' hands and feet throughout the world. Diverse peoples of all backgrounds need to find their place in local church communities using their gifting to build up the body of Christ. Such diversity inevitably brings with it confusion and conflict. This is not an excuse to avoid such diversity but rather a call to intentionally maintain the unity achieved for us by Christ's death on the cross. His death broke down the walls that divided us and kept us hostile with one another and his Spirit has united us together into one new 'man' making peace possible among all nations and types of people.

It's this 'peace' that the world needs to see and that we are called to display. Such unity reflects the unity of our God and such unity manifest brings glory to his name. God's church is called to love better than the world around us. The world may be content to remain separate and love those who are similar to us but we must not. Let's dare to go further in our efforts

to make disciples of all nations and see the nations saved
and added into churches that demonstrate for all to see how
the walls that once separated us; race, culture, class, money,
education and status, have all come tumbling down!

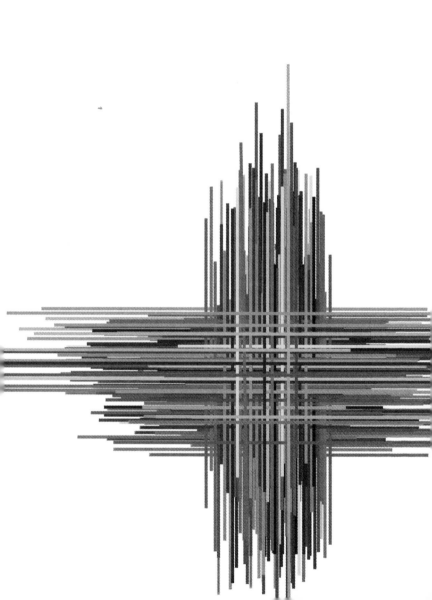

6 Daring to go further

> 'There has been considerable debate in recent years whether a local church could or should ever be culturally homogenous. A consultation on this issue concluded that no church should ever acquiesce in such a condition… Every homogenous unit church must take active steps to broaden its fellowship in order to demonstrate visibly the unity and the variety of Christ's church.' [186] (John Stott)
>
> 'The new humanity is not a trend or when a church is known for attracting one particular kind of demographic, like people of this particular age and education level, or that particular social class or personality type. There's obviously nothing wrong with the powerful bonds that are shared when you meet up with your own tribe and hear things in a language that you understand, and cultural references are made that you are familiar with, but when sameness takes over, when everybody shares the same story, when there is no listening to other perspectives, no stretching and expanding and opening up – that's when the new humanity is in trouble' (Rob Bell and Don Golden)
>
> 'The living witness of the Christian community is intended to demonstrate the future of the world that has arrived in the person of Jesus Christ'. [187] (Jim Wallis)

Lisa is a fantastic hairdresser. Over the years she has worked in top-class hair salons, won hair-dressing competitions, taught hairdressing at a college and slaved many long hours on magazine and movie shoots. In more recent years with the arrival of our two children Ben and Katey, Lisa set up her own hairdressing business that she runs from our home, giving her the time and flexibility to work as and when she pleases. Consequently, I've had the opportunity to watch her at work and have since discovered an amazing and bewildering truth – going to the hairdressers is not primarily about going to have ones hair cut!

It is in fact about ladies (and men) coming and revealing their deepest and most intimate secrets. Lisa has great power in her hands! I cannot believe what people will talk to her about as she snips and chats away, exercising her creative skills. There seems to be no topic untouchable and no secret so secret that cannot be shared. Fears, doubts, insecurities, marital problems, sexual infidelities and so much more are openly and honestly revealed and spoken about. Consequently, Lisa has had many opportunities to give counsel, pray for people and share about her faith in Jesus.

Rather annoyingly, despite my frequent casual attempts to loosen some juicy news out of her, Lisa is frustratingly good at keeping confidences. However, on occasion she may chat to me about some interesting conversation she had that day. One day not long after we left Jubilee church to start Khanyisa a lady spoke with her about her cross cultural struggles. [188] She was quite upset and told Lisa that she had thought that since a group of people had left Jubilee to be part of the new church plant, things would have returned to 'normal'. She anticipated that she would no longer have to sing Xhosa songs and her children wouldn't have to mix with Black children in their children's ministry. This did not happen as Jubilee had in fact continued to grow cross culturally, despite many Black folk leaving to join Khanyisa.

Lisa tried to give her advice on pushing through some of the pain barriers of cross- cultural community, but despite her attempts the lady decided to leave Jubilee to find a more comfortable church where she could mix with people who were more of her own kind. Homogeny for this lady was more preferable than diversity. Not long after this we came across a similar situation while visiting with a church in the UK. The pastor of this particular church told us about a South African family who had left the church to join an Afrikaans-speaking only church in London. They too felt more comfortable being with their own people. Homogeny for comfort reasons is definitely high on some peoples' agenda.

The most segregated hour

This, of course, is not just a recent phenomenon or one totally unique to South Africa. In 1963 Martin Luther King was invited to speak at Western Michigan University in America where he commented on homogeny in God's church. In his speech he shrewdly observed that, 'the church is still the most segregated major institution in America. At 11am on Sunday morning when we stand and sing that Christ has no east or west, we stand at the most segregated hour in this nation.' I wonder if much has changed in the last forty years when we still hear talk of Afro-American churches and White churches, student churches and children's churches, rich churches and poor churches? Homogenous churches and racially divided churches are still a common sight to behold. One reason for this in the United States, argues J Daniel Hays, is that 'a large majority of Christians in that country are probably identifying themselves more with their racial background, with all it's cultural baggage, than they do with Christ and his gospel'. [189]

Homogenous evangelism

Another reason perhaps influencing the prevalence of homogenous churches, as well as individuals desiring to be part of predominantly homogenous communities, is the factor of church growth, mission and evangelism. In the late 1970s Donald McGavran (1897-1990), an early exponent of church growth, stated a principle that had already been used extensively in cross-cultural mission. He said, 'People like to become Christians without having to cross racial, linguistic, or class barriers'. [190] This insight, based largely on rural mission where villages were usually fairly culturally homogenous, led McGavran to develop a 'people-group' approach to evangelism in order to penetrate the mission fields of the world. He was interested in meeting people on their own turf and identifying with the seeker. McGraven noted that 'like reaches like' and that this was more effective when people were not required to leave their homogenous unit and join other people. He also observed that people preferred to join churches whose members looked, talked and acted like themselves and that people became Christians fastest when least change of race or clan is involved. This principle became known as the 'homogenous unit principle'. [191]

Seeker-sensitive churches

This homogenous unit principle has had significant consequences for the church and has played an important part in the modern church growth movement and influenced the development of many churches with a heart for mission. Bill Hybels, the pastor of Willow Creek Community Church, for example, one of the largest churches in the United States, decided to target a particular people group when he planted his church in Chicago. His focus group was primarily un-churched middle to upper class, middle-aged, family, professional people who populated the suburbs around the church. The church, and in particular the services, were designed around the needs and desires of this group, and success was rapid. People flocked into the church and many became Christians. It could be argued that Bill Hybels was simply applying the homogeneous unit principle that people will more easily become Christians if we offer them the gospel in their language without extraneous cultural barriers to overcome. 'The resultant seeker-sensitive movement', comments one author from the Queensland Baptist College of Ministries, 'has influenced churches worldwide'. [192]

Observation

Without doing any empirical studies of my own, my guess is that much of what McGravan and Wagner have argued for is probably correct. Most of us naturally find it easier to relate to those who are most like us and with whom we have things most in common. It makes logical sense that people will more likely become Christians if they are not taken out of their comfort zones too much. It makes logical sense that homogenous churches will grow faster if that most readily meets the needs and desires of the people they are reaching. Certainly most large churches that I know are fairly homogenous either in age, socio-economic group or ethnic group. In Cape Town I know of one church that is targeting the rich and wealthy of the city and they are growing nicely. Another is targeting the students, who in the words of its pastor are the 'cream of the crop' of society. A colleague of mine from Bible College is building a French-speaking Congolese church targeting the ever increasing influx of refugees flowing into Cape Town. A further acquaintance is targeting the middleclass Coloured population of his particular community. All are growing nicely!

In other parts of the world, however, there are many examples of larger fast-growing churches that are claiming heterogeneity because of the many different cultures represented in the congregation. But, in reality it could be argued that many of them are relatively homogeneous because the different cultures represented seldom interact. Their programs, small groups and even church services tend to minister to different cultures and therefore separate the cultures into homogeneous units. [193]

What is the problem with homogenous church?

Even if this is the case – what is the problem with that? What is the problem with homogenous evangelism and in turn, homogenous church? If more people become Christians this way does it really matter? What's the problem with having a church largely for ex-drug-users, or one that is largely upper middle class business people? 'Surely we need to bare in mind the changes in modern life?' says Tim Chester in his examination of the homogenous unit principle. [194] Traditionally, a church congregation was defined by two things that they held in common – the gospel and their locality. Today many urban people live in dormitory suburbs in which they do little more than sleep. There is little sense of neighbourhod. Today community is defined in other ways – overlapping communities of work, family, leisure and shared interest. If the community of people with whom I work is more significant to me than the community among whom I live why not have a church of my work place? If community is defined by common interest rather than common location then why not have interest group churches? What's the problem with homogenous church? Three main criticisms can be suggested:

1 Christian discipleship

One problem is that homogeny misses out on the fullness of Christian discipleship. Homogeny in and of itself is not a sin. It's not wrong for the youth to come together or just the ladies or just the men. It's not a sin for students to want to fellowship and have fun together. There is a place for the old to gather, as well as business men with other business men. Invariably it can be helpful and beneficial for single people to have their point of contact with one another, as it is for married couples. Similarly, those who speak a particular language will want to gather with others who can understand them.

However, there is something we are missing out on if we just walk the homogenous route. If all that people get is from those who are the same as them or similar to them then something is amiss. Rob Bell and Donald Golden remind us that it's a dangerous thing when,

'…a church becomes known for being hip, cool and trendy. The new humanity is not a trend or when a church is known for attracting one particular kind of demographic, like people of this particular age and education level, or that particular social class or personality type. There's obviously nothing wrong with the powerful bonds that are shared when you meet up with your own tribe and hear things in a language that you understand, and

cultural references are made that you are familiar with, but when sameness takes over, when everybody shares the same story, when there is no listening to other perspectives, no stretching and expanding and opening up – that's when the new humanity is in trouble.' (Bell & Golden 2008:156) [195]

Homogeny weakens Christian discipleship. While people may be more likely to become Christians without dealing with their cultural differences, they are less likely to grow spiritually unless they deal with, learn from and embrace these differences. A homogeneous church cannot easily offer the richness and challenge of life that flows from being part of the body of Christ. As Jean Vanier says,

'God seems pleased to call together in Christian communities people who, humanly speaking, are very different, who come from very different cultures, classes, and countries. The most beautiful communities are created from just this diversity of people and temperaments. This means that each person must love the others will all their differences, and work with them for the community. These people would never have chosen to live with each other. Humanly speaking, it seems an impossible challenge. But it is precisely because it is impossible that they believe that God has called them to live in this community. So then the impossible becomes possible. They no longer rely on their own human abilities or natural sympathies, but on their Father who has called them to live together. He will give them the new heart and spirit which will enable them all to become witnesses to love. In fact, the more impossible it is in human terms, the more of a sign it is that their love comes from God and that Jesus is living: 'By this all men will know that you are my disciples, if you have love for one another' (John 13:35). When he created the first community of the apostles, Jesus chose to live with men who were very different from one another: Peter, Matthew (the publican), Simon (the Zealot), Judas, and so on. They would never have come together if their Master had not called them. And when they were together they spent a lot of time squabbling about who was the most important amongst

them. Yes, community life is definitely not easy! But it becomes possible because of the call of Jesus. We shouldn't seek the ideal community. It is a question of loving those whom God has set beside us today. They are signs of God. We might have chosen different people, people who were more cheerful and intelligent. But these are the ones God has given us, the ones he has chosen for us. It is with them that we are called to create unity and live a covenant. We choose our own friends, but in our families, we do not choose our brothers and sisters; they are given to us. So it is in community life.' (Jean Vanier 2001:45) [196]

2 Preferable for salvation

A second problem with targeting specific sociological or people groupings is the subtle danger of deeming certain types of people to be of more benefit for the gospel than others (something that we examined in more detail in chapter four). Suffice it to re-emphasise that though it may not be biblically wrong to develop evangelistic strategies that target specific people groups or people types; if this in any way excludes and overlooks other types of people in the process, or makes them feel to be of less value and worth; we are in great danger of compromising on the very heart of the gospel. Few would probably admit to such a charge, yet it is amazing how many church leaders feel 'led' to target the upwardly mobile of society, but so few put the same effort into reaching the poor. Many will 'unashamedly' target the 'cream of the crop' of society, but ignore the oppressed and overlooked of their communities – the very ones that Jesus, if anything, was bias towards.

3 The reconciling nature of the gospel

A third problem with homogeny in God's church is that it denies the reconciling nature of the gospel of Jesus Christ. Gordon Fee, renowned New Testament scholar, argues that there was no place in the apostle Paul's thinking for homogeneous churches. Such a concept he says lies totally outside Paul's frame of reference' as homogenous churches,

'..cannot maintain the unity of the Spirit that either Ephesians 2 and 4 or 1 Corinthians 12 call for. God by his Spirit has formed into one body a radically new eschatological fellowship that transcends both race (Jew and Gentile) and socioeconomic status (slave and free).' (Fee 1996:70) [197]

The unity of the Spirit therefore, and the expression of 'one new man' in Christ is not just a calling for the church universal but for every local church as well. It is no good having homogenous communities of 'same sorts' demonstrating wonderful fellowship with one another – then they in turn express 'church unity' with different homogenous churches singing 'Simunye' – we are one! The unity of the Spirit needs to be visibly seen in local expressions of church – communities united in diversity. Rich and poor together, old and young, male and female, Black and White, Jew and Gentile, slave and free together in proximity and fellowship with one another.

Such heterogeneous church communities will astound the world. Such diverse communities will act as a signal to the nations of the knowledge of God. One day the whole of God's creation will be brought into community in Christ. [198] In the meantime the church should be eager and aggressive to demonstrate the beginning of that great reconciliation now. As Jim Wallis says, 'The living witness of the Christian community is intended to demonstrate the future of the world that has arrived in the person of Jesus Christ.' [199]

Counter arguments in favour of homogeny

Some people would argue, however, that there is place for homogeny in the church. Tim Chester is one such author who has attempted to come to some form of healthy compromise in the debate between homogenous and heterogeneous church communities. He gives several suggestions that people have raised as to where and how homogeny might be 'acceptable' in the church, and thus not deny the reconciling nature of the gospel as argued . [200] I'd like to briefly examine his suggestions and give a few comments on them accordingly:

1 Firstly, some would argue that homogeny is a principle
   of mission, while reconciliation is a principle of church. In
   other words, it is argued that homogenous groups are valid
   when they are in the context of mission, but as people
   are converted and discipled they must be integrated into
   a church which is diverse in character. A weakness of this
   approach, however, is that it makes a strong distinction
   between mission and church – a distinction which fails to do
   justice to the essential missionary nature of the church.

2 A second suggestion is that the racial mix of a church
   should reflect the multi-cultural pattern of how people
   are relating outside the church. In other words if people,
   for example, in a mixed urban centre are comfortably and
   intentionally relating with one another then we should build
   multi-cultural churches that reflect this. However, if there is
   animosity and hostility amongst different peoples outside
   the church and especially if there are different languages
   involved, it may be wiser to evangelise such groups
   separately and build separate churches that are designed
   for each groups styles and preferences. Such thinking,
   though, seems to forget that the church has a 'ministry of
   reconciliation' (2 Corinthians 5:18), not only between God and
   man, but among different peoples as well.

3 Thirdly, some have argued that the churches of the
   New Testament may have been networks of household
   churches and it is possible that these churches were fairly
   homogenous reflecting the homogenous nature of their
   social connections. The reconciling nature of the gospel
   then found expression in the city wide identity of these
   household churches. This structure then would have allowed
   the apostolic churches to express both homogeny, as well
   as multi-cultural and ethnic reconciliation. For example,
   McGraven and Wagner say, 'The biblical teaching is plain
   that in Christ two peoples become one. Christian, Jews and
   Gentiles become one new people of God, part of the body

of Christ. But the one body is complex. Since both continue to speak separate languages, does not the oneness cover a vast and continuing diversity?'[201] In other words it's okay for local churches to be homogenous provided we express general unity together throughout our cities and nations.

One problem with this argument is that even if the early church did relate in this way, it omits the diverse nature of 'slave and free' found within New Testament households. That in itself would have brought diversity into the church communities. Secondly, it doesn't fully take into account the obvious close interaction of diverse peoples witnessed in the New Testament and the benefits of discipleship that can only happen with diversity as mentioned above. For example, a person struggling with racism can never be discipled into total freedom by remaining in a comfortable homogenous unit and choosing to like those who are different from a distance. True freedom is tested and worked out in close proximity with others different to oneself.

4 A fourth suggestion is that although a homogenous church consisting of a socially powerful group is wrong, there is a place for churches of the socially marginalised in order to prevent further social marginalisation happening in the church. Tim Chester quotes a Tearfund representative in the UK who said, 'When middle-class people come in they destroy the confidence of my people just by the state of their hair'.[202] In other words, it is argued that we shouldn't bring poor and rich together because the rich will inadvertently oppress the poor even further. This, however, seems to be a fearful and somewhat lazy argument that blatantly undermines the power of the gospel. Inevitably there will be very real and potentially difficult dynamics encountered whenever people of diverse cultural and socio-economic backgrounds are brought together. However, just because difficulties are real, that does not mean we avoid diverse community – rather we need to exercise great wisdom in the

way we build community and bring people together. The socially dominant have issues they need to repent of and be set free from, just as the socially marginalised have areas in which they need to experience the healing and freedom found in Christ. God's answer – diverse community!

Every local church should be cross-cultural

All local churches should seek to cross, pull down and destroy the racial and economic divides of society. Cultural and socio-economic diversity are essential ingredients for healthy working local church communities that will astound the world. Diversity in and of itself does not guarantee that there will be unity, reconciliation or genuine relationship and fellowship. Community is more than just gathering a group of different people together in one room. The divisions seen in early church communities are proof enough of that, which is why unity was continually stressed and fought for. Diversity and unity must go hand in hand. The unity brought about by God's Spirit between us needs to be eagerly laid hold of and maintained to form a community of the Spirit that glorifies God. This is a New Testament essential that all local church communities should prioritise to lay hold of and visibly demonstrate for the glory of God.

Such is the endorsement of John Stott and other leading theologians who agree that the church must exhibit its '...multi-ethnic, multi-national and multi-cultural nature. There has been considerable debate in recent years whether a local church could or should ever be culturally homogenous. A consultation on this issue concluded that no church should ever acquiesce in such a condition... every homogenous unit church must take active steps to broaden its fellowship in order to demonstrate visibly the unity and the variety of Christ's church.' [203]

Such is the exhortation of this book – that we as individuals and local churches should take 'active steps' to broaden our fellowship and love better than the world around us. Unity in diversity demonstrates something of who God is – the Triune God! The glory of God is at stake and our witness to the nations is at stake. Many churches may feel burdened with a particular sociological grouping or even specific indigenous communities. However, we will not be serving those people well if we fail to help them grasp God's heart for other nations of this world and people who are different to themselves. True discipleship of the nations will lead the nations into fellowship and relationship with other nations. Homogeny may be comfortable and appeal to peoples' likes and preferences, but it never fully leads us into discovering the greater depths of the knowledge of God. To build totally homogenous church communities fails to lead people into the freedom, healing, love and joy that can only be found in communities that build across racial, cultural and socio-economic divides. They also fail to fully demonstrate Christ's reconciling work on the cross and dim the churches' signal to world of the power of the gospel.

Dare to go further

Does this mean that if a local church community does not express this diversity and evidence of being 'one new man in Christ'; then it is not a true genuine church community? No, as John Stott also says,

'All of us are agreed that in many situations a homogenous unit church can be a legitimate and authentic church. Yet we are also agreed that it can never be complete in itself. Indeed, if it remains in isolation, it cannot reflect the universality and diversity of the Body of Christ. Nor can it grow to maturity.' (Stott 2006:290) [204]

There are many genuine examples of homogenous church communities throughout the world that I believe genuinely love God and love one another. I see God's favour upon these communities. These communities may display 'one-fold' of the glory and splendor of God but not fully enter into to displaying the many-folded, multi faceted aspects of the glory of God. To such churches I say – dare to go further. Dare to glorify God more than you are doing already. Be eager to visibly demonstrate the unity of the faith. Don't love as well as the world loves, love better than the world. Dare to love as Jesus loves. Have faith to walk the uncomfortable path of diversity.

What if a church is genuinely is located in an area where there are no different nations? The reality is in the modern world there are very few remaining single-nation communities. If, however, you so happen to come across one I can guarantee you will still encounter diversity; in education, status, class, sociological divisions, male and female, old and young. The opportunities to shock the world and glorify God with his new tribe are endless. As John Piper tells us, 'the strength and wisdom and love of a leader are magnified in proportion to the diversity of people he can inspire to follow him with joy'.[205] Diverse, united communities will tell this world how great our leader is – King Jesus! Let's go out of our way to bring glory to his name!

7 Becoming faithful friends

> 'Becoming faithful friends is an adventure into personal
> vulnerability. It is not always easy. Often there are
> misunderstandings and unmet expectations. Like any adventure
> the outcome is seldom a foregone conclusion. However
> when we are with someone who accepts us as we are, listens
> attentively to what we share and is committed to mutual
> interaction, courage is given for the first steps in the life-sharing
> experience.'[206] (Trevor Hudson 1995)
>
> 'The unity of the Spirit that is achieved when diverse peoples
> of different backgrounds become Christians should not be
> underestimated. Rich and poor, Black and White all have
> something in common together as followers of Jesus – God's
> Holy Spirit. It should therefore come as no surprise to know
> that that author of cross-cultural diversity is more than able
> to assist in the development of deep, intimate and close cross-
> cultural friendships.' (Nigel Measures)

Being schooled and raised in Elsie's River it was not uncommon
for Lydia Mhlanga to play in the streets together with children
of all racial backgrounds. The implementation of the Group
Areas Act in the early 1960s changed all this when she and her
family were forced to move to Bishop Lavis, a newly designated
Coloured area on the outskirts of Cape Town. The upheaval was
immense and made worse by the difficult home circumstances
that had forced her to leave school to find domestic work,
cleaning White peoples' houses with her mother. Bishop Lavis,
however, became Lydia's home and it was here she remained,
eventually meeting and marrying her first husband Nicholas
Olivier in the summer of 1964.

Family life was immediately thrust upon her as she instantly
became the step-mother of three active boys. The family

increased with the arrival of seven children, as well as an adopted baby girl. Today as a 'mama' in her mid 60s, she has 22 grandchildren and 10 great-grandchildren to keep her busy.

Defending the rights of the oppressed

1976 was a turning point for Lydia when her teenage stepson came home announcing that his friend, Chris Nissen, had been expelled from school. He was accused of being a terrorist. His crime was that of stirring up the passions of Coloured teenagers towards the plight of Black teenagers struggling for the right to receive education in their mother tongue – one they could understand. Lydia and the mothers of Bishop Lavis were shocked. They knew Chris to be a quiet boy who certainly was not violent or aggressive. How could he be a terrorist for merely standing for the rights of his peers? If this could happen to him – it could also happen to their children. They decided to go and visit the principal of Ramsey High School to ask him to give an account for his actions. Unsurprisingly, he was not happy at having his decision challenged but, despite his angry protests, he was forced to relent and Chris was allowed to remain at school – victory number one!

Motivated and energised by their success Lydia went on to fight for the rights of others in her community. Her next challenge was to petition for the Bishop Lavis residents to have electricity in their homes. This was a much longer battle and it was only three years later that they saw the first electric light bulbs enter their homes. This was victory number two, but no sooner had this happened Lydia and her growing family moved away.

Hit with a Sjambok

An opportunity had arisen to move into a three bed-roomed house in Atlantis, 50 kilometers up the West Coast from Cape Town. Though they were now living further away from the city, Nicholas was able to continue his work as a labourer on the railways and Lydia was able to continue her involvement in community issues. Papers had been served on nearly 430 residents who were about to be evicted from their homes for non-payment of rent. [207] It did not take Lydia long to become a community representative and help initiate a protest march to the rent office to stop the evictions. All did not go to plan and the march never happened. Somehow the police heard what was going to happen and before residents could start to move, the police turned on the crowds and used 'sjamboks' [208] to beat both men and women across their backs and chests. Many were hurt that day. Doctors and lawyers involved in the 'struggle' [209] were called for and detailed descriptions of people's injuries were recorded as evidence. Lydia did not need any more encouragement – she was now officially involved in the underground resistance to the apartheid government.

Code name Ten

Lydia's friend was thin – like the number 1 while she herself was more rotund like the number 0. Out of this joke between friends Lydia developed her secret code name Ten (10). It was 1986 and Lydia had to go into hiding from security police for her involvement in politics. Lydia had founded the Federation of South African Women (FEDSAW), a cover organisation working to support women and families of those involved in the struggle – namely within the underground structures of the then banned United Democratic Front (UDF) and African National Congress (ANC). Lydia's responsibilities took her throughout the Western Cape supporting women whose husbands had been detained. She would teach gardening and business skills so families could survive. She helped mothers make arrangements for their children to be taken care of should they ever be arrested. She would train people how to make and throw petrol bombs, as well as remove rubber bullets in the event of being shot by the government forces.

On the run

For three years Lydia lived a life on the run – always using her code name ten in telephone conversations, never using her real name in case the phones were tapped. Wanted by the police she couldn't stay in any one place for too long and frequently moved between hotels and houses of those loyal to the struggle. They were hard and difficult times and Lydia's anger and hatred towards White people grew.

Things did not improve when in the September of 1986, she was unable to attend the wedding of her daughter Mattie. The security police were watching to see if she would turn up and all she could risk was a quick five-minute liaison a few hours after the wedding had finished. It was heart-breaking season for Lydia and made worse when, at the end of that year, her husband died of cancer. Unable to hold the funeral in Cape Town she was forced to secretly bury him in Durban, thousands of kilometers away from home. Bitterness towards the police and White people were by now deeply rooted in Lydia's heart.

Move to Tambo

The following year – still in hiding, Lydia met her second husband Chris Mhlanga (nick named Zizi), a Xhosa man, who was a commander for the 'marshals'[210] in the Western Cape. Her children and family were nervous of her marrying a Black man and even more so when they discovered he lived in a shack area called Tambo Square. Lydia however was determined and, not wishing to crush her husband's dignity, made the move to live in a shack. It was difficult at first adjusting to life in a corrugated iron 'hokkie' with no inside running water and only a bucket for a toilet. However, Lydia soon adapted to carrying water on her head, as well as washing her clothes with the other township Mama's at the nearby stand pipes.

Lydia was readily accepted in Tambo Square due to her involvement in politics and knowing many residents active within the ANC. Of course, it was not long before Lydia was on her next assignment – building a crèche and soup kitchen to accommodate Tambo Square's children while their parents were out at work. On its completion, this not only became a place of refuge for children during the day, but also a useful meeting point for the newly formed Tambo Housing committee. It was here that Lydia and other committee members had strategised to 'sit-in' at the nearby council offices to secure land for Tambo residents to build houses[211]. It was also here that Lydia, in the January of 1992, first met a strange White lady called Angela Kemm – someone whom at first she was not inclined to get on with.

Proudly English speaking

Angela's background couldn't have been more different to that of Lydia's. Born in Mossel Bay along the southern coast of South Africa she, like many South Africans, had been brought up a racist, not allowed even to speak to a person of Colour let alone have them as friends. To complicate matters further, her parents were proudly English speaking and prejudiced against Afrikaners and the Afrikaans language they so readily promoted – racism was in Angela's blood.

Books in brown paper bags

On leaving school Angela trained as a psychiatric nurse for six months before changing careers and entered the world of banking, quickly climbing the corporate ladder and excelling in what she did. Living in Cape Town she met and married her husband Greg in the December of 1972 and three years later they both became Christians. As a recently married couple they moved to the new area of Rondebosch East, which had historically been a Coloured area and was now proclaimed White. Much to their shock and dismay they moved into their house only to find they had been tricked – Coloured people were still living in the area.

God was to use this trickery to change Angela's heart and attitude. Since they were now living in a mixed area, the local Baptist church that they attended re-allocated them to a new home-group led by a Coloured couple called Roger and Wendy Arednse. Roger set about challenging Angela by giving her books to read – political books that were banned under the apartheid government. Hidden within brown paper bags he would secretly pass them to her, which she would later read and return. Questions would fill her mind as she struggled to reconcile politics with Jesus, but through the process slowly found her eyes opening to the suffering people of colour were experiencing in South Africa – even within the very neighbouredhood in which she lived. To the bewilderment of her family and even herself, Roger and Wendy persuaded her to petition door to door for the Coloured people NOT to be forcefully removed from their area – a major turn around from when she first moved in!

Unexpected visitors

Angela's passion and gifting was evangelism and by 1985 she was regularly using her Saturday mornings to go onto the streets and share the gospel. This she would now willingly do within the historically classified White and Coloured areas, but fear still kept her away from the townships and so-called Black areas.

A year later this would change when one evening in 1986, Roger and Wendy unexpectedly brought a Black couple called Themba and Lavinia to the Wednesday night home group. It was the first time any Black person had been inside Angela's house. Lavinia was a health worker and explained how their shack had been burned down and they were temporarily staying with another couple in the group, Howard and Joy de Smidt until their shack was rebuilt. At the end of the meeting, Angela thanked Themba and Lavinia for visiting her home not expecting the reply that she would receive.

Crossroads – where white people die

Lavinia expressed that in her culture, now that she had visited with Angela, it was only right that the compliment be returned. Angela must now come visit at her home in Crossroads (once it was rebuilt)! Verbally Angela agreed to go but secretly thought inside her head, 'No way – that's where White people go to die!'

Joy de Smidt, however, had been to Crossroads once before and offered to take Angela along. Reluctantly, with her excuses squashed, Angela had no choice but to comply with the plan. When the morning arrived she asked friends to collect her three daughters from school just in case she didn't come back alive. Such was the fear and the trepidation she experienced in the process.

What was intended to be a once-off visit somehow back-fired. Shaken by the impoverished living conditions that she witnessed and the amazing love and acceptance shown towards her, she unexpectedly found herself returning the following week to be part of a ladies Bible study. Being an evangelist she came prepared to speak on John 3:16, 'For God so loved the world' but was immediately humbled when one lady spoke from 1 Peter 5:7, 'Cast your burdens onto him because he cares for you'. Her heart was broken and this was the start of the journey that would lead Angela into the townships for the next twenty years.

Phone taps

The relationships Angela made in Crossroads were lasting so it was only natural, when some of her friends moved to Khayelitsha 35 kilometres out of Cape Town, that she would go there as well. Such friendships, however, did not come without cost. The Security Police would frequently stop her, wanting to know what she was doing and where she was going. Angela recalls how one day;

*'They spat on me and said that they wished the 'K****** would kill me as I was a K***** lover and not worthy of them wasting their breath on. They bullied and threatened me regularly and left me feeling unclean by the things they said and did. I would have to go back regularly to God for healing'.*

One day, on hearing a silence followed by a click before getting a dialing tone on her home telephone, she realised her phone line was being tapped. Unperturbed, Angela used the opportunity to speak on the phone about Jesus and give the gospel in as much detail as possible. What Satan meant for evil, God meant for good.

The two meet

In January 1992 Tata Mgijima, a church pastor from Guguletu, took Angela to speak with community leaders in a small shack community called Tambo Square – and so Lydia and Angela met for the first time.

Attracted by the ANC slogans proudly displayed on the shacks of residents, Angela was keen to ask permission to be allowed to make friends within the community and to speak to people about Jesus. The leaders were naturally suspicious – after all she could have been a police informer, a spy or even mad! Surprisingly, much to the upset of her fellow comrades, Lydia found herself granting Angela's request saying, 'Our people need the light'. She later paid for her impetuous response by being assigned the dubious task of following the White lady to see what she was up to.

And so began a journey where the lives of two people from very different worlds began to cross. Lydia kept her distance at first. If Angela gathered ladies in the community to pray, Lydia would remain in the crèche seeming uninterested, but surreptitiously standing close to the open window to hear what was going on. The housing committee continued to meet regularly in the crèche and it was not long before Angela was drawn in. She was asked to help with fund raising, which in turn led to meetings with builders, ministers of housing, lawyers and politicians. Lydia and Angela were increasingly spending a lot more time together.

Finger in the face

Besides housing, several factors were influential in bringing Angela and Lydia closer together. One was their united resistance to the old apartheid government by clashing with security police. On one occasion The ANC woman's league carried out a 'sit-in' at the local council offices. The fight on this occasion was not the Tambo housing but the right for Guguletu tenants to own their houses. Angela was asked to bring the protesting mamas some food to eat – a task easier said than done when a disapproving policeman threatened to put her in prison for being there. Lydia immediately went to Angela's defense and put her finger in the man's face telling him to, 'leave Angela alone' and, 'leave my people alone'. Their protest was a success, and some tenants who had been renting for more than 30 years, had their houses signed over to them. They were now proud house owners for the very first time.

The Green VW Beatle

Perhaps the key defining moment in their relationship, however, came one evening while talking together in Angela's old but reliable green VW Beatle. Curiosity had gotten the better of Lydia and she asked Angela if she could visit Jubilee, the church that she had heard so much about. Angela, knowing how political Lydia was, nervously took her to one of their meetings hoping that no one, at what was then a predominantly White church, would do anything stupid to rock the boat. All went well and they both came out alive.

Their conversation afterwards was deep and honest. Lydia opened her heart and spoke about many painful things that had bothered her for years. Angela listened and also shared some of her story, struggles and of her faith in Jesus. The two connected openly and that evening Lydia became a Christian accepting Jesus as her saviour – right there in the car. Their friendship was now further sealed by their common faith in Jesus.

Lasting friendship

Lydia and Angela started off as two women of different colours, cultures and backgrounds, yet ended up as two women who loved God and had a passion to see the oppressed set free and dignity restored to the poor. In the process of partaking in a shared mission together, they became friends, sharing of their lives and their families. In so doing they also shaped one another to be the women they are today. Lydia helped Angela cross culturally, often speaking directly to her with 'no beating around the bush.' Angela in turn helped disciple Lydia spiritually and in her walk with God.

Today Angela lives in central London in the UK working with Newfrontiers churches and leadership teams stirring up gifts of evangelism and helping people to believe God to move in signs and wonders. Lydia is a key leader at Khanyisa church and still actively involved in community transformation. Once a month they will phone one another and, though they are living in different parts of the world, their friendship has withstood the test of time. When they are together they continue where they left off – as if they had never been apart. Such is the dynamic of any true and close friendship.

Is it really possible to have deep and intimate relationships across cultural and socio-economic divides?

Angela and Lydia's testimony is a definite yes. But, for some of us however, though we hear stories like this, we can still have our doubts. Are they not the exception rather than the rule?

Tough cross-cultural questions

I've never been to the States but I love following the comments on faith, politics and culture in America carried out by Jim Wallis and the Sojourners team[212]. In 2008 Ryan Roderick Beiler, the web editor for Sojourners, started a discussion blog raising some tough questions and comments made by his friend Bart Compolo regarding cross-cultural church community. Bart, who leads the cross-cultural Walnut Hills fellowship in Cincinnati had held a church retreat with the theme of building relationships across racial, cultural, ethnic and economic divides. At the retreat some of his comments generated strong reactions and so with Bart's permission, Beiler put them out on the web for discussion:

'Bart asserted that while forming relationships across barriers is important… it is unrealistic to expect the kind of intimacy and understanding in those relationships that one might reasonably seek and enjoy in relationships within one's culture of origin. Bart's point then and now is that, even as we reach out across racial and cultural barriers, we shouldn't feel guilty about staying rooted in mostly homogenous core communities, nor should we feel compelled to seek essentially unnatural diversity within those core communities. While we shouldn't automatically exclude different people from our inner circles, we shouldn't feel obligated to change our group dynamics to suit them either. According to Bart, it is difficult, if not impossible, to build a core community that meets the deepest needs for intimacy and understanding of people with radically different backgrounds and seeking to do so almost always results in painful divisions and burnout. (Bart does note the exception of cross-cultural marriages, where sexual intimacy enables people to overcome otherwise insurmountable barriers – but even then often only with significant challenges.) Instead of feeling guilty about this limitation we should accept it and resolve to use the strength we draw from our core communities for the important work of reaching out to build authentic cross-cultural relationships, wherein we learn from, teach, nurture, challenge, protect, mentor, and work together for justice with one another. Such relationships are not superficial – just not intimate.

In Bart's community, that means hanging out with your mostly white, formerly middle-class inner circle, doing stuff white people like on Wednesday nights, so that you can completely relax and be energized for the demands of higher maintenance cross-cultural relationships with your mostly black, underclass neighbours at community dinner on Monday nights… In his view, the goal is authentic interrelation – not integration – so that it's OK to maintain predominantly white and predominantly black institutions, churches and communities, so long as all of them relate meaningfully and authentically with one another.' (Beiler 2008) [213]

Bart has raised some very helpful, pertinent and thought-provoking points regarding cross-cultural friendships and the dynamics of building diverse church communities that will be useful to discuss.

1 Are deep friendships really possible?

According to Beiler's blog, Bart asserts that while cross-cultural friendships are desirable it is unrealistic to expect the same kind of intimacy that one would get from relating with people of one's own culture. In other words, it is possible to have good relationships cross-culturally, but not necessarily intimate relationships. In fact, it is not really possible to have deep and meaningful relationships with people who are so different to us (unless in a cross-cultural marriage). Angela and Lydia's testimony above would refute this, but are they the exception to the rule? Is it, therefore, not worth bothering trying to get too close to someone from a different cultural background as it will never be the same as with someone of one's own culture? To answer this I'd like to make a number of comments and observations.

Intimate friendships

Deep and meaningful friendships could perhaps be described as those relationships where people feel the most relaxed and can truly be themselves. They are the kind of relationships where there is great intimacy and understanding between one another. A number of varied factors can, of course, be attributed to the formation and development of such friendships. For example:

- Being part of something together such as the same family, a sports club, a local church, a political struggle or a university course.

- Doing things together such as travelling, church camps, mission teams or working in the same job.

- Having something in common together such as sharing a similar experience, coming from the same place or becoming Christians. In the New Testament diverse and separate people (Jew and Gentile, slave and free) were brought together because they became followers of Christ and were united by the one and same Holy Spirit. Though they previously had nothing in common together, they now had something that could connect them – their shared faith in Christ Jesus and the Spirit of God.

- Struggle. Many close relationships have come about because they have passed the test of time and withstood misunderstandings, hardships, difficulties and challenges. In some cases it is because people have gone through such things together that close friendships have developed.

- Time. Most close friendships do not happen overnight – they take time to develop.

To suggest that it is not really possible to have the same levels of intimacy within cross-cultural friendships as with same culture relationships is too unrealistic and dogmatic to be true. The same factors that help with the formation of same culture relationships apply across cultural and economic divides. Crossing cultural boundaries can of course add a number of unforeseen challenges to the relationship-building process. Problems like, racism, culture, money, education, superiority, inferiority, geography and language, may not necessarily be encountered when making same culture friendships. Yet of all these obstacles none are insurmountable. All can in fact be overcome if there is willingness by both parties to do so. As Trevor Hudson says;

'Becoming faithful friends is an adventure into personal vulnerability. It is not always easy. Often there are misunderstandings and unmet expectations. Like any adventure the outcome is seldom a foregone conclusion. However when we are with someone who accepts us as we are, listens attentively to what we share and is committed to mutual interaction, courage is given for the first steps in the life-sharing experience.' (Hudson 1995) [214]

With such commitment, intimate cross-cultural friendships are more than possible. Furthermore, the unity of the Spirit that is achieved when diverse peoples of different backgrounds become Christians should not be underestimated. Rich and poor, Black and White all have something in common together as followers of Jesus – God's Holy Spirit. It should therefore come as no surprise to discover that the author of cross-cultural diversity is more than able to assist in the development of deep, intimate and close cross-cultural friendships. The question, perhaps, is whether we will allow and ask God's Holy Spirit to help us with the friendships that we make.

High maintenance relationships

We all have and need a variety of types of relationships that operate in different ways and to different levels of openness, closeness and vulnerability. We are not best friends with everyone and in fact we wouldn't want to be so. We have acquaintances, work colleagues, peers, people we know to speak to and neighbours as well as family-type relationships such as brothers, sisters, mothers, fathers, aunts and uncles. Beyond this we also have group friendships, school friendships, church friendships and sports friendships – and so the list can go on. Of these relationships it would only be fair to comment that there are people who we find encouraging and life-giving to be with. We also have those who de-energise us and drain the life out of us. Lisa calls such people 'dementors' after the fictitious creatures in Harry Potter, who suck all life and happiness out of all those they approach.

The same is no less true cross-culturally. To classify all cross-cultural friendships as hard work or high maintenance, compared to same culture relationships would be unrealistic. Yes, some relationships, as within ones own culture, can have dementor-like qualities, but others are as equally life-giving and invigorating.

Circles of friendships

Most people have several inner circles of friendships that could be described as intimate. I, for example, have a deep and meaningful relationship with my parents that I would say is close. It is a different kind of relationship to that of my wife and children which in turn is different to the friendship I share with my friends in the church. They are all different but could all could be described as deep and meaningful. We can expect the same cross-culturally and cross-economically.

Mother and father friendships – The Bible depicts church as family. One shouldn't be surprised then to find levels of family type relationships as we interact cross-culturally. Dominic Mabikwe a Black Xhosa man, is 81 years old and is one of the elders at Khanyisa. He is truly my friend but it is a kind of father and son relationship. Frequently we go out for coffee together and I unburden my soul letting him know my concerns and frustrations. We cry together, pray together, have meals together and do mission trips together. My relationship with him truly enriches my life as I believe my life enriches his. I don't necessarily, however, talk to him in the same way that I might talk to my friend Siviwe who is my peer – it's a different sort of friendship.

Peggy Lande, a Black Xhosa mama, is like a mother to me. She knows some of my and Lisa's deepest struggles, insecurities and secrets. The same is true for Lydia mentioned above – she is our Coloured mother. We have deep and close friendships with both of them. They pray for us and love us as their own children. They encourage us and confront us when they are concerned about things that they see. They speak the truth in love to us as we do to them. We will have meals together and chat for hours together (especially with Peggy who loves to talk!).

Sons and daughters – Lisa and I also have cross-cultural sons and daughters, brothers and sisters. Mabhuti, Mno, Mzukisi, Monwabisi and Dumani are our friends, our sons and our brothers. Lucy, Nontsikelo, Nokwanda, Nokuzola, Luleka and Unathi are our friends, sisters and daughters. We joke together, talk together, do things together, have meals together and encourage one another. In one sense we are their parents but in another sense we are also their friends, brother and sister. They will challenge us as we will challenge them. Are our friendships close – yes, but they are different kinds of friendships to the ones I've mentioned above.

Thus, as we build friendships with people of different cultures and backgrounds to ourselves, we should not only be open to the best friend circles of friendship, but to mother/father and son/daughter relationships as well. This is to be expected if we are truly involved in making disciples of all nations.

Casual acquaintances – Besides best friend and inner circle friendships we must not undervalue the importance of more casual cross-cultural relationships. Lisa and I have hundreds of cross-cultural acquaintances that we know from a variety of settings – through church, through funerals, through community organisations, through visiting and through business. They are people we will stop to chat to, whom we know by name and whom we know a little about their lives and they know a little about our lives. We may have had tea together in their houses, been in church meetings together or involved in projects together. We may not be best friends with them or socialise together, but through them we have learned about culture, about poverty, about the goodness of man, the sinfulness of man, about ourselves and about God. They are relationships in which, as Bart rightly says, we learn from, teach, nurture, challenge, protect, mentor, and work together for justice with one another. Such relationships have enriched our lives as I believe we have enriched theirs. These relationships may not be intimate but they are invaluable.

Don't miss out

All these levels and types of cross-cultural relationships are necessary and beneficial. Let's be open to them all whether intimate or casual and not miss out on the life-enriching process. Let's also be careful of just seeking cross-cultural friendships with those who are the most similar to us perhaps in class, age, education and economic background. Real friendships can cross the different circles of relationships mentioned above.

At Khanyisa, for example, where perhaps about 75% of our congregation are Black Xhosa-speaking people, I have noticed an interesting observation in the way other cultural groups attempt to build relationships with them. Invariably our young White people will immediately look for best friend type relationships with other similar aged Black or Coloured men and women in the church, or those from a similar class background. Frustration and disappointment may occur if such close friendships don't happen within a certain time period. As I chat to them further about the depth and variety of different types of relationships that they have developed they suddenly realise they have gained a wealth of mothers, brothers, sisters and fathers that they are thoroughly enjoying. They have established healthy diverse relationships and friendships, but they did not recognise it at first because they were not the best friend type relationships they were hoping for. The best friend relationships that they desire inevitably do come about, but patience is required for them to happen.

In our desire for intimacy therefore, we must be careful of missing out on the wealth and depth to be gained from other seemingly less-intimate type diverse relationships within God's church.

2 Interrelation but not integration?

A second point raised by Bart Compolo, is that our goal in building diverse communities should be authentic interrelation rather than integration. In other words it is okay to maintain predominantly White and predominantly Black institutions, churches and communities, so long as all of them relate meaningfully and authentically with one another. As such we shouldn't feel guilty about staying rooted in mostly homogenous core communities, nor should we feel compelled to seek essentially unnatural diversity within those core communities. In turn, we shouldn't intentionally seek diversity in the church or go out of our way to build church community across racial and cultural lines. If it happens then that is great but we mustn't beat ourselves up if it doesn't happen.

If you have read the preceding chapters in this book my hope by now is that you would be convinced otherwise. Diversity is not a periphery issue within God's church to be taken or left according to whim or fancy. Diversity is a reflection of the very nature of God and crucial to his purposes in the world. Jesus died and rose to create a new and reconciled community – his church. In doing so Jesus reversed the flow of fallen sinful history. As John Stott says;

'The Old Testament is the story of human scattering, of nations spreading abroad, falling apart, fighting. But the New Testament is the story of the divine ingathering of nations into a single international society.' (Stott 2006:289) [215]

This ingathering needs to be visibly and practically seen by the world around us. Unity in God's church is more than building separate essentially homogenous communities that relate well and authentically with one another. The new humanity needs to be seen and reflected in every local church body thus revealing God's multi-coloured wisdom to the world. A manifest reconciled community is therefore an absolute essential and priority for God's church – God's glory is at stake.

Intentionality then is crucial to developing cross cultural relationships as well as demonstrating radical diverse church communities. Just as Jesus was intentional in seeking cross-cultural reconciliation between God and sinful humankind, so we too need to be intentional in seeking diversity in God's church. It doesn't happen by chance. It is to this point that we will explore further in the next chapter as we examine some of the practical dynamics of choosing to enter the worlds of those different to ourselves.

Last words

My last comment and observation on the topic of cross-cultural friendships is that of 'sharpening'. True friendships are more than just those people we feel the most relaxed with or those with whom we feel free to be ourselves. They are also those people who sharpen us in the way we live our lives and in our relationship with God. As I examine my own relationships for example, inevitably those closest to me challenge, provoke and sharpen my thinking and actions. They are those who speak the truth in love to me and I can speak the truth in love to them. They are those who have walked with me through thick and thin and in spite of arguments, disagreements and fights we have overcome. This is true for Lisa my wife, but also many diverse friends as well. Those who have sharpened me the most have been very different to me, but through them I have grown the most and discovered more of God.

The question therefore, as we close this chapter is, 'Who is sharpening you?' Are you mainly sharpened by people similar in culture, thinking, background and class status to yourself? This, of course, is wonderful, but there is another level of sharpening that arguably can only occur as we dare to inter-relate to those different to ourselves. I would urge us all seek to enlarge our circles of friendships and dare to go further in crossing cultural and economic boundaries than we have ever gone before.

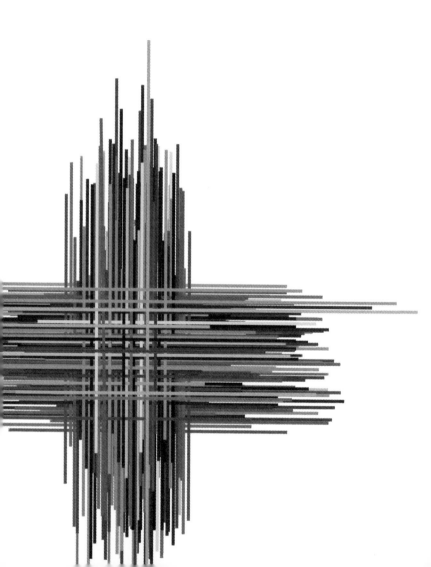

8 Seeing as others see

> *'We discover togetherness in community and that difference is not a threat but a treasure.'*[216] *(Jean Vanier)*
>
> *'It may be difficult to teach a person to respect another unless we can help people to see things from the other's point of view' (Kohei Goshi)*

I was the only White man in the place and could feel every eye boring into me as the plate was passed around and landed on my lap. Before my eyes I had witnessed an old man take a large piece of sheep's intestine that had a yellow/green tinge. This wasn't just any old piece of sheep's intestine – it was 'isandlwana', an especially soft and juicy section of the intestine reserved for honoured guests and older men, who with little or no teeth, may struggle to chew upon the tougher and harder sections. The old man had lifted the dripping innards out of the pot and proceed to rub his fingers down its length, and in so doing squeezing out various loose and unwanted raison like pellets – the last remaining remnants of the beasts' faeces. With the task duly completed the slimy green inner tube-like piece of sheep gut was now before my eyes and I was expected to eat it.

'See what I do for you Lord,' I prayed quietly as I nervously lifted the innards to my face. I somehow felt I was representing the entire White male human race. It was a test of the White man and what I did at that moment in time could have an impact on White/Black race relations for generations to come. I had no choice in the matter, and so discovering a will-power I didn't know I had, I chewed and swallowed it, resisting an overwhelming urge to vomit in front of over a hundred men. The deed was done, I had conquered, I had won, I was the victor, the champion and the hero – what a man I was. No one seemed that impressed – it was after all only a bit of sheep intestine – what's the big deal?

The occasion for this feast and celebration was Sabelo, who
at the age of about 17 or 18, had just become a man. He, as
is typical of the Xhosa tradition, had a few weeks earlier been
circumcised, cutting off any remnants of boyhood and entering
a new season of manhood. This was the day he'd come out
from the 'bush' where, for the past three weeks, he'd had time
to heal as well as being taught and discipled by older men in
the community, various aspects of what it means to be a real
man. His training was over, he had returned home and we were
celebrating the occasion together bringing gifts and final words
of encouragement before he continued the next leg of his
journey in life. As I thought upon these things the Isandlwana
seemed like a small thing in comparison to being circumcised. I'd
eat slimy green sheep gut in my cross-cultural identification, but
there is no way I'd go as far as having my foreskin chopped off!

Cross-cultural identification

Building cross-cultural relationships is about being willing
to enter, however briefly, the world of someone different to
oneself. How far do we go with this? In Acts 16 we witness
a remarkable incident that I'm sure would be frightening for
most of us. The apostle Paul took Timothy and 'circumcised
him because of the Jews who were in those parts, for they
all knew that his father was a Greek' [217]. Paul therefore, for
the sake of the gospel and his desire to see all nations come
to know Christ, asked Timothy to be circumcised. Timothy
willingly did this, not for salvation purposes, but rather to
assist him in building cross-cultural relationships and open up
doors for the gospel to be heard and received. I wonder how
many of us in our attempts to reach the different nations in
our midst would be willing to do that?

Entering the worlds of others forces us to get out of our
comfort zones. This is something that is as equally challenging
for Black people as it is for White, for poor as it is for rich.
Dumani Domo, for example, a Xhosa leader at Khanyisa was

invited to the wedding reception of a White South African friend who was getting married. He arrived at the reception with his girlfriend only to discover that he had been invited, but his girlfriend had not. The tradition of inviting someone to a wedding was an alien concept to him, as according to his culture everyone would naturally have been welcome to attend. There was no space for his girlfriend at the table so he found himself awkwardly re-arranging chairs to give her a place to sit, feeling very self-conscious in the process. Being invited to a 'White' wedding was as equally challenging for him as was my experience eating sheep's intestines in Khayelitsha.

Building cross-cultural friendships and reaching out to people of other nations therefore, will inevitably involve some action on our part that will be inconvenient, difficult or downright embarrassing. This may cause some of us to shy away from attempting to enter someone else's world. We'd rather let them enter our world but we're not so sure about entering theirs. What practical advice then can be given that will encourage all of us to dare enter the worlds of others?

Practical advice in building cross-cultural relationships

Many years ago while doing a cross-cultural seminar at a leadership conference in Bloemfontein, a lady stood up and shouted at those of us who had been speaking, wanting to know why we were always talking about the Black people but didn't ever focus on Coloured people. I quickly handed over to John Jacobs – who is now one of my fellow elders at Khanyisa and who conveniently happens to be a Coloured man. He quickly clarified the heart and purpose of what we were trying to get across and that we had no desire to offend any specific culture or people group. We were merely attempting to examine principles that could be applied to various cultures and people groups throughout the world. She very graciously received our apologies and she, along with her husband have since become very good friends of Lisa and myself.

With the risk of being shouted at again, I want to give practical principles that all of us as individuals can learn from in building genuine relationships across cultural and socio-economic divides.

Lessons from Jesus

The greatest example of breaking down the dividing walls that separate us, entering other people's worlds and interacting with those different to ourselves, is Christ Himself. Jesus the perfect, majestic, glorious Son of God was willing to become a first-century Galilean Jew. He is the Word that became flesh and made his dwelling among us [218]. He is Christ incarnate (God becoming man). This is arguably the most spectacular instance of cultural identification in the history of mankind. You can't get more cross cultural than that – God entering the world of sinful man!

A paraphrase version of Philippians 2:5-11 says this;

'Let your cross-cultural perspectives have as their vantage point the life of Christ. For Christ belonged to a celestial culture where he fitted in perfectly enough to rank among the best. But he put that aside and entered a terrestrial culture carrying with him no extra baggage, no sense of superiority, no chauvinism, no presumptions. He joined its peoples and became one of them until he not only could see from their point of view, but could live their kind of life. His identification was so complete that he died for their cause. God noticed and honoured the venture by making Christ the universal focal point in whom all people can have common vision.' (Philippians 2:5-11) [219]

Jesus is our model for reaching out and making friends with people of other cultures and economic backgrounds different to ourselves. Let's examine some principles of entering someone else's world from the life of Christ.

1 Intentionality

Jesus was intentional about breaking cultural divides. Jesus did not find himself in a situation where he was left with no choice other than having to relate to sinful man. His hand was not forced by unforeseen circumstances thrown his way. He didn't just find himself sitting next to a bunch of sinners and think, 'I'd best do what I can to get on with this lot.' No – it was a deliberate plan strategised before the foundation of the world. Choice was involved.

We mentioned Bart Compolo's comments in the previous chapter suggesting we shouldn't intentionally seek diversity in the church or go out of our way to build church community across racial and cultural lines. It's fine if it happens, but we shouldn't intentionally try and make it happen. The action and example of Jesus, however, seems to contradict this. He was very intentional about crossing dividing walls to have a relationship with us. Any friendship is a choice. To build genuine friendships with someone of a different culture is a choice we have to make and a commitment we must stick to. They don't just happen. We have to choose to make them happen, especially in a world where there is so much that would keep us apart.

There are many excuses and reasons we could give as why we should not cross racial and economic divides:

- It is not easy
- It takes effort
- It can be embarrassing
- It can be frustrating
- People might disappoint me
- It's inconvenient
- It's uncomfortable

Ultimately we are our own biggest hindrance to entering the worlds of those different to ourselves. It takes deliberate choice on our part to follow the example of Christ and enter the world of others.

Why choose?

It's on God's agenda – We choose because we are convinced
God wants us to. We choose because Christ is our example
and we are convinced that in the same way the Father sent
him so he is sending us. We choose because we are convinced
that diversity is something central to the purposes of God in
the world. We choose because we long for the multi-coloured
wisdom of God to be manifest to the world. We choose because
the glory of God is at stake. We choose because actually we have
no choice as not do so would be a compromise on the very
heart of the gospel.

Too much choice – We choose because the prevalence of
homogenous groupings and the separation of people groups
demand that we make a choice. If we look at the early church
communities as seen in Scripture, there was little or no choice
involved in making cross-cultural friendships. The context was
one of immense racial, cultural and economic diversity. Among
the Jews there were diverse factions of people from Pharisees,
Sadducees, Zealots, Herodians and Essenes. Politically there were
those committed to Rome and those against Rome. Then there
were the Greek Hellenists, slaves and free, proselytes, Samaritans,
Greek Gentiles and Roman Gentiles and so the list goes on. With the
formation of new church communities all were thrown together
and there was little choice involved as to who mixed with who.

Today things are very different. It's similar in the sense of the racial,
socio-economic diversity and divisions – yet it has changed due to
the availability of different kinds of church communities for people
to choose. People today choose church like they would any other
commodity. People choose church according to the personality
of the pastor, the size of the congregation, the kind of songs sung,
length of service, number of services held and anything else that
suits their needs. We choose to relate with those we want to relate
with. This is a dangerous situation to be in and one only we can
choose not to comply with.

We are missing out if we don't – Those who 'stay with their own' and don't choose to embark on the adventure of building cross-cultural friendships are missing out. We miss out from release from captivity, on having our broken hearts bound and our darkness turned to light. We miss out on our mourning turned to joy and our heaviness turned to praise [220]. Such is the work of Christ today but his method for doing so is through diverse relationships in his multi-coloured church.

In Luke chapter 7, for example, we witness an astonishing encounter between Jesus and two people from very different backgrounds. Jesus had been invited for a meal at the house of a wealthy Pharisee called Simon. He seemed to have had his suspicions about Jesus and did not extend to him any of the common courtesies his culture demanded – namely having someone to wash Jesus feet. A prostitute came uninvited to the meal and full of love for Jesus, proceeded to kiss and wash his feet, wetting them with her tears and anointing them with her perfume. Simon looked with disdain on this lady and on Jesus who obviously was just a 'nobody' by the very fact he had allowed this woman to do this.

There was something Simon could have learned from this lady had he been willing to get to know her and hear her story and dare to discover a little bit of her world. But no – he was too high and mighty for that – what possibly could he learn from a dog like her? Jesus spoke into the situation to try to get Simon to open his mind and realise that this woman had done a marvelous thing and he would benefit by following her example. He told a parable about two debtors – one who had been let off repaying a very large amount of money, whose love and gratitude was overwhelming. The other had only been let off repaying a small amount of money and hence his appreciation was not so great. The implication of course is that the one debtor was the woman while the other debtor was Simon himself. [221]

Not only did Simon miss out on an opportunity of relating with Christ, he missed out on an opportunity to embrace a relationship with someone very different to himself. There is much we can learn and discover about God and ourselves by being willing to relate with people who come from very different backgrounds and environments to us. If we don't choose to do so – we miss out on life-changing opportunities and lessons.

2 Willingness

Not only was Jesus intentional about breaking cultural divides but he was willing to identify and be associated in every way with sinful man. Several years ago I found myself in Wynberg magistrate's court supporting a lady in the church who was taking out a safety injunction against her husband. Her marriage was turbulent and on several occasions she was very concerned for her safety. As we sat outside the domestic violence court waiting for her case to be called, I once again had the feeling that all eyes were on me. In looking around the waiting area I noticed that I was the only man there – all the rest were ladies who were presumably also suffering to some degree under the hands of their respective partners. I felt an overwhelming urge to stand up and defend myself, to shout aloud and exclaim, 'I'm a happily married man, I'm not a wife-beater, I'm only here to help someone!' I did not want to be misunderstood and perceived to be someone I was not.

How unlike Jesus who was so willing to be misunderstood and associated with me and my sin. He was willing to become poor. He was willing to get out of his comfort zone (my guess is that heaven is a fairly comfortable place) and walk a difficult path. He was willing to look a fool in the eyes of others. He was willing to identify totally with all aspects of those he related with – their good and their bad. Jesus' identification was so complete that he 'became sin' dying on the cross in our place. He paid the price that we deserved. The apostle Paul shows a similar willingness as he writes to the Corinthians,

'For though I am free from all men, I have made myself a slave to all, that I might win the more. And to the Jews I became as a Jew, that I might win Jews; to those who are under the Law, as under the Law, though not being myself under the Law, that I might win those who are under the Law. To those who are without law, as without law, though not being without the law of God but under the law of Christ, that I might win those who are without the law. To the weak I became weak; I have become all things to all men, that I may by all means save some. And I do all things for the sake of the gospel, that I might become a fellow partaker of it.' (1 Corinthians 9: 19-23 NASB)

Paul was willing to take drastic measures to relate to and identify with people of different cultures and backgrounds to himself – all for the sake of the gospel. Willingness is a key to building relationships cross-culturally. We need to be:

Willing to associate with a person of another culture – This was an issue for many people when we first started Khanyisa. There was a cost to Black people to be associated with White. Some were scorned, ridiculed and accused of being traitors by family members and neighbours. Our White folk and those from other nations also faced challenges. Why did they go to the townships? Didn't they know it wasn't safe? Their motives for being part of the church were questioned and regularly misunderstood. Entering the worlds of others requires a willingness to be seen with, fellowship with and identify with people of very different cultural, class and socio-economic backgrounds to ourselves.

Willing to get out of our comfort zones – We need to be willing to leave that which is familiar and dare to experience that which is unfamiliar. We need to be willing to have a go at new languages, try out new types of food and even make a fool of ourselves. The first funeral I ever led in South Africa was an open-air service held among the shacks of Tambo Square. It was a baking hot day and I was struggling with a bad chest and various allergies that were causing me to cough and sneeze. Trying to

be clever and impress people I had, the night before, got out my
Xhosa dictionary to learn a few sentences and phrases. When
I stood up to speak I gave my general introductions which all
went well, then tried to explain to people about why I was
coughing. What I tried to say was, 'My chest is very sore' (Isifuba
sam sibuhlungu), but ended up saying, 'Amabele am abuhlungu,'
which means my breasts are very sore. I'd picked the wrong word
for chest out of the dictionary. For a long time afterwards I was
known as the pastor with sore breasts!

Entering the worlds of others will take us out of our comfort
zones. Sometimes we will make fools of ourselves, but we need
to be willing to be laughed at and even laugh at ourselves. We
can't take ourselves too seriously when relating cross culturally.

**Willing to go to places we previously would never have gone
to** – We need to be willing to go to a part of town we have
never been to before in order to enter the worlds of others.
We need to be willing to deal with our fears in the process. I'm
reminded of Philip Yancey's testimony in his book, 'What's so
amazing about grace?' He tells the story of his friend who came
'out of the closet' declaring himself to be homosexual. Philip
loved his friend even though he disagreed with the lifestyle
he was pursuing. Philip willingly went with his friend on gay
marches and associated with the people his friend was mixing
with – he wanted to learn about his world [222]. He was willing
to go to places he never would have gone to in his efforts to
know and reach out to those who were different to himself. He
was also willing to be severely misunderstood in the process.

Willing to make mistakes and get it wrong – We will make
mistakes and get things wrong – that is just par for the course.
Fear of getting it wrong or past mistakes made should not,
however, hinder us from going forward. Similarly, when we
do make mistakes or unintentionally offend others, we need
humility to hear correction and a willingness to be challenged
about what we do. On one occasion a lady expressed to me

how hurt she was because I had repeatedly not greeted her on a Sunday morning. Unaware of what I was doing I had unintentionally been insensitive to the importance and value of greetings as in her culture. I immediately asked her forgiveness and have since attempted to be more sensitive to others, hopefully learning from my mistakes.

Willing to listen and learn – We need to listen to people and hear what they are saying, not what we think they are saying. Similarly, we must be careful of presuming to know all about another culture and how people think or why they do the things that they do. When I first came to South Africa I already had my own opinions on things like lobola, circumcision, African beer, witchcraft and ancestral worship – as well as the theological implications of how such things should be handled in the church. So much of what I thought I knew to be right was wrong and I had to take time to learn, ask questions and be taught by others.

It's important, therefore, to be teachable, hungry to learn and ask questions of one another. We should ask others to teach us and explain more about themselves to us as this demonstrates humility, our need of the other person, a willingness to learn and a desire to genuinely know about that person's world. We should also be willing to get books, listen to new music, learn about unfamiliar sports, read literature and even newspapers that may not naturally be our first choice of reading material. In Cape Town, for example, we have a variety of free local newspapers according to different areas and communities. By reading these we can catch a glimpse into the world of others and get a little more understanding of some of the issues and challenges they face.

Willing to take time – My culture is fast, furious and functional as we speed in and speed out from one thing to the next. We miss out on so much because we are unwilling or unable to spend time with people. Time is one of the biggest killers of relationships in the modern western world.[223] If we truly desire to enter the worlds of others we must be willing to give of our time.

Willing to persevere – A frequently sung song in many township churches is this, 'Never give up, never give up; never, never, never, never, never – never – never – never give up.' This seems to be resonant of Jesus' repeated exhortation to overcome to the seven churches of Asia Minor in the book of Revelation.[224] It is also good solid advice for building cross-cultural friendships. Perseverance, overcoming, pressing through the pain barriers and never giving up are essential qualities in entering the worlds of others.

Willing to see as others see – Jesus entered our world and was willing to see as we see. The book of Hebrews says, 'We do not have a high priest who cannot sympathise with our weakness but one who has been tempted in all things as we are, yet without sin.'[225] That's why we can come to him with freedom and confidence because we know he understands us. He can see as we see and he knows where we are coming from. We all see and look at life through our varying cultural-lenses and perspectives. Entering the world of others means being willing to have our world-views challenged as well as attempting to understand the world-views of others.[226]

Willing to open the purse – South Africans are very curious people and invariably like to know what is going on. If for example, they come across a road traffic accident, not only will cars slow down and pull over onto the hard shoulder, but vehicles travelling in the opposite direction will also slow down and stop. Everyone wants to get involved, sometimes resulting in major traffic jams.

This reminds me of the story of the Good Samaritan where, in contrast to South Africa, only one person was willing to stop and help. His involvement, however, was quite extensive, even to the extent of opening up his purse and sharing his money and possessions.[227] We too, in entering the world's of others, will be required to share of what we have; our money, our cars, our houses and our possessions. This inevitably will put our attitude to such things to the test and can expose a whole number of rotten motives in the process. We'll examine such things in more detail in Chapter 12, but suffice it to say at this stage, crossing racial boundaries stretches as far as our wallets.

Willing to tackle racism – In daring to enter the worlds of others my racism, prejudices, assumptions and stereotypes have been revealed. I hate seeing this in my own life and I hate seeing it in others. Many of us don't even know it is there. In fact, it's not until we start interacting with others different to ourselves that we see such dross come to the surface. As we cross the racial and economic divides of our societies, we need to be willing to deal with this in our own lives, as well as facing it in others. [228]

3 Attitude

The way Jesus chose to enter our world was important. His attitude was one of pure humility with no sense of superiority or patronising attitude towards those he was relating with. His attitude was not that of, 'I'm God and I'm coming to show these sinful people a thing or two.' He humbly embraced us with all our cultural differences to him treating us with respect, dignity and value. Such is the attitude that we too are encouraged to model as we dare to embrace those different to ourselves.

Jesus never imposed – even though Jesus was fully anointed, gifted and capable – he was after all God. He did not use his 'Godness' as a right to impose on peoples' lives. He was as Philippians says 'in very nature God but did not regard equality with God a thing to be grasped.' [229] In fact, he emptied himself and took on the form of a servant. He was the most gifted and anointed person of all and had a right to tell people what to do, where they must change or force them to bow the knee and honour him. Yet Jesus never did so. Instead, he chose to invite relationship and offer his gifting to any who would receive him. He never enforced or imposed his will onto those who did not want it.

Similarly, in our cross-cultural endeavors we must not force ourselves, our opinions, our will or our gifting upon people – even when we know it to be right. Some of us by nature or cultural upbringing are more forceful than others. Others of us by nature, cultural upbringing or due to a history of cultural exploitation and rejection are more timid and more vulnerable to be exploited. Not long after I came to South Africa, for example, I had the privilege of leading a witchdoctor called Gogo to the Lord. I had my own ideas of how such things were meant to be handled and so immediately tried to force her to get all her 'dirty things' and burn them publically for all to see. She was an old lady and slightly fearful of talking to me since I was a White man (and a church pastor at that), so she did not express some of the concerns she was facing. I, insensitive to her situation, continued to pressurise her to burn her things, until one day she suddenly burst into tears as I was talking to her. She explained how her brother had paid for all her equipment (a sizeable amount of money) and that he would not allow her to burn them as they did not belong to her but the family. In fact, he had taken the things off her and would not give her access to them. Gogo was petrified that she could not become a proper Christian as a result, and was also saddened at the thought of disappointing and upsetting me.

I felt ashamed of how ignorantly I had handled the situation and my insensitivity to her and all she was going through. We never did have a 'burning,' but I learned a hard lesson that day about how to treat people. Gogo is still in the church today and passionately following Jesus.

More recently we have had another lady start attending our Sunday morning meetings. I've known her for many years, from our days in old Tambo Square – and she too was a witchdoctor that I frequently used to visit and drink tea with. I hadn't seen her for a long time and was pleasantly surprised when I saw her attending our church meetings. My guess was that she was still doing her 'old things' so I started to pray for the right opportunity to talk to her.

A couple of months later some of the ladies in the church came to me distraught – we have a witchdoctor in the church! Didn't I know who she was and what was I going to do about it? I explained that it was important that she knows that she is loved and accepted by people, and that in the right time God will show us how and when to talk to her. We didn't have to wait long as that week she invited me to her house for tea. On going there I gently raised the subject of her witchcraft. She explained to me how she had come to a place where she didn't want to do those things any more. In fact, she had already told her 'ancestors' that they mustn't come and talk to her in dreams any more as she now wanted to follow Jesus. That day I led her to the Lord and the following week she was baptised in water. She also brought her 'things', which at her own suggestion, she publically burned outside our church building. How wonderful it is when we try to apply the attitude of Jesus towards others we relate with.

Jesus was humble and open to receive from others – Jesus did not see himself as so highly anointed and above us that there was nothing he could receive from his relationship with us. Though he came to humankind and had much to give to us, he also willingly and gladly received from those he had made. Jesus gave to sinful people, but also had his needs met by sinful people – it was a two way relationship!

In one sense of course, there was nothing that sinful man could input into Jesus life as he had it all – he didn't actually need them as he was totally secure and content in himself and his relationship with his Father. Yet Jesus willingly and gladly received from us having his physical, emotional and even spiritual needs met through others:

- Jesus not only comforted others but others comforted him.
- Jesus not only prayed for others but allowed and needed others to pray for him.
- Jesus not only fed others but allowed and needed others to feed him.
- Jesus not only gave joy to others – but others gave joy to him.

Cross-cultural relationships must always be two-way involving both a giving and a receiving. Superiority needs to be discarded throwing away any thoughts that we are doing people a favour by gracing them with our presence. Similarly, inferiority must be challenged and any ungodly subservience broken. Our attitude should be rooted in humility, not seeing the relationship as 'me doing something for them', but recognising that 'I need them as they need me'. It's having the attitude of the Aboriginal woman we mentioned in chapter 4 who said, 'If you have come to help me you are wasting your time, but if you have come because your liberation is bound up with mine, then let us work together.'

A test of this attitude is seen in whether we are open and able to receive from those different to ourselves. Are we able to receive encouragement and let others know when we are feeling discouraged? Are we able to receive prayer and allow others to pray for us or must we be the ones who pray for others? Are we able to receive advice and teaching and willing to ask others for their opinion?

Let's humbly share our lives with one another, enjoying our differences; giving, learning and receiving from one another. Let's grow in our appreciation of one another and in so doing provoke one another to a greater and more passionate love for God.

Jesus motive was pure – Jesus never used people for his own selfish purposes. He didn't enter our world so he could have a ministry with sinners in order that he could look good amongst the angels in heaven or impress his Father and Holy Spirit. His heart and motive was love – for God so loved the world![230] Our motives for wanting to cross cultural divides need to be discerned. Various wrong motives can include:

Seeking a ministry and finding a 'work for the Lord' – It is possible to want to cross cultural divides in order to seek a ministry rather than genuine relationships. People of different cultures can be regarded as an area of ministry within the church, which if we give ourselves to, will help us fulfill our calling and spiritual growth in God. This may be to look good among peers or to be seen to be successful by doing something for God. It can also be viewed as a useful experience beneficial for our long-term walk with God – where working with; the youth, with kids, with the poor or with refugees will give us good experience for the future. Such a motive, however, is all about us and not about others or Jesus. We then make plans for people (which we don't necessarily communicate) and become frustrated if they disappoint us or have alternative plans themselves. In building cross-cultural relationships don't seek a ministry – seek a friend.

Romanticism – Some of us can have a romantic idea of mixing with someone from a different culture. It can seem like a nice thing to do. I was a romantic when I first came to South Africa having somewhat of an 'only Black is beautiful' concept and didn't really want to mix with White people. It was only after I got held up at gun point in Khayelitsha that my bubble was burst and I started to get a more sober perspective, realising there is beauty and ugliness to be found among all peoples of the earth.

I borrow the term 'romantics' from David Dennington, who was my pastor while I was a young student living in Chertsey. He has many good friendships among the gypsies in England and is frequently asked by people to take them to see the gypsies or have a look inside of one of their caravans. David calls them romantics because of their tourist-like curiosity, wanting to visit with another culture in the same way one might want to visit Table Mountain or the Great Wall of China.

Romanticism sounds nice, but often is very patronising. We can talk down to people viewing them as sweet, nice, or lovely, but not quite as equals. David says this about some of the patronising attitudes expressed towards gypsies in the UK:

'Many (of the gypsies) may not know what the word patronise means but they certainly know when it is happening to them and they do not like it. It is not a matter of accent or using special language. They may not always be very literate but they have normal intelligence and are used to dealing with folk from all levels of society through their work and daily living. They can quickly sense if people are afraid of them. They are used to being rejected and discriminated against so when they are spoken to as an equal person they just respond well and want to share their lives.'

We must be careful of viewing cross-cultural relationships as a nice idea and thus fall into the trap of patronising people in the process. Let's reach into the worlds of others because it is a privilege to be able to do so and because we see others as of great value in the eyes of God.

Obligation – Lastly, some of us may be tempted to cross cultural divides because we feel we ought to do so. We see others in the church doing it and therefore feel we should do the same. We can feel guilty when we see those who do not have as much as us, or we become aware of how past atrocities have harmed others. Our motivation to relate, therefore, can be more out of guilt or obligation rather than a genuine desire to do so, or a sense of following God's lead. Such motives may feel honorable, but will not sustain us in the long run. Faith and vision are necessary for the long-haul.

Motives then for wanting to mix with other cultures are varied and many, and possibly very few of us are 100% pure in our desires for crossing cultural divides. Fortunately we have a God who knows the very intentions, motives and thoughts of our hearts and is more than able to cleanse and purify them when they are skewed. Let's seek and desire to take on the same attitude in our relationships that Christ has shown towards us. Let's embrace one another with joy genuinely appreciating the differences between us. Let's lay off any sense of superiority and humbly regard others as more important than ourselves. Let's take our cross-cultural perspectives from the life of Christ and experience the joy and delight of entering someone else's world.

A few last pieces of advice on entering someone else's world:

Don't say 'I can't'

- Don't use a bad experience you may have had with someone of a different culture as an excuse not to push through.
- Don't put people all in the same bracket
- Don't use language as excuse, 'I can't speak the language.'
- Don't be intimidated by other Christians whom God has led to do 'strange things' that you feel you could never follow eg Timothy getting circumcised (Acts 16:1-5).
- Don't be hindered by fear of making cultural blunders. You will make them. Being genuine, humble, full of love and willing to say sorry goes a long way.

Start where you are at – You don't need to get on a plane and fly thousands of kilometres to find another culture. Start with people you meet regularly – in the same church, cell group, at work, neighbour, student etc

Pray, pray and pray – Ask God to help you and fill you with his Holy Spirit. He is after all our helper and comforter. Just as Jesus only did what he saw the father doing so we need to ask of him and seek his face for wisdom and direction in all that we do. he is passionate about this and more than able to help.

Fun, fun, fun – Evan Rogers wrote a children's song called, 'Fun in the Son'. This is solid advice for cross-cultural relationships. Let's have some fun together. There is great joy and fun to be had in entering the world's of others.

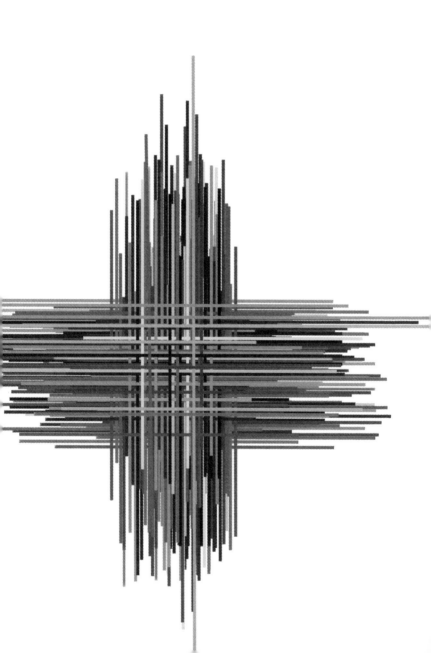

9 Building together

> *'Multi-cultural churches are local communities of believers that are intentional in their efforts to embrace diverse types of people across racial, cultural and economic divides; are committed to racial reconciliation and demonstrating genuine loving community that magnifies the oneness of believers in Christ and brings glory to God in the nations.'*
> *(Nigel Measures)*
>
> *'In that band of Christ-followers, believers loved each other with a radical kind of love. They took off their masks and shared their lives with one another. They laughed and cried and prayed and sang and served together in authentic Christian fellowship. Those who had more shared freely with those who had less until socioeconomic barriers melted away. People related together in ways that bridged gender and racial chasms, and celebrated cultural differences.'*[231]
> *(Dr Gilbert Bilezikian)*

Cape Town has a wonderful restaurant called Moyo that offers it's customers an African experience and a gastronomic feast to die for! It's a place I'd whole-heartedly recommend for all visitors to our beautiful city. On entering the restaurant, one is graciously welcomed and seated either at the sturdy tables in the heights of the towering lush tree canopies, or under the Moroccan style tents close to open wood-burning steel braziers. The atmosphere is electric as one's hands are washed, faces painted and a multitude of African dancers and singers entertain nearby. Then, of course, there is the meat – an abundance of meat that would challenge even the most committed of carnivores! On the few occasions Lisa and I have been there we inevitably crawl out of the place on our knees having over indulged on delights such as; springbok, kudu, sheep, cow, warthog, chicken, ostrich, buffalo and even crocodile. It's a place where many Africans like to say 'we eat the meat and spit out the bones'. Such is my advice as we continue this chapter grappling with some of the practical dynamics of building multi-cultural church communities. There is no 'one-size-fits-all' approach to be duplicated in any locality as no two churches will be made up of the same groups of people. It's worth examining, however, what is being practiced elsewhere to help discern possible implications and change in our own situations.

Radar screens

Increasingly the subject of multi-cultural churches is entering the radar screens of topical conversation, comment and consideration. More and more local communities of believers are considering the dynamics of what it means to build radical and relevant church communities in our increasingly racially and economically divided societies. Unsurprisingly, motives and factors driving church leaders and congregants to think along these lines are varied and diverse.

a) Vision, faith and theological conviction – For some, like Lisa and myself living in Cape Town, the post-apartheid South African context was a major factor influencing our desire to build a multi-cultural church community. Apartheid intentionally separated people groups, tearing down established communities and sowing seeds of mistrust and hatred towards one another. We intentionally wanted to see the 'broken walls' repaired and the reconciling nature of the gospel visibly demonstrated, allowing God's healing love and grace to come to a hurting nation. Though initially motivated by our context we were increasingly influenced by deeper theological reasons, convinced that this was what God wanted us to do and genuinely believing that diversity was on God's heart for all of his church. It is this faith and vision that has sustained us when the going has gotten tough.

b) Need and Relevance – Others of us have been faced with the rapid multi-cultural growth rates occurring within the many towns, cities and urban centres of the world where we live. Some predominantly homogenous local churches therefore, have felt the need to wake up and go with the flow or risk no longer being relevant to their communities. Reverend Ken Davis says that in the United States over 85% of Americans live in cities. In the 2000 US census it was estimated that the ethnic population of America was over 100 million people, representing more than 500 people groups, speaking more than 630 languages and dialects. Davis observes that if homogenous churches do not change there are at least four types of people whose needs will not be met:

- Inter-racial couples and families
- Ethnic people who prefer speaking English
- Urbanites who appreciate living, working and ministering in the midst of ethnic diversity
- Generation-Xers who often despise racial separatism (Davis 2003: 114) [232]

c) It's happening anyway! – Elsewhere, some of us have been faced with uninitiated cross-cultural change happening within our local churches, leaving us with little choice other than to address the matter. This is a phenomenon noted by Owen Hylton that prompted him to write his book on cross cultural diversity, 'Crossing the Divide.' He and a number of other British leaders observed a growing trend of ethnic minority people starting to attend their local churches. In most cases he noted, 'The vast majority of these churches that I am aware of began predominantly with white people attending, who have been joined by people from ethnic minority groups.' [233] As such, many church leaders needed to examine reasons for these changes in their midst, as well as handle the practical implications of such changes. Certain ethnic minority people, for example, had expressed a growing frustration in having to travel long distances to their own-type churches and therefore wanted to rather mix in local churches closer to home. For others, children were the initiating factor provoking parents to change. Many families had noted that diversity was a natural part of their everyday lives and so began questioning why this had not been their experience in church. [234]

Minefield of thinking over cross-cultural church

Regardless of these varying motives, change is happening in God's church and many local churches are exploring, perhaps for the first time, some of the dynamics around building multi-cultural church communities. This is encouraging news, though as we'll see, having a vision or desire to build such communities is one thing, but what it means in practice is something else altogether.

Naturally, many of us may be tempted to examine how others are going about this elsewhere. In the United States especially, much has been written about cross-cultural or multi-cultural churches and there are a great number of models being offered for willing and searching learners. In studying such models, however, one embarks along a confusing path and potential minefield of conflicting thought and practice that can leave one bemused, harassed and bewildered. What is being practiced and presented as cross-cultural church is all so different. I'd like to enter this minefield and comment on four common examples or ways of building multi-cultural church that are frequently presented as the way to go forward. [235] Before doing so it would be helpful to know what it is that we are talking about or what is it that we should be aiming to build? I'd like to present a working definition of what a multi-cultural church is or should be in order to help us comment upon and evaluate what is being practiced elswhere.

A working definition of cross-cultural church

I base this definition partly on research made by Davis and Peart with a few added twists of my own;

'Multi-cultural churches are local communities of believers that are intentional in their efforts to embrace diverse types of people across racial, cultural and economic divides; are committed to racial reconciliation and demonstrating genuine loving community that magnifies the oneness of believers in Christ and brings glory to God in the nations.'[236]

Four common approaches to multi-cultural churches

1) Multi-congregational model

In this example churches will hold multiple services (normally held at different times of the day within the same church building) that are each geared towards the different ethnic and people groups. Each congregation will have its own leaders that will work together as part of the larger umbrella church. In such churches everyone technically is part of the same local church community but little interaction, cross-pollination or relationship occurs outside the services. These churches can also be practiced along sociological lines having for example, student services, family services and business-men services etc.

2) Multi-language satellite model

This example is similar to the multi-congregational model above, but in this case each congregation will meet in different parts of the town or city as opposed to using the same facility. Each congregation could be geared towards different people groups doing things in 'their style' and in their particular language. Again the congregations will have their own leadership teams that would work together as part of the larger umbrella church.

3) Cell-celebration model

In this model, as is typical of many so-called cell churches, life is geared around the cell groups (small groups) of the church. The members will also come together for various weekly or bi-weekly celebration gatherings, but the main focus of building community, such as discipleship, mission and evangelism, is designed to happen with the small group context. With this model each cell can be designed for a particular ethnic, language or generational group. Most examples of this type of church will have diverse celebration meetings though they will usually be held in one dominant language (commonly English). The cells will commonly be more homogenous bringing like and like together.

4) Multi-ethnic church model

In this example local churches will be culturally and ethnically diverse communities that meet together as one congregation. They will utilise one connecting language (commonly English) but will design their worship services and ministry for a variety of cultural groups. Such communities tend to gather with ethnic people who have a low ethnic consciousness. They are generally socio-economically upwardly mobile, who prefer to associate with Anglos and other upwardly mobile ethnics. [237]

Comments on such models

This of course is by no means an exclusive list and many other models or examples could probably be mentioned. In my own church, for instance, I would not see us falling into any of the categories above. My point, however, is not to raise a set of models as helpful examples for others to copy, but rather to use them to navigate through some of the diverse thinking and complexities around building diverse church communities. I'd like to start by making a number of comments and observations on these commonly practiced models, and then examine some of the practicalities that many of us will be faced with when building diverse local churches.

a) Diverse examples

Perhaps the first thing to note from these models, is what we've already stated – that there are major differences in thinking, opinions and practice about how to build diverse multi-cultural churches. What is practiced by model one appears very different to what is demonstrated by model four. Within the models above, some churches could be multi-language while others are English-only churches. Others yet could have separate homogenous congregations, while still others have a single combined service. What is practiced is very diverse, but all would claim to be cross-cultural.

This is important to recognise, as there could be a tendency to merely copy what is done elsewhere, with no real forethought and prayer into what is right for one's own local situation. If there is any model to be copied outright then let that be the example of Christ whose attitude was always to do the will of his Father in heaven. In John's gospel Jesus said, 'I tell you the truth, the Son can do nothing by himself; he can only do what he sees his Father doing, because whatever the Father does the Son also does. For the Father loves the Son and shows him all he does. Yes, to your amazement he will show him even greater things than these… By myself I can do nothing; I judge only as I hear, and my judgment is just, for I seek not to please myself but him who sent me.'[238]

Jesus did not, for example, choose 12 disciples because it was a decent strategy and good model to copy – he did it because they were the ones the Father told him to choose and he felt God's leading in the matter. Jesus prayed, 'I have revealed you to those you gave me out of this world. They were yours; you gave them to me and they have obeyed your word. Now that they know that everything you have given me comes from you'.[239] We too should seek to learn from this as we look at our own local church situations and see what it means for us to build radical diverse communities that glorify God.

b) Homogenous practices

Secondly, it is worth emphasising how homogenous thinking and practice is still very prevalent within the way many multi-cultural churches are building community. As we examined in previously, many leaders approach church with the underlying premise that their churches will grow best if people don't have to cross racial and cultural barriers. They may attempt to heterogeneously match the racial diversity of their surrounding communities by placing people within separate homogenous groups within the church. In other words, they are using homogeny as a means of bringing people closer to the heterogeneous ideal. The key perhaps in evaluating this, is to examine the levels of diverse interaction happening outside of the homogenous groupings in the church, as well as the extent to which genuine, meaningful and reconciled relationships are occurring among different people types.

c) Location

Thirdly, it's fair to point out that most of these models are geared towards urban and inner-city contexts. One mustn't be blind, however, to the unique, diverse and widely varying local contexts within which our churches are situated. Khanyisa, for example, is a local church rooted in a specific township community called Tambo Village. We are intentionally building with other non-township people from outside that particular community. As such, we face various unique challenges that other churches located in more neutral areas may not have to face. Some so-called city-churches may not be rooted in any specific people areas but rather meet in neutral zones gathering diverse people from the quarters of their city. A church located within a council estate of London would need differing wisdom in its cross-cultural endeavors compared to one gathering at a cinema in central London. Both may be intentional in seeing racially diverse communities established, but their methods and strategies could vary immensely. The impact of location must not be underestimated.

d) Economics

Fourthly, none of the above models take into account crossing the economic divides that separate people. As stated in earlier chapters, building community with people of differing economic, class or education levels can be as equally cross-cultural as with different race groups. Churches may be practicing large ministries to the poor but giving little effort to building community with people of different socio-economic standings, wealth, class and education. In building diverse local churches I would encourage all of us not to forget the poor!

e) What cross-cultural church is NOT

Perhaps, the fifth point to reinforce comparing practice to our working definition is to clarify what cross-cultural church is NOT. I would suggest that in building multi-cultural churches the goal is not any of the following:

Assimilation – Where one culture merely blends into another culture (usually the majority one). In my own context, for example, the goal is not for all to adopt and blend into the dominant Xhosa culture. Rather that mutual appreciation, recognition and enjoyment of one another would occur. Similarly for more English-dominated churches, the goal is not to anglocise ethnic minorities so they become more English, westernised, middle-class and easier to relate to. Among African traditionalists in South Africa, one of the worst insults a Black African can call a fellow Black African is 'Eurocentric' or a 'coconut' (black on the outside but white on the inside). The implication is that they may look like a Black African but their thinking and practice is White Western. They are like a bucket that has leaked all of their own culture and embraced an entirely different (White Western) culture altogether.

The complication in Africa, of course, is that Christianity by many is associated with westernisation and first-world thinking and practice. Christianity, as we know is not a White, western, middle-class religion and we need to be very clear that in becoming Christians we are not calling someone to take on a western cultural approach to life. We all, in responding to the gospel, will have to leak aspects of our own cultures as we submit our thinking and practices to the Word of God. In turn, we should all be willing to embrace aspects of other cultures, valuing and appreciating God's multi-coloured people among us. Nevertheless, our goal or expectation should not be to see coconut churches with minority cultures leaking all aspects of their identity, embracing the dominant culture present, while the majority culture does no leaking or embracing on its part. We need a healthy appreciation and respect for one another and genuine willingness to enter the worlds of others in our midst.

Assembly – Where we are just open to everyone to come and having as many different nations together in one place as possible. The goal is not to have nations for the sake of having nations. It's not a competition among church leaders to see who has the most types of people in their congregations or to have the largest number of nations in a room at any one time. Bringing many different people together is of course good, but it is not a good thermometer as to the state of health of the relationships between those people. A church can be multi-cultural in terms of different people present, but not truly cross-cultural in terms of heart attitudes with one another. We should desire, create and encourage contexts where real relationships and friendships can develop allowing genuine fellowship, integration, social interaction, and reconciliation to occur.

Syncretism – Where we bring together two or three cultures to create an entire new culture. The goal is not to become a new culture-less community losing all flavour and spice that is incredibly tasteless, offending and satisfying no one. Rather all that is good, glorious and wonderful from all our respective cultures will be added into the pot enriching one another's lives, enriching church community and glorifying God. We are not after McDonalds type franchise churches that we can go to anywhere in the world, knowing exactly what we'll get, but lacking the flavour and personality of its local communities. We should expect local churches to have their own personality reflecting the diversity of gifting, personalities and types of people making up the body of Christ.

Practical help in building diverse church community

It's important for church leaders and congregants alike to have a clear vision for their local churches. Having briefly explored some of the diverse thinking 'out there', my hope is that we'll be able to more effectively sift through this thinking, taking out the meat and spitting out the bones, for what God is saying to us in our local church contexts.

For the remainder of this chapter, I'd now like to give practical thoughts, comments and suggestions on some of the many choices and decisions likely to be encountered when building diverse church community.

To translate or not to translate – that is the question?

I'm a firm believer in the importance of diverse types of people coming together to worship God. This, of course, in many of our contexts will mean people of varying languages coming together. How then do we handle this as obviously we want people to be able to understand what is going on? Some churches will opt for multiple services gearing each service to differing language groups. Others will take a more technological approach utilising headphones for simultaneous translation from behind the scenes. Others, like my own church, will have upfront translation with a translator working alongside the speaker. Still others may have more than one upfront interpreter translating for different sectors of the congregation. All have their advantages and disadvantages but let me highlight a few of the generally contested points:

Time and length – One of the common objections to the use of translation is the extra time it can add on to a service making the meetings too long and increasing the possibility of boredom. Length does need to be watched and for those of us with 'long stomachs' translation could be a potential hazard. Such a problem is not insurmountable with careful thought and effort on behalf of leaders. In some ways translation is something that people need to learn to adjust to and invariably ends up feeling normal. Experienced translators can in fact work very quickly and efficiently adding fun and new dynamics to the proceedings challenging any opportunities for boredom. Also, if people are taught and envisioned as to why translation is important (which is essential!), this will help them push through any of their initial discomforts and press into the fullness of all that God has for them in the local church.

Simplicity – Others would argue that the use of translation means sermons have to be simplified and therefore deep theological truth cannot be tackled. In other words translation means you can only preach simple messages. I resist this argument, though I do admit it does demand fresh creativity and openness to change on behalf of the preacher and listeners alike. Preaching with translation is different to normal preaching. If there is an unwillingness to change – we will struggle. However, if we are willing to adapt, translation can in many ways add a whole new depth to preaching. It can be interactive, fun and offer new creative expression within the traditional preaching context. Sermons may need to be adjusted but they do not need to be simple or lacking in depth. Preachers, humbly aware of the possibilities of misunderstanding, may in fact be driven to handle the Word of God with greater care resulting in clearer and more effective preaching of God's Word. Furthermore, simplicity in itself is not a sin where the art of good preaching should be to communicate the deep truths of God in a manner all can understand.

Lost in translation – Linked to the objection above is the suggestion that truth, meaning and understanding can be lost in translation. Some words, for example, cannot be translated directly from one language to the next. This of course is true, but again such problems are not insurmountable with careful work and preparation on behalf of the preacher and translator alike. We must also not be fearful of misunderstanding. It's not a sin to be misunderstood – people commonly misunderstood Jesus. Misunderstanding can in fact create healthy discipleship opportunities to speak into one another's lives.

Mutual appreciation – One of the reasons I am in favour of the use of translation is that it provides a visible expression of our love towards others in our midst. It communicates a message to people that we value them enough to want them to fully participate in all that is happening. If we truly do love one another surely it is not a big deal to adjust to translation for the sake of the wider body of Christ? Also, being on the receiving end of translation (in my case someone speaking in another language and it being translated in English), it gives one some sense of what others experience on a regular basis. Translation therefore, demonstrates a willingness on all sides to enter the worlds of others, to see how they see and feel like they feel. One should encourage a give and take attitude among church members! At Khanyisa for example, where most of our translation is done from English into Xhosa (with a bit of Afrikaans as well), we will on occasions do it the other way round so others get a feel for what it's like when 'the slipper is on the other foot'. Translation then can be a good discipleship tool to test where one's people are at. Those most resistant are probably more selfishly interested in their own comfort and not as far down the discipleship track as they perhaps first thought.

Cross-cultural worship

We all have styles and types of music that we prefer with some liking jazz more than classical, or rock more than house. Similarly, in church many of us have our natural preferences – some liking deep and meaningful hymns more than repetitive choruses, or loud and 'vibey' praise more than quiet and gentle worship songs. This should not mean that we all just stick to what we prefer. It's important that we all learn to push through our natural preferences and explore more deeply the depths of God and expression of worship of him. Diverse forms of style, song, dance, music and instruments offered in praise to Jesus only enhance the greatness and splendour of the God we worship. Being willing to get out of our comfort zones and offer unto him new forms of worship will only magnify the sacrifice of our praise.

Just as we are exhorted to 'Sing unto the lord a new song,' so we should realise that this can include songs in different languages or styles to our own. Many of us have been conditioned to believe and expect that we can only meet with God in a certain way with the right kind of music. This of course is not true as God is so much bigger than our styles or preferences. Re-education is needed. It is possible to learn to worship God in a different language and still experience his presence, though it will require some patience, faith and renewing of our minds on our part. I would encourage all churches in expressing their worship to make it God-centred, Holy Spirit filled, participatory and reflective of the diversity of people in their congregation. We should expect the Holy Spirit to be at work among our people using their diverse personalities to write and sing new songs of all languages. We should also encourage people to pray and express themselves to God in their own languages, tongues and dialects.

Besides enlarging our appreciation of God, cross-cultural worship can also be fun, strengthening fellowship and encouraging our understanding of one another. On one occasion at Khanyisa I saw some of my young men laughing during the worship overhearing an English lady in her efforts to sing a Xhosa worship song. Instead of singing 'Uyingcwele Baba' (You are Holy Lord), she sang, 'Uyitswele Baba' meaning 'You are onions Lord'. Though a little embarrassing, this broke down barriers, opened up doors of conversation and over time allowed good friendships to develop. This lady later commented how learning to sing in a new language gave her an understanding of what others go through and how they might feel.

Encouraging genuine community

How then can we encourage genuine interaction and relationship among diverse people in our churches? I'd like to suggest various things that we do and have done at Khanyisa over the years that have proved very helpful.

Participation in teams, groups and activities – Several years ago we held a church camp mixing everyone in the church together into various teams. [240] Each team had to wear their own coloured bandana, as well as come up with a team name, flag, motto and drama. The teams were in competition with each other, seeing who could serve the meals most creatively or wash the dishes afterwards the best. There were team tasks to be completed, as well as information team members had to find out about one another. The highlight of the camp for me was watching an 82-year-old Xhosa mama doing a karate-chop on a blonde haired, 28-year-old female 'Moses', acting in a short drama together. It was an intense weekend away that resulted in story-telling, laughter, tears and so much more, and relationships were established that have continued until today.

Returning from the camp I became convinced of the importance of teams. In church life we have many teams and encourage everyone to get involved with as many as possible; from the setting up teams, welcome teams, worship teams, tea and coffee teams, sidewalk teams, children's teams, discipleship groups, mission teams, visiting teams, cell groups, soccer groups, fellowship groups, leadership teams, dance groups, choirs, learning language groups, bible groups, HIV-support groups, house repair teams and so the list can go on. Not everyone gets involved of course, and teams don't automatically guarantee real relationships, but being involved in a common purpose together can really help establish foundations, break down dividing walls and give opportunities for deeper relationships to develop.

Story-telling – It is helpful, in as many contexts as possible, to encourage story telling and the sharing about one another's lives. This doesn't just have to be with new relationships where perhaps people are meeting one another for the very first time, but also with established relationships and friendships. On one occasion Lisa and I started a 'couples' group, gathering several married and courting couples in the church. We started the group by asking each couple to share their story of how they met and came together. When Dumani and Luleka (whom we've known for many years) shared their story, I nearly fell off my chair with admiration. If there was ever an example of perseverance and not giving up, Dumani gets the prize – having hunted his 'prey' incessantly for more than three years till Luleka eventually surrendered. Story-telling opens up windows of insight into the lives of others encouraging faith, love, understanding and mutual respect.

Fun activities – Doing fun things within certain cultures can be perceived as childish and immature, yet at the risk of offense we have pushed through with this being convinced that fun and laughter can bring the strangest of people together. At Khanyisa we have held dances, parties, plays, fear factor events (eating sheep's head and chicken feet), combined meals, bring and share, fashion shows, quizzes, and many other things encouraging fun and fellowship together

Training and feedback – Teaching and training courses to do with cultural diversity need to be built into the building blocks of church life. Everyone benefits from theological teaching and practical insights that promote mutual understanding of one another. It's also helpful to create contexts where people can freely discuss, comment on and give honest feedback on how 'we are doing as a church' in the various areas of diversity, such as old and young, rich and poor, different cultures etc.

This, of course, demands wisdom and careful handling, but it is essential to rather err on the side of revealed honesty as opposed to hidden frustration and anger.

Advice to leaders

Be theologically convinced – Theology must influence all that we do. We need to be as theologically convinced in the area of God's heart for diversity as we are with our theology of the Holy Spirit or the person and work of Christ. A strong theology of diversity, grounded in vision and rooted in faith will help us push through the hard times and lead God's people into his purposes for the church.

Be Intentional – Rarely do diverse, cross-cultural churches just happen as there is much in this world that would keep separate people. Furthermore, we face a real enemy who would be glad to keep us all apart. It demands intentionality by everyone in the church, especially leaders, to make it happen. Leaders set the pace and show the example. If leaders don't get it, then there is little hope for the rest of the church. As the famous saying goes, 'Everything rides and falls on leadership'. Leaders must be intentional in prayer, intentional in discussion, intentional in communicating vision, intentional in mission statements, intentional in preaching sound theology and intentional in laying hold of the values they proclaim. As the saying goes, 'we do what we value and we value what we do'. If diversity, racial reconciliation and unity are our values we will allow such values to shape us, our ministry and every part of church life.

Be open to change – Churches should always be changing as they are by definition alive and growing local bodies. Change, of course, rarely happens overnight. It requires patience and perseverance on the part of leaders to hear Holy Spirit promptings to renewed thinking, changing traditional ways of operating and adopting new wineskins that will encourage diverse church community. The leaders must also be willing to hear the opinions, thoughts and suggestions from those of different cultures in their congregations. It's amazing what wisdom and answers can be found from within the body, even from those we might least expect. This requires humble openness to hear criticism, not getting defensive and graciously admitting when we get it wrong.

Develop diverse leadership teams – Lastly, we need to be active in building diverse leadership teams, as well as discipling people of all nations. Diversity of gifting and people types within our pastoral and eldership teams is exceedingly healthy giving added wisdom and renewed perspectives that enable better leadership oversight of the church. It is essential for this to happen if the church is to be taken seriously and seen as genuinely diverse. This again will require humility on part of the main church pastor, willingness to change, as well as openness to different ways of doing things and to different leadership styles. If obvious 'other culture' leadership is not yet apparent we should ask God to show us those in our midst that we can pull under our wings and get down to the hard work of discipleship. Training of new leaders should not be confined to those we naturally relate to the best, nor should we be tempted to merely import the right person from elsewhere.

Other things

A number of others issues will commonly raise their heads whenever diverse types of people are interacting in community:

- Cultural differences and varying political and other worldviews, which can lead to misunderstandings, confusion and potential conflict.

- Economic differences among people which can cause a variety of problems including theft, resentment, jealousy and guilt.

- Racism, prejudices and stereotypical thinking, which are commonly revealed leading to hurt, anger and strife.

■ Children often become a stumbling block for many parents
– they want to be cross-cultural but what about their kids?
How do we raise our children to celebrate diversity?

These are all real and pertinent issues that require more detailed discussion and insight. It's to these topics therefore that the remaining chapters of this book will be given, allowing greater exploration of the practicalities of building multi-cultural church communities. Suffice it to say, let me finish this chapter with a quote by Dr Gilbert Bilezikian who, in talking about the early church, reminds us of what can be achieved through genuine multi-cultural church communities. He comments;

'In that band of Christ-followers, believers loved each other with a radical kind of love. They took off their masks and shared their lives with one another. They laughed and cried and prayed and sang and served together in authentic Christian fellowship. Those who had more shared freely with those who had less until socioeconomic barriers melted away. People related together in ways that bridged gender and racial chasms, and celebrated cultural differences' (Dr Gilbert Bilezikian). [241]

This truly is a compelling vision of the church that we should aim to demonstrate in the nations today.

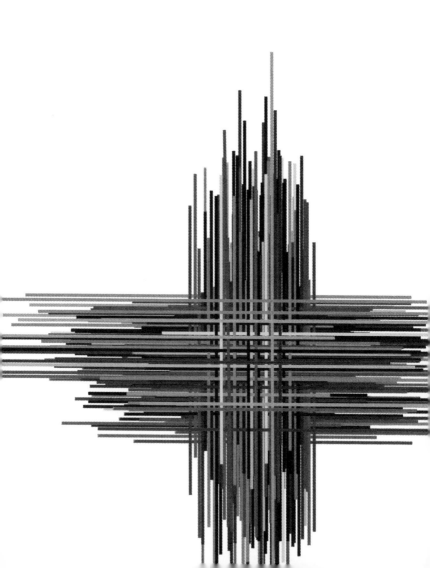

10 Cultural tapestry!

> *'Culture is ambiguous because man is ambiguous. Man is both noble (because made in God's image) and ignoble (because fallen and sinful). And his culture faithfully reflects these two aspects.' (John Stott)*
>
> *'Each of us is a cultural creature. We have drunk in our cultural inheritance with our mother's milk. The way we think, we walk, talk, dress, work, play, the way we do everything is conditioned by our cultural inheritance. Culture is a man-made structure… It's the glue, if you like, that keeps any society together. Nature is what God gives us, culture is what we do with it…' (John Stott)*

One of the first interactive cross-cultural workshops I ever attended was in Cape Town, led by a Zulu man from Pietermaritzburg. The group, unsurprisingly, was a diverse bunch of people and it wasn't long before we'd been divided into two teams and given our first task to complete. One team member was given a pencil and paper while the rest of us were each given a piece of a chopped-up picture. We had to describe our piece of the puzzle to one another (without showing it to anyone), and work out between us what the completed picture was. The scribe then drew our team's completed picture for all to see. It was all a matter of clear and efficient communication.

The picture was of a Rastafarian man wearing John Lennon style glasses and playing a guitar. Next to him was a hat into which an unseen person was donating a few coins. As the exercise progressed it was soon clear that one team was doing well while the other was struggling badly. Communication was a problem. One man described his piece of the picture as a pair of curtains, though he did, in fact, have the lower part of the Rastafarian's body showing his trouser legs. No matter how hard other team members described their conflicting explanations, he adamantly insisted that he had a pair of curtains and so somehow that had to be drawn into the picture.

Within the same group, another team member had been given the head of the Rastafarian, revealing his long dreadlocks and a pair of round John Lennon style glasses. She insisted that she was seeing a naked lady with two big 'boobies' sitting in a palm tree. Despite the conflicting explanations from the rest of the group, this too is had to be drawn. The completed picture was a naked lady with two big boobies sitting in a palm tree on top of a man's body playing a guitar. Beneath the guitar was a pair of curtains and next to the curtains was a pair of boots and a hat with a few coins inside it. The atmosphere was raucous. Tears of laughter ran down our faces as we gazed at the absurd drawing in front of us. The 'curtain' man and 'booby' lady, unfortunately, were not so amused and felt humiliated in front of everyone else in the room.

In hindsight I am ashamed about the way I and others made these two people feel. Neither the man nor the woman were fools by any means of the word. Both in fact were highly respected leaders carrying major positions of responsibility within their respective communities and organisations. Our approaches to problem solving and analysing information were simply very different. We did not go about things in the same way! Awareness of this factor could have helped us in our approach and understanding of one another and enabled us to work together towards a more satisfying conclusion.

Handling cultural differences

Our world is full of cultures in conflict. For the church to be fully effective in making disciples of all nations, crossing cultural boundaries and establishing cross-cultural church communities, we must endeavor by all means possible to understand the worlds of those we are interacting with. In chapter eight, we gave advice on entering the worlds of those different to ourselves. In this chapter I'd like to give specific attention to some of the practicalities of handling cultural differences.

1 Recognise that we all have a culture and worldview

We first need to recognise and acknowledge that we have all been shaped by our cultural and economic backgrounds, whether we realise it or not. Each of us were born into a particular family, race, culture and social context where we've inherited and grown up with a certain way of viewing the world, a way of behaving and way of evaluating other people's behaviour in terms of what we perceive to be normal. These basic assumptions about reality are what we might call our worldview. The way we think, walk, talk, dress, work, play, the way we do everything is all evaluated and conditioned by our worldview and cultural inheritance. To make my point, try answering this culture test below:

I believe in: Yes/No

- Using a knife and fork to eat with
- Paying a dowry (lobola) for my wife
- Looking someone in the eye as a mark of respect
- The importance of ancestral spirits
- Washing my hands before every meal
- Using first names to show friendliness
- Circumcision as a rite of passage for young men
- A young woman making her own mind up as to whom she must marry
- The TV being turned off when we have visitors
- Using a tissue to blow your nose
- Serving older people first before younger
- Children referring to adults (non relatives) as auntie or uncle
- Children going to bed early before the adults
- Tea being drunk in a china cup (and pouring the milk first!)

How we have answered these questions above tells us something of our cultural background and different worldviews.

Cultural leakage – You will notice that, in relation to the gospel, some of the thinking and practices outlined above are positive and directly in line with Christian values, some are negative and in need of transformation by the gospel, while others are relatively neutral and can be embraced without any qualms by Christians. For example, whether one eats with a knife and fork, a spoon, one's fingers or a pair of chop sticks is neither wrong nor right – they are simply reflective of cultural practices and worldviews. Though it's interesting to note as one commentator has wryly quipped that, 'Jesus was killed because of the way he ate.'[242] One must not underestimate the potential for cultural offense through something as simple as what and how we eat.

There are aspects of our cultural inheritance and thinking that we can hold onto that reflects the beautiful tapestry of the way God has made us. In turn, there are aspects of cultural inheritance of others that we can honour, admire and even willingly embrace as our lives are enriched by the diverse people God puts our way. Other aspects, however, need to be 'leaked' and repented of as they are contrary to the gospel. This is true of all cultures – including western culture, which some Christians can incorrectly assume to be Christian culture. The key perhaps is being willing to evaluate our own cultures and traditions before the throne of God, discerning what is honourable and to be enjoyed and what is dishonourable and needs to be leaked. As John Stott says,

'Culture may be likened to a tapestry, intricate and often beautiful, which is woven by a given society to express its corporate identity. The colours and patterns of the tapestry are the community's common beliefs and common customs, inherited from the past, enriched by contemporary art and binding the community together. Each of us without exception has been born and bred in a particular culture. Being part of our upbringing and environment, it is also part of ourselves, and we find it very difficult to stand outside

it and evaluate it Christianly. Yet this we must learn to do. For if Jesus Christ is to be Lord of all, our cultural heritage cannot be excluded from his lordship. And this applies to churches as well as individuals.'
(John Stott) [243]

2 Acknowledge the limitations of our perspectives

Having recognised and acknowledged that we each have a cultural heritage that has shaped and molded us over time we must not assume that our culture or worldview is right. We should be willing, like John Stott expresses above, to 'stand outside it and evaluate it' under the watchful eyes of the Holy Spirit. Problems arise when we judge and interpret the actions of others through our own cultural lenses, when we wrongfully assume that our way of doing things is the correct way, and when we fail to recognise and give credence to the differences in the worldviews of others. Under such circumstances, cross-cultural conflict, misunderstandings and hurt will undoubtedly occur. As such we must humbly acknowledge the limitations of our own perspectives.

In one culture, for example, children may be put to bed at seven at night and get up early in the morning following a fairly disciplined routine. In another culture families may let their children stay up till midnight. The former could judge the latter as being undisciplined and ungodly parents on the basis of not doing things the right way. This would be a wrong judgment based on evaluating and interpreting another cultural practice through a particular cultural lens. In crossing cultural and economic boundaries, it is imperative therefore, that we learn to see as others see and hold back on hasty judgments that invariably lead to wrong and generally negative conclusions. Following Christ's example, our approach should be to enter and better understand the other person's world, rather than requiring them to enter into our world. This means being willing to learn their cultural forms, perspectives and language.

3 Be aware of the seen and unseen aspects of culture

Certain aspects of culture will commonly spring to mind when contemplating cultural differences such as; language, clothing, food, literature, customs, history or folklore. Like the tip of an iceberg such things are obviously visible, above the surface and are generally the cultural differences that we are most consciously aware of and more easily prepared to handle. When I first came to South Africa I anticipated and was prepared for cultural differences with Black Africans. There were obvious differences in language spoken, traditions practiced and so forth for which I readily prepared myself. I was taken by surprise, however, by cultural differences with White South Africans. On the surface there were many similarities between our cultures in certain traditions, kinds of food eaten etc, and as such I thought our cultures were basically the same. Following several months of annoyances and misunderstanding I soon realised I was experiencing cross-cultural conflict. The areas of cultural differences, however, were not so immediately apparent and took me much longer to recognise, process and handle appropriately.

Icebergs – There are aspects of culture that are not so immediately obvious, things hidden beneath the surface that don't commonly spring to mind and can, like an unseen iceberg, take us by surprise. These areas could include styles of communication, role expectations, values and priorities, what is good and what is bad, and what is appropriate and inappropriate and so forth (see the diagram opposite).

A healthy appreciation and awareness of such cultural differences can help us avoid some of the unseen and potentially 'Titanic' disasters along the way. As such, I'd like to comment on a few of these hidden icebergs to help get the point across.

Communication styles – Within more Western cultures of the world, communication style is direct, fast, forceful, focused and gets straight to the point. Elsewhere, it is more indirect, meandering and slow. To the former the latter can come across as frustratingly long-winded, not knowing what they are talking about and seemingly talking about pointless facts and information. To the latter the former come across as fast, rude, impatient and difficult to understand.

The iceberg concept of the nature of culture [244]
Aspects of culture we are consciously aware of:

- Literature
- Manners
- Customs
- Language
- History
- Folklore

Aspects of culture we are less aware of:

- Communication style
- Non – verbal communication
- Patterns of interpersonal relationships
- Approaches to carrying out a task
- How tasks are assigned
- What motivates people
- Attitude towards commitments
- Attitude towards/concern for planning
- Ways of establishing rapport
- Negotiation styles and handling conflict
- Attitude towards authority
- Perceptions of professionalism
- Role expectations
- Values and order of priorities
- Work and learning styles
- Attitude towards words
- Concern for efficiency
- Tempo of work
- Politeness and etiquette

In my own church we encounter these dynamics in a number of contexts. In our home groups, a lady might share a testimony of God's provision in her life. To her the details of the story are important and will expound on all the ins and outs, emotions and feelings of her journey eventually getting to the main point where God came through for her. To her the process is as equally important as the end result. If it was me, I would have skipped most of the detail and gotten to the end result. Those like myself learn to give time to listen to others, not be in such a hurry, and enjoy the journey of listening and walking with others!

As an eldership team we have had to learn to give grace to one another in our communication styles. Dominic Mabikwe one of the team who is now 82 years old, would describe me as fast and quick thinking and he has learned to allow me to express my exuberant summary-point thoughts and ideas. I have also learned to allow him a few days to ponder about what I have said. He will not respond straight away but will come back to me days later to clarify certain points and give his input in the conversation. I have also learned in listening to his stories (which at first-glance may appear unrelated), that he always pulls them together and makes some very profound comments and remarks. Patience and grace are key to mutual understanding and appreciation of one another.

Conflict resolution – Linked to communication styles is the related topic of conflict resolution. The Western approach to handling conflict tends to value a direct, confrontational, one-on-one approach. Even the idioms we use can reinforce such thinking. Things like:

- Don't beat around the bush
- Put your cards on the table
- Lay it on the line
- Give it to me straight

Though some may fall into the camp of avoidance, giving-in, or compromise, individual and direct confrontation is the preferred method. We like straight, clear and direct communication. If someone is not straight forward with us we judge them to be devious, deceptive, evasive, guilty and trying to avoid the truth. Most other cultures of the world, however, do not place high value on direct face-to-face confrontation. Such directness is considered crude, harsh, uncultured, disrespectful and at times cruel. 'Saving face' or not causing another to feel shame are central values to many cultures and as such, people prefer to handle conflict indirectly, circuitously and obliquely. [245]

If in a teamwork context, for example, someone was not pulling their weight, the group may be called together and the problem indirectly addressed to everyone – exhorting everyone to pull together and work harder. This way the message gets across to the person in question and he escapes the public shame of being singled out as directly responsible for the problem. To the Western mind this would not be fair – why should everyone be blamed when only one person was responsible? Even language that people use can reflect this value of saving face. Where Westerners might say, 'I broke the plate', other cultures might say, 'The plate fell and broke'.

Such indirect methods of handling conflict can often be misinterpreted by the Western mind as;

- Lack of courage to confront a person
- Unwillingness to deal with the issue
- Lack of commitment to solve the problem
- Refusal to take responsibility for one's actions

In fact, as the American author Duane Elmer says in his book on cross-cultural conflict, 'the person may be displaying both courage and commitment, but in ways that are not understood by those of us who come from a culture that values directness.' [246]

Biblically, passages like Matthew 18:15-17 seem to approve the more direct approach of handling conflict;

'If your brother sins against you, go and tell him his fault, between you and him alone… If he does not listen, take one or two others along with you, that every charge may be established by the evidence of two or three witnesses. If he refuses to listen to them, tell it to the church…'

The text seems clear that direct, face-to-face confrontation in a caring, loving way is the biblical approach to conflict. Many Christians would argue, therefore, that this is the only biblical approach and must be applied in all contexts and with all cultures. What is not so clear from the passage above, however, is whether this is intended to be the only approach to conflict or whether it represents one good approach. [247]

I would like to suggest that it would be unwise to totally regard direct confrontation as the only way of handling conflict. At the very least we need to be aware that not everyone thinks in the same way that we do, and to be sensitive to these dynamics when relating cross culturally. Biblically, there is evidence of more indirect conflict resolution techniques that would be well worth considering when encountering disagreements and conflict in the church. [248] Jesus, for example, in handling the woman caught in adultery in John 8:1-11, remained silent when the Pharisees brought their direct accusations. He disarmed the accusers with a simple question diverting the focus from the woman's sin to their own sin. On another occasion in Mark 9:33-37, when Jesus' disciples were arguing over who was the greatest, he did not confront them directly or shame them publically. Rather he pulled a child forward and shared a short parable to give indirect teaching and correction to them. Direct confrontation is not the only way of resolving conflict.

Politeness and etiquette – Cultural world-views regarding politeness and etiquette vary considerably. To demonstrate this point I'd like to share a conversation that Sarah Lanier had with some fellow passengers while travelling on a flight to New Mexico. Sarah was conversing with an American lady who had asked her what it was like growing up in the Middle East. Eavesdropping on their conversation was a Lebanese lady called Aida who had been living in the States for eight years;

(Sarah) 'Well, I grew up in a variety of cultures. The Jewish and Arab cultures are vastly different… In the Jewish culture, you say what you think. It's direct, and you know where you stand with people. The Arab culture, on the other hand, is much more indirect. It's all about friendliness and politeness. If offered a cup of coffee, I say, 'No, thank you.' The host offers it again and I decline again with something like, 'No, no, don't bother yourself.' He might offer a third time, and I'd reply, 'No, I really don't want any coffee. Believe me.' Then my host serves the coffee and I drink it.'

'You've got to be kidding' she (the American lady) said incredulously. 'No, really', I assured her. 'You're supposed to refuse the first few times. It's the polite thing to do.' 'Then, what if you really don't want the coffee?' she asked. 'Well, then there are idioms you can use to say that you wouldn't for any reason refuse their kind hospitality, and at some point in the future you'll gladly join them in coffee, but at the moment you really can't drink it.'

Now Aida got into the conversation. 'Incredible! I didn't know that' she said as our heads turned her way. 'Aida,' I replied, 'what do you mean you don't know that? You're Lebanese for heaven's sake'. 'Yes', she said, 'but I mean I didn't know this was not normal. I've been in the United States eight years already, and did not realise it was done differently here. That explains so much. I've been lonely since moving here and now I know why. When people in the office would ask me if I wanted to go to lunch, I would say 'no' to be polite, fully expecting them to ask me again. When they didn't and left without me, I thought they didn't really want me along and had asked only out of politeness. In my culture it would have been too forward to say 'yes' the first time. For this reason I've had few American friends. After all these years now I know why' (Sarah Lanier).[249]

As I ponder the sadness of this story, I am challenged to the importance of daring to understand different world views – no one should have to suffer like that simply because they don't understand the culture of another.

Priorities and values – Another potentially unseen aspect of cultural diversity is that of cultural priorities and the things cultures consider to be of importance and value in life.

Allocation of finance – If you came into some extra money do you buy a big car, go out for a meal, do work on your house, help family members or go on vacation? Different cultures will have different values about such things. Among the Xhosa people of South Africa great importance is placed on having a decent and honourable funeral. Many people as such, including the poorest of the poor, would prioritise paying into a monthly funeral policy over and above buying something for one's house or other 'essentials' of life. To an outsider this may be perceived as being foolish, but merely reflects a different value system.

Which is the greater sin – lying, stealing or losing your temper? In the West, high value is placed on accuracy and truth so lying and stealing are generally looked down upon or more readily disapproved than an outburst of rage. Outside the Western world, for most part, greater value is placed on relationships. Losing one's temper is a more grievous sin because it represents a rupture in relationship.

Duane Elmer recalls an encounter he had while asking for directions at a petrol station in Amanzimtoti along the Indian coast of South Africa. In seeking to know how to get to a local church where he was due to preach, the petrol attendant gave him verbal directions. Several minutes later a frustrated

Elmer found himself even further away from the church than before, and was bemused as to why the attendant had apparently deliberately led him astray. Clearly the man was either irresponsible, dishonest or downright devious. Elmer later discovered that in Zulu culture great value is placed on courtesy to the stranger and help to the needy. He qualified as both. The last thing the attendant wanted to do was disappoint someone looking to him for assistance. Rather than disappoint Elmer by not being able to help, and rather than risk him thinking poorly of him, he gave Duane his best effort. In this context relationship was valued over truth. Furthermore, to admit that he did not have what Elmer needed would have brought shame or loss of face upon himself, another cultural taboo that had to be avoided at all cost. [250]

Community versus individualism – How we allocate our time is a good indicator of the things we value most. The Western world does not place a high premium on community. For those of us with a more individualistic mindset, time allocated towards community needs (including church community) can be easily sacrificed for personal preferences. Within other cultures, however, priority of time willingly allocated towards extended family, local community, and even church community may be of higher importance over and above personal and individual requirements. Such differences in priority can be a source of misunderstanding and conflict when not recognised and discussed.

At Khanyisa, for example, some cultures will think nothing of giving a whole day to attending a funeral, a wedding or even a church event. To our people with a more Western mindset, however, such a thought would be inconceivable unless one was totally psyched and prepared. We recently held a wedding for a young couple in the church called Nikelo and Gcobisa Mandondo. One of our White young men kindly volunteered to drive Gcobisa and her bridesmaids to the church. He failed to realise, however, that the driving would be a whole day affair taking the couple for photographs afterwards, as well as visiting various family members. Such a thing apparently didn't need communicating as naturally this is what one does for one's community. Community is highly valued and therefore worthy of allocating many hours of time. Michael, the young man in question, was not used to such a thing happening, and naturally assumed the wedding would be over within the 'normal' couple of hours and consequently had made plans to go on a date with his girlfriend later that evening. Community triumphed resulting in Michael having to buy several bunches of flowers to appease his rather disgruntled girlfriend. Some interesting conversations followed the event between Michael and Nikelo regarding expectations and communication![251]

Patterns of interpersonal relationships – How we relate with one another, our non-verbal communication and our means of expressing friendship, love and appreciation to one another are further cultural examples with the potential to take us by surprise.

Looking someone directly in the eye is commonly regarded as a mark of respect within my culture. If my children are talking to me I would expect them to look me in the eyes. If they didn't I would think they were being shifty or have something to hide. Such would be my immediate thoughts when talking to others or pastorally counseling people within the church. In other cultures such a thing is inconceivable. Respect is shown by lowering ones head and NOT looking at someone directly in the eyes. Misunderstandings can frequently occur in this area if we are not aware.

Expressions of friendship are culturally defined. Duane Elmer as an American recalls, 'In North America we have defined ways of showing friendship and love. One of those ways is to invite someone to my house for an evening meal together; we set a day and time for this meeting. Both parties understand this as a friendly, if not loving, act and something that will strengthen our relationship. But in many parts of Africa, an invitation to come to my house at a designated time may not be interpreted as friendly and loving. In fact, it might be interpreted as a sign that I want a formal, distant relationship. Why? In Africa one shows friendship by stopping in unannounced, perhaps at a mealtime. If a time, place and agenda for meeting have to be prearranged, the relationship cannot be open and spontaneous and evolve naturally, or so the reasoning goes.'[252]

Such has been my experience in my own church context where many of my more Western people question why they don't get invited for meals in the townships? I tell them to just show up and see what happens!

Expressing love and praise – One year, following a three-day leadership conference held in Bloemfontein, I witnessed a heated debate between a number of leaders from varying cultural backgrounds. One leader had expressed his shock seeing some young ladies dancing and worshipping God at the front of the meeting hall, shaking their chests and gyrating their bottoms in a very distracting and suggestive manner. Another leader argued that this was totally culturally acceptable and was not suggestive in any way. He, on the other hand, had been more offended by seeing married and dating couples in the congregation sitting next to each other, their arms around one another and at times publically kissing one another. This, he exclaimed, was far more offensive and unsuitable behaviour than any gyrating of hips. Though we may struggle to agree, let's be careful how we judge one another and dare to examine situations through the eyes of others.

Perceptions of professionalism – We once had a guest speaker at Khanyisa who recalled his experience preaching at a conference in Johannesburg. He was highlighting the importance of time-keeping and recalled his shock and dismay when a small group of Malawians arrived at the conference not one hour late, not five hours late, not one day late, but three days late! He proudly exclaimed how he had travelled from New York and managed to get there the day before, why then could these people not arrive on time? Such people were obviously not serious for the Lord, lacking in commitment and in great need of some sound discipline. To make matters worse, a group of Khayelitsha youngsters arrived late in our meeting only to add fuel to his fire and be on the receiving end of his disapproving glare.

I could feel my blood boiling. Did he know how far Khayelitsha was from Guguletu? Did he have any idea what it was like relying on public transport waiting to catch taxis to get to a church meeting at that time of night? The fact that these youngsters had made it at all impressed me greatly, showing great commitment and eagerness to learn. Did he have any idea what it was like to travel by road from Blantyre to Johannesburg enduring potholes, numerous tyre punctures and waiting for trains and buses that may or may not arrive and frequently break down even when they do? The Malawians should have been honoured for their commitment and seriousness to the Lord, their willingness to endure such hardships and travel great distances for the sake of the gospel. Perceptions of professionalism and excellence can vary greatly from culture to culture! For those of us from the West, where time has the potential to control our lives, can I humbly suggest we loosen up and not take it or ourselves quite so seriously.

4 Recognise our need of one another

Such examples of the hidden nature of culture are, of course, a mere drop in the ocean and it would be unrealistic, if not next-to-impossible, to examine every aspect of every culture in the world. They do highlight, none the less, that we are not all the same. Most cross-cultural conflicts and misunderstandings are not intentional. Most are inadvertent, occurring because underlying cultural values are not understood. What is surprising is not that we have so many conflicts and differences, but that given all of our cultural centeredness, there are not more conflicts and misunderstandings. Such is the grace of God on our lives. It is important to remember that we are each children of God, made in his image, and in that sense are more alike than different. That should be our starting point.

In turn, we must humbly recognise our great need of one another. We cannot reach out across the cultural divides on our own – to see as others see, we need their help. There is a limit to how much we can single-handedly prepare ourselves to learn and understand another culture. No matter how well prepared we are, or how much we read and study about another culture (something I would encourage us all to do), it will never be enough. There will always be some hidden cultural aspect that will take us by surprise. Such unforeseen differences, along with their potential to create confusion, misunderstanding and upset, cannot be resolved by resorting to a book. We are left with no choice but to journey into the mess of developing deeper and genuine relationships with each other. We must create contexts to meet, relate, discuss and ask questions. When we fail to understand we don't give up but ask again. We share our lives and our stories together, pray together and slowly learn to see as others see.

Lastly, we must rely on God. We have fellowship with the Holy Spirit who unites us all together. His glory is revealed through our living together in unity, and there should be no doubt that the love and the power of God is available to us. He is the one who will grant us the ability to respect our human and cultural differences, overcome misunderstandings and not allow them to disrupt loving and genuine fellowship with one another. Let's seek God in our own situations with the knowledge that he who has begun a good work in us will bring it to completion.

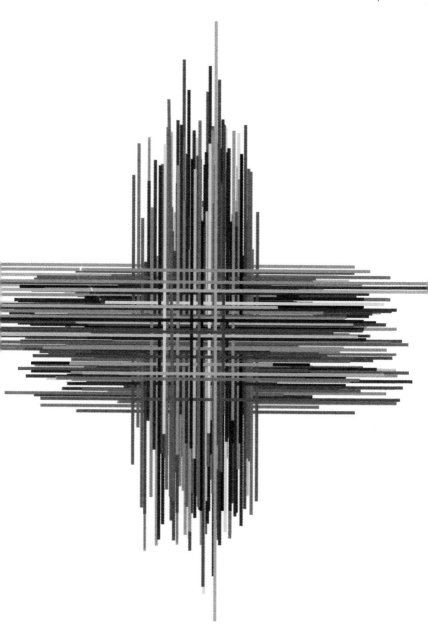

11 Breaking the silence

'Confronting the barriers of race, class, culture and gender was perhaps the major social drama of the New Testament Church. Overcoming those divisions was seen as a primary test of spiritual authenticity. If the churches would reclaim the call to spiritual warfare, this time against the principality and power of racism, how might the battle against racism be transformed? We might finally begin to estimate the enemy adequately.' (Jim Wallis) [253]

'The issue of racial prejudice and snubbing and suspicion and mistreatment is not a social issue; it is a blood-of-Jesus issue.' (John Piper)

We are all tinged by racism and I am no exception to the rule. I came to South Africa in 1994 with a smug sense of English superiority subconsciously ingrained in my thoughts. I never would have said so at the time, but my actions over the subsequent months would expose more clearly the hidden motives of my heart. Deep down a number of false assumptions and stereotypical thoughts governed what I did and how I viewed people:

Black is better than White – I had a somewhat 'Black is beautiful and White is ugly' type of thinking. I deliberately put all my effort and time going into the townships and building relationships with Black and Coloured people while actively avoiding too much contact with my fellow 'Whities'. I prided myself on the fact that I could travel all around Khayelitsha and Guguletu but could not tell you how to get to the cable car at Table Mountain or go to the sandy beaches of Clifton. Subconsciously I separated myself from White suburban life judging my paler-coloured friends for their past, their fear, their wealth and their ignorance.

Somehow I was in a different league to them as I had never been under apartheid. Like Jonah I was willing to enter the world of certain people – but not others. [254]

South Africans live in fear – I especially judged and looked down upon White South Africans for what I saw to be their fear. It seemed to me that many White people were too scared to go into the townships and most seemed to lock their car doors the moment they got into a vehicle. I would judge them for their lack of faith and trust in God and deliberately made the point of NOT locking my door whenever I was in a car. I tried to make a point by cycling into the townships, demonstrating that I wasn't governed by fear and that I was protected by God. After all I had wandered the streets of Khayelitsha all by myself in 1988 and I was perfectly fine [255].

Held up at gun point

Two events in particular would challenge my attitude in this regard. The first incident occurred one day while visiting with friends in Khayelitsha. I was driving the Jubilee church 'bakkie' [256] and as usual my door was unlocked, my window down and my seat-belt off. As I reversed around a street corner a man appeared from nowhere, opened my driver's door, put a gun to my head and screamed for me to get out. Without thinking I continued to reverse the vehicle knocking the man out of the way in the process. The lady in the car with me, Mavis Mthandeki, shouted Xhosa obscenities like I'd never heard before and fortunately for us, the bullet that I anticipated to come our way never did. Duly shaken I made the point of locking my door for the rest of my journey home, something I'm still in the habit of doing today.

Knife attack

The second incident occurred returning home from a visit to the dentist. I used to cycle to Bible College on the Klipfontein Road close to Tambo Village. Afterwards I would then ride my mountain bike into the townships to visit friends in Tambo Square. One day having also cycled for a check-up at my local Guguletu dentist, I decided to take the long route home past the Fezeka council offices and over the railway bridge on Lansdowne road. As I crossed the bridge a group of youths ran into the road and knocked me off my bike. One man then proceeded to chase me down the road with a knife in his hand, while the other youths ran off with my bike. I was scared and genuinely thought I would be stabbed. The man eventually got hold of me and took the rucksack that was strapped to my back. Unharmed bar a few cuts and bruises, I shakily made my way home.

Attitudes exposed

God used these incidents to expose my stupidity and the terrible motives and attitudes I was harbouring in my heart. Suddenly Black was not as beautiful as I'd first idolised and White wasn't as bad as I'd first judged. I became more willing to hear White peoples' stories and enter their world attempting to see things from their perspective. My vision changed from being a missionary doing something for these poor oppressed Black people to one of cross-cultural diversity and reconciliation. God wanted to bring healing to this amazing but hurting nation and didn't need another Englishman bringing judgment on the periphery.

My racism to Black and Coloured people was also exposed. I somehow thought they needed me as I was the missionary from England coming to help them. With time I came to see that such an attitude was steeped in superiority where I judged them of less worth, perhaps because of education or poverty and lack of wealth. This was a humbling and painful season in my life. I realised that if I was going to see God's Kingdom advance in the lives of others and in the communities where I was serving, I also had to allow it to come in my heart as well. Crossing racial boundaries has forced me to do this and I'm grateful to God for the many people he has used and continues to use in the process.

Willingness to look at racism

In crossing racial and economic boundaries it is only inevitable that at some point or other we will come face to face with the reality of racism and prejudice – whether in ourselves or in others. Uncomfortable as this may be, it is something we must be willing to look at if we genuinely desire to take the gospel to all nations of the world. Furthermore, if we want to build dynamic church communities across racial and economic lines we must be prepared to look at the way racism has shaped (and continues to shape), has wounded (and continues to wound) both people of Colour and those who are White.

Not only must we face this individually, but we must face it in the church as well. As Rick Joyner says;

'The world is losing control of its racial problems. The cause is a spiritual power that no legislation or human agency can stop. Only that which is bound in heaven can be bound upon earth. If the church does not face this problem, overcoming racism within its own ranks, so that we can take spiritual authority over it, the world will soon fall into an abyss of chaos, destruction and suffering of unprecedented proportions – all from racial conflict.' (Rick Joyner) [257]

Assumptions, stereotypes and prejudices

Let's be honest – none of us can function without making assumptions, judgments and stereotypes about others – we all do it. On a daily basis we make judgments about people based on a whole variety of external factors, opinions and presumptions. For example:

- Wealth means success while poverty means failure. 'I've worked hard for what I've got – they are obviously lazy.'
- The poor only see what they can get from you.
- Working class is inferior to middle class. 'Times and Telegraph' readers are better than 'Sun' readers. [258]
- White is better than Black – this can be perceived by people of all colours all over the world.

- City is better than rural – 'Can anything good come out of Nazareth?' (John 1:46)

- Accents – hearing certain accents we judge people to be common, uneducated or stuck-up.

- Prejudices such as 'Cretans are always liars' (Titus 1:12); The French are…; The Germans are…; The Irish are…; Pakistani's are…; Polish Immigrants are…etc.

- My quality of life is reducing because of 'all these immigrants'. Things are not like what they were before!

- First world (White) is better then Third World (Non White). Even terminology such as Third World Countries and First World Countries, can reinforce this stereotypical thinking.

- White churches will get better teaching than Black churches. We are more confident in White leadership than Black leadership.

- Black songs are simple while White songs are deep and meaningful.

And so the list can go on. Such values are rarely taught to us. Rather they are attitudes and perspectives we have unconsciously absorbed and are then sustained through the language that we hear and use, the media, professional values and even our political and legal systems.

Discrimination and racism

Inevitably if we act on these assumptions, stereotypes and prejudices, discrimination and racism occur. Racism is specifically discrimination that happens based upon a persons colour, culture or ethnic origin. This can be either direct, indirect or simply a reluctance to challenge or change the status quo.

A helpful definition of racism comes from a report that came out of the UK following the death of Stephen Lawrence who was killed in a British racist attack in the early nineties. It defines general racism practiced by individuals as consisting of;

'…Conduct or words or practices which disadvantage or advantage people because of their colour, culture or ethnic origin. In its more subtle form it is as damaging as in its overt form'. [259]

It's important then to recognise that racism is sustained by individuals personal attitudes, prejudices, bigotries and biases. These extend to every level of human emotion and thinking as well as EVERY society and culture.

Racism, however, is not just carried out by individuals (ourselves and others) but can also occur within institutions such as businesses, schools, universities, local churches, denominations, local councils and even governments. The Lawrence report defines such institutional racism as;

'…the collective failure of an organisation to provide an appropriate and professional service to people because of their colour, culture or ethnic origin. It can be seen or detected in processes, attitudes and behaviour, which amount to discrimination through unwitting prejudice, ignorance, thoughtlessness and racist stereotyping which disadvantage minority ethnic people.' [260]

This is no small thing. It is as Rick Joyner says, '…not just a demon or even a principality – it is a world ruler. It is one of the most powerful strongholds on earth and it has sown more death and destruction than any other one.' [261]

Comments on racism

Racism is a much debated and highly contested topic for which time and space don't allow us to engage in this book. Suffice it to say I'd like to make a few hopefully helpful comments on the topic before moving on to examine practically how we deal with this in the church.

Economic roots – It is worth noting that historically much racism has an economic root. In America for example, racism developed in thinking and action to justify the slave trade from Africa. The slave was seen as less than human – an animal or piece of property to be bought and sold. This has been even more so in Africa with colonialism and where racism developed out of a desire for economic gain by the West from theThird World. It's only fair to say then that the English, like myself, have benefited from the structure of racism whether or not we have ever committed a racist act, uttered a racist word or had a racist thought (as unlikely as that is).

Perspectives – Racism also has to do with power to dominate and enforce oppression. Generally speaking on a global scale, power that inevitably comes with wealth is in the hands of the so called White Western World. Some would say that there is no such thing as Black racism as generally speaking throughout the world Black people do not have the power to enforce that prejudice. This is controversial and I don't want to argue that point,[262] only to emphasise that it's a fair observation to make that much power, control and wealth in the world is in the hands of White people. It's worth remembering then that one's views and perspectives on the topic of racism sitting behind the desk (in a place of power) can be very different from those sitting on the other side of the desk.

Racism has thus been defined by some as, 'prejudice plus power'. Individually this is not always a helpful way to look at racism as many White people and especially White women may feel that they have no power and are therefore not racist. White women may also feel that they can identify with People of Colour as they too have been discriminated against, without realising the depth of prejudice that Black People and others live under.

Control – Linked to power is control. Many of us from our backgrounds and upbringing (and colour of our skin) are just used to being in control. We are used to making decisions and telling people what to do. In short term mission we as churches can go into communities or countries to do good or give the gospel. However, the way we do this can merely reinforce the feeling of control – especially if we hold the purse strings. Even in discussions together on racism we can define the problem and put a solution together not really having heard or listened to other people in the room. One Black youth leader in Cape Town gave an example of control while participating in a Newfrontiers discussion on race led by Gary Welsh in 1996. He shared how when he had been in meetings to discuss things with White people, such as the annual youth summer camp, he had a feeling that he had just been invited as 'window dressing' but was not really part of what was going on. When asked if his opinion had been asked for in these meetings, he replied;

'Yes but the 'skeleton has already been decided before hand' – all they want to do is put a bit of flesh on the bones. Our opinions are not asked and we are not involved in helping set the direction and structure.'

On another occasion a White woman leading a team complained that she found it difficult when Black women challenged what she was saying. 'They want a democracy and not a theocracy,' she said. What this lady failed to understand was that the other ladies also wanted to be part of the process of hearing from God. They had been so used to White people coming to them and saying, 'God said,' as though he speaks to White people only. There must of course be the right respect for the authority and gifting of the leader, however, it's important to listen to the view points of others – especially in a cross-cultural context.

Superiority and Inferiority – Though the consequences of racism are many, there are two related resultants that are inseparably linked; superiority and inferiority. On the one hand racism makes certain people see themselves as culturally superior to others based on the firm belief that their way is right. This acts out with a know it all attitude and a portrayal of confidence and having everything held together. It can further be revealed by a patronising attitude of 'these people need me' or 'I'm coming to do something for them' – the us and them language!

On the other hand racism can make others feel very inferior ie 'what can I do; I'm not educated and don't have money'? Within church evangelism some will 'take it' not wanting to offend the person of another culture. They feel that they cannot match up to the pressure put on them by the other culture to conform to their way of thinking – which is portrayed as best. They may feel like children having to answer to their parents and this may make them feel angry, helpless and dependent.

Trying to be cross-cultural – We can attempt to break these prejudices by trying to be cross-cultural and or holding multi-cultural evenings to find out more about one another. While this is good and invariably is enjoyable and enriching, having more knowledge of another culture doesn't automatically mean that prejudices will be done away with. They can, if we are not careful, appear patronising and can even fool one into thinking that more is being achieved than actually is.

How do we respond?

How then do we respond to such a real but highly emotive topic where there is so much potential for hurt and misunderstanding? It can feel as Owen Hylton says, 'like you are entering a minefield without the aid of body armour'.[263] At the risk of being blown up I'd like to give some suggestions on going forward overcoming racism in our own lives, relationships with one another and in the church.

1 Racism is a blood of Jesus issue

It's important first of all to remember that we have a God who is passionate about this topic. This is not merely a topic reserved for left-wing political people and those with issues in the church. God also has issues in this area. As John Piper says; 'The issue of racial prejudice and snubbing and suspicion and mistreatment is not a social issue; it is a blood of Jesus issue'.[264] Christ went to great lengths not only to see reconciliation between God and man but also to reconcile different people groups one to another in the body of Christ. Ephesians tell us that;

'..you who once were far off have been brought near by the blood of Christ. For he himself is our peace who has made us both one and broken down in his flesh the dividing wall of hostility by abolishing the law of commandments and ordinances that he might create in himself one new man in place of the two, so making peace and might reconcile us both to God in one body through the cross thereby killing the hostility.' (Ephesians 3: 13-16 ESV)

Through the blood of Christ, through his flesh and through the cross Jesus paid a terrible price not only to reconcile us with God but also to reconcile us with other races – previously separated and hostile races now united together as one new man in Christ. In other words Jesus paid a major price to deal with racism.

Revelation tells us he, 'purchased for God… men from every tribe and tongue and people and nation' (Rev 5:9 NASB). This means all the terrible attitudes that we hold in our hearts to one another like jealousy, suspicion, anger, superiority, hatred, prejudice, racism and all the things that cause us to have animosity towards people of different skin colour. All of this was purchased by Christ's blood so we would be united together in love in his church! Wow – Christ did a lot to deal with this issue of racism.

Jesus takes this issue seriously and so we should as well. We should allow the love of Christ to compel us forward if we ever feel tempted to avoid dealing with racism in our midst. It's a costly and uncomfortable business, but that shouldn't surprise us when we think of how much it cost Christ.

2 Recognition of the issue

We need to recognise that racism is still alive and kicking and as such be open to talk about it, not dismissing its existence with clichés like, 'let's put the past behind us'. As Beverly Daniel Tatum says,

'We need to talk about it at home, at school, in our houses of worship, in our workplaces, in our community groups. But talk

does not mean idle chatter. It means meaningful, productive dialogue to raise consciousness and lead to effective action and social change.' (Tatum 1997: 193) [265]

Talking about it, however, is easier said than done. It may generate discomfort, cause offense or incur the wrath of others. As such we risk rejection and misunderstanding, a risk for which many of us may be tempted to avoid by remaining silent. Silence, however, is a danger that should be avoided at all costs. As Tatum goes on to say,

'Unchallenged personal, cultural and institutional racism results in loss of human potential, lowered productivity, and a rising tide of fear and violence in our society. Individually, racism stifles our own growth and development. It clouds our vision and distorts our perceptions. It alienates us not only from others but also from ourselves and our own experience.' (Tatum 1997: 200) [266]

Recognising racism in ourselves, each other and in the church will require a willingness to be challenged and corrected by Scripture. Again this is easier said than done as for many of us it is easier to admit to other sins rather than this one called racism. We also need to acknowledge, as we saw in the previous chapter, that we each have a worldview that influences how we think and do things. Our worldview can even affect how we read, see and respond to the Bible. Robert MacAfee Brown argues that those of us brought up in comfort and privilege hear a different message to those brought up under oppression and poverty. Some of us, from our social backgrounds, can screen out passages of Scripture that call into question our values or threaten our comfort and lifestyle.

Furthermore, besides individual racism and prejudice, we should also recognise and be prepared to face racism in the church and in our leadership structures. This will require a willingness to examine our leadership teams, the types of people we are discipling, our leadership styles and our ways of working with people. It will also mean being willing to talk, preach and pray into racism as well as allowing forums where people can openly speak and not be judged or have their theology corrected. Avoidance is not a leadership option and we should learn from mistakes made by churches in the past that have done this. Many leaders in South Africa, for example, says CW du Toit;

'…distanced themselves from the injustices of apartheid and would not admit to anything that questioned the credibility of their ministry over many years. In the minds of ministers, they had preached the love of God as well as the imperatives of neighbourly love and justice. Most of them also tried to abstain from politics in their preaching and pastoral work. They may have felt uncomfortable with some aspect of apartheid but felt it was a political problem, while they were called to preach the kingdom of God. Evangelism was the only way in which to better society.'[267] (CW du Toit)

We must resist the status quo and recognise that for the world to change, it starts within the very systems we are part of – including our local churches.

How do we recognise prejudices in ourselves?

Here are a few questions to think about that can help us begin to recognise some of the racism and prejudice in all our hearts. Once recognised we are then in a much stronger position to deal with it.

- Have you found yourself saying: 'I am not a racist but…' then follow on with a derogatory racial remark? (I'm not a racist but I don't go to the beach anymore, it is too full of 'other' people).

- Do you find that you have all the answers to problems presented to you by people of another culture, and then get upset when you find that no-one has acted on the answers you gave them?

- Do you find that as you are listening to people of another culture present their problems, hurts and frustrations to you, you are already formulating a response in your mind as you listen, not to their hurt and pain, but to their 'sin' of anger, not to mention their 'bad' theology which you need to put right?

- Do you find that when looking for people in your cell group, ministry or organisation to promote to leadership you seem to automatically go for those of the same culture as you?

- Do you expect people to live up to your standard and do things your way?

- Do you want someone from this culture to pray for you rather than that culture as this culture appears to have more power?

- How do you feel as a leader when someone from another culture corrects you or makes you aware that you may have just made a mistake or said the wrong thing?

- Do you walk in anger against another race or cultural group?

- Do you find that you'd rather stick to your own cultural group as you don't 'understand' the other cultures and don't want to bother finding out about them?

- Do you feel inferior in the presence of other cultural groups?

3 Struggle

Rooting out racism doesn't just happen overnight or by trying to change a few things in our lives. For many of us we need to settle in our hearts that we may be dealing with this over a long period of time. We need stickability and a commitment not to give up.

This can be tiring and exhausting. Being aware of race dynamics can cause one to become conscious of every word one says so as not to upset or cause offense. Similarly we can analyse every action we make wondering how it will affect those around us. Lisa once made this observation and asked someone how long she might have to keep doing this. The reply given was, 'It may take for ever – but that is a small price to pay for the suffering that we have gone through over many years, during which we have had to keep quiet.' Oops – not an easy answer but it was also very healing. At least we now knew what was expected and how long it would take!

Listen – We must make time to talk, share stories and listen to one another, open to hear the things we don't want to hear. We need to let one another talk without butting in, making judgments or even trying to give an explanation for something we feel has been misinterpreted. Humility is a basic characteristic that makes us open to listen and not defend, allowing us to extend grace to one another. God after all 'gives grace to the humble'. (James 4:6)

The following comments are examples of some of the things that I have heard shared by people from various cultures in our interactions with one another in South Africa around race and racism. [268] Many of these comments could be perceived to be hard hitting – but none the less we have felt it important, to keep healthy contexts where we can share openly and freely with one another. Sometimes it is not a question of being right or wrong in what we say but merely having someone listen to us, genuinely hearing what we say and loving us all the same.

The following comments were made by People of Colour [269]

- I often feel that White (western) people do not listen to what I have to say.
- I found that there was more excitement when a White leader planted a church than a Black leader.
- I find that White (Western) people appear to be thinking for me and talking about what is best for me but have not bothered to ask what I think and in this way my dignity is taken away.
- When thinking about competency, I feel that if I fail it would be seen as a Black person failing but if a White person fails it is just seen as a mistake.
- I grew up thinking that White was good and if you are not White then you are sub-standard.
- As a Black man, I get up in the morning, look in the mirror and know that I am black and wonder who is going to use this to judge me in some way. White people won't understand the concept of looking at their colour every day. It would never enter their thinking.

- Whites can sometimes feel that they have not done anything wrong, especially the younger leaders – but both sides need to recognise that there is much to do.

- In Newfrontiers Black people have been put up front to lead but this has been for the sake of it. People should not be put in positions just because of the colour of their skin.

- The White middle class wish to hold onto their identity as a white middle class church. There is intolerance and white people don't wish to give on their side. Whites are happy as long as all remains middle class.

- Who defines the quality of Black leadership? Western standards are set as the goal posts. Where do values come into our standards? One Black person in Newfrontiers got up to preach and afterwards a White pastor went to him and pulled his sermon apart. He was criticised not on theological issues or any great error but on style because he didn't do the intro and three-point sermon. Who says this is not quality?

The following comments were made by White people [270]

- I invite Black people to my house but they don't even come or phone to tell me they are not coming.

- I make effort to get to know people but it is not reciprocated. Black people won't invite me to their house for a meal and no one says thank you.

- I feel like I'm being used, always giving people lifts but it is not appreciated.

- Black people don't seem to show any initiative and won't speak up in meetings. Why won't they say anything?

- Some people will listen to me because I'm White but how do you know when they are listening because of one's gifting and not the colour of one's skin?

- I feel that some Black people look at me with the attitude, 'There is a White person, what can I get?'

- I'm tired of having the race card always thrown in my face.
- This is a lot of nonsense which I haven't got time for. The world is dying for lack of hearing the gospel and I am supposed to contemplate my navel and wonder whether I'm a racist.
- I always feel condemned and feel ashamed to be White.
- Black people are cruel to their animals – I saw some boys kicking around a live rat and then laughing about it.
- Why should I have to pay the price for what other people did – I was never part of it?
- Some Black people will say yes to do something but then they don't do it – they don't seem to be able to take responsibility.
- We are all tarred with the same brush. I feel like people are always looking at me as privileged and that even though I'm giving my best it is still not good enough.
- I get offended when the Black women dance at the front and shake their 'boobs'.
- I have a nice house so I struggle to invite people around as I feel embarrassed that I have and they don't. I don't know how to handle it.

As you can imagine hearing such comments can be difficult, requiring much wisdom, love and grace with one another. As leaders we may feel that our authority is being questioned or feel criticised and a failure in the church. None the less we need the humility to listen and humbly discern how to respond.

- Some comments come out of pain and hurt requiring no further action other than love, understanding and God's healing grace.
- Some comments should provoke us to greater awareness, understanding and sensitivity towards one another.
- Some comments demand repentance, giving and receiving of forgiveness, action, intentional change and practical steps to be made in the way that we do things.

4 **Confession and repentance**

The time will come when we will need to be still before the Lord and ask him to reveal what is in our heart. Many of us will need to confess that we are racist (call it what it is) or that we have racist tendencies. This, of course, is a hard confession to make but it is very cleansing and releasing once it is done. The first letter of John 1v9 says, 'If we confess our sins, he is faithful and just and will forgive us our sins and purify us from all unrighteousness.' Worship the Lord and praise him for beginning the healing process in you and helping you to move from being a cripple into being a whole and healthy person.

Forgive – We also need the courage to ask forgiveness of one another. Some of us have genuinely hurt and offended others and need to face up to the truth of that and the pain we have caused. We should dare to confess such things to each another and have the grace to get on our knees and pray for healing for one another. We need to remember that God is passionate for genuine reconciliation and he is more than willing to help us and give us his Holy Spirit.

Renewal of our minds – Lastly, we must realise that though we are forgiven we still have to walk through the process of renewing our minds in this area. If we find racist or prejudicial tendencies cropping up in our lives we must confess them immediately and ask the Lord to change us. We can also ask others to be honest with us and point out when our racism or prejudice is showing.

5 **Be colour conscious and not colour blind**

In South Africa it is common to hear people talk in terms of colour. When I was first in the townships one lady tried to tell me about a friend of hers of whom she was convinced I must know. 'You know the Black one with the long stomach, she lives next door to that White mama with demons,' she explained to me now certain I would know who she was talking about. 'Eh? What do you mean the Black one living next door to the White one – you're all Black?' I was confused. It turned out both the ladies were in fact Black, only one was blacker and the other paler in skin colour than the other. Talking in terms of skin colour can get one into trouble. I mentioned in chapter eight how, while doing a cross-cultural seminar in Bloemfontein, one Coloured lady got up and shouted at us saying, 'We are always talking about Black people but forget about the Coloured people'. Some, like the lady above, are proud to be Coloured and want to be identified in such a manner. Others would rather be associated with other people of colour under the general heading Black.

Shaped by skin colour – Whatever our feelings are on colour, one thing can't be denied – we are all people of colour to one shade or another. Our skin colour cannot be denied (or changed) and to various extents we have all been shaped and molded to be who we are today by the colour of our skin. It's often said, 'When I look at you I don't see colour,' but as someone once replied, 'But if you don't see my colour you don't see me, my history, my culture, my pain, the injustice of racism.' [271]

White people often don't think about how the colour of their skin affects them or shapes them. As a White man myself I have had to come to terms with the colour of my skin. At one stage I felt ashamed to be White and would rather have been Black, or at least a darker shade of pale! However, no matter how hard I protest, God put me in a white skin and that's the way it's going to be until the day I die. I've had to deal with the shame of what White people have done and deal with hostility shown towards me. I've had to come to a place of being happy to be White, knowing God loves Black and White equally.

Benefited by the colour of my skin – I've also had to come to terms with how I have benefited from being White. I've been greeted with respect in the market places and offered the best seats at the banquets. [272] Entering a London restaurant one day, the waitress politely spoke to me but blatantly ignored the Black person with me. On another occasion a Black friend of mine went into a bank and was totally ignored, but when I came and stood next to him the attendants fought for our attention. I've also used my skin colour to push to the front of a potential three or four-hour queue at the Red Cross Children's hospital. I wasn't prepared to wait and got away with it – after all I was White. This, of course, is not even to mention how I've accepted and enjoyed the benefits and rewards of what my British forefathers achieved with their racist and colonial exploitations (but that is a controversial topic to be discussed elsewhere).

These are just a few of my own struggles of the realities of walking in a white skin. Reading some of the comments above by people of Colour perhaps also gives a microscopic insight into some of the realities of walking in a Black skin. My point in all of this is to encourage us to be colour conscious in our relationships with one another, and not colour blind. It would be naïve to think that skin colour has no relevance or impact within the dynamics of evangelism, mission, cross-cultural relationships and cross-cultural church.

Last words

Racism, therefore, is not a topic that can be avoided if in any way we are attempting to cross the racial boundaries of our societies. We will face it and continue to face it in one form or another – whether in ourselves, in others, on the mission field, in our communities, in our work places and even in our local churches. My friend Siviwe, in proof reading this chapter, asked me whether I still see myself as a racist. My answer was yes. Even after years of walking with God and wrestling with issues around cultural and economic diversity, I still at times recognise racist attitudes, reactions and motives in my heart. Yet I press on in my goal of loving Jesus and those he has put around me. We will make mistakes, yet I have found as Beverly Tatum says, 'that a sincere apology and a genuine desire to learn from one's mistakes is usually rewarded with forgiveness'.[273] Let's not avoid or remain silent on this painful topic, but rather recognise it for what it is, deal with it accordingly and advance the Kingdom of God.

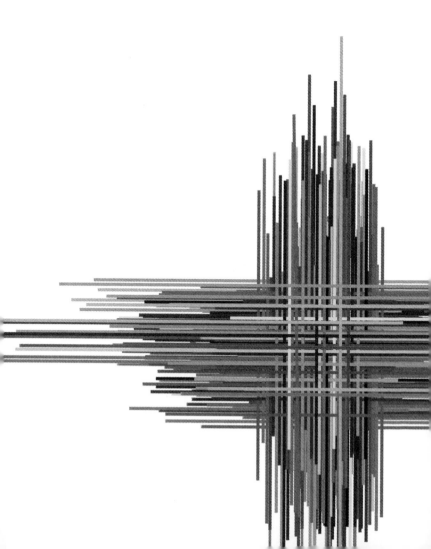

12 Go and do likewise

> *'The Christian lifestyle is not an individualistic one, for as Jesus arranged much of his teaching around the love of one's neighbour, so Paul believes that a valid Christian lifestyle must be worked out in the context of a commitment to the Christian community. Christ has broken down the barriers between nationalities, social classes and the sexes, he has brought his people together into complimentary relationships in which they care for one another.'*[274] *(Peter H Davids)*
>
> *'A big problem needs a big vision to sustain those who are brave enough to tackle it. Poverty is a massive problem but the vision of the Kingdom of God is equal to it. It provides an adequate end for all human effort because it is ultimately rooted in a heavenly future. It sustains effort now because the king has promised to be with his disciples in the heart of the conflict. Because the king is endowed with indestructible life we can be sure that even if we lose our own life in his service that our self sacrificing service will not be in vain.'*[275] *(D Hughes)*

A turning point in my rather nervous start to a career within the British Police Force was an encounter I had with a dead body by the river Thames. I'd only been on the job a few months and was working in the Weybridge area of Surrey on night patrol. At about 3 o'clock in the morning a call came over the radio reporting that a fisherman had overheard a loud argument occurring between a man and a woman down by the river. Things had since gone quiet and he was feeling rather concerned for the woman's safety. The Walton-area patrol car was assigned to investigate. A few minutes later, following a quick search of the scene, a frantic call was made by the officers appealing for urgent assistance. The woman had been found badly beaten and injured, but the reported man was nowhere to be seen. An ambulance was immediately deployed, but unfortunately by the time it got there, the lady was declared to be dead. This was now an official murder investigation. The superintendent was informed, dog and light units were called for and all remaining officers were quickly deployed in the hunt for the offending man. I was eventually summoned to the scene and given the dubious task of guarding the body, and logging every person who approached the scene of the crime.

It wasn't long before I found myself alone in the dark, with a dead body at my feet (covered in a blanket), as my colleagues were systematically called away on various errands. Being a 'good Christian', I contemplated praying for the body to be raised from the dead, but the best I could manage was a small prayer inside my head. As I nervously stood there, I heard what sounded like a deep guttural groaning noise 'Urrrrgh' coming from the body. I shone my torch down for what felt like an eternity, but no, definitely no movement. Perhaps it was the death groan that dead bodies have been known to exude as various gases are released from the corpse. A few minutes later, now whistling to calm my nerves, I heard the groan again. This time I was sure it was coming from the body. I cautiously reached down to lift the blanket and as I did so up it leapt.

Astonishingly, there before me was not a stranger. Instead it was a woman police constable whom I vaguely knew to work out of the Addlestone radio dispatch. The whole thing was a set-up! My colleagues, who were supposedly hunting for the missing man, burst out of the bushes laughing hilariously. They patted me on the back and advised me that I'd been well and truly conned. Experiencing a sudden sense of humour failure, I proceeded to speak a number of unrepeatable explicatives over the police radio, my good Christian witness going far out of the window! I became the rookie joke for many months to come.

The positive outcome of all this was that people got to know me and it opened up doors for many conversations about the incident, and also my faith in God. On this occasion the incident in question was a hoax, though in my remaining years in the police that was not to be the case as my eyes were quickly opened to another side of British life. Though different to anything I would later experience in South Africa, I experienced first hand the impact of poverty and crime in England, and was faced with the complications of traversing socio-economic divides. I would one day be interrelating with street-sleepers, while on the next with the wealthy and so-called elite of society. On one occasion I entered the house of a young family living in a poorer part of town only to discover piles of dog faeces (days old) lying on the carpet inside the house. Such lives and lifestyles seemed worlds apart from my own life and way of living. I saw the reality of drug and alcohol abuse, domestic violence, unemployment, broken homes, and homelessness, and had to establish my response as a Christian. I heard the way some colleagues would speak of those from the council-estates or local gypsy communities, and had to make choices based on my own values.

Rich and poor together

At that stage of my life, my interaction and involvement across such socio-economic divides of my country was very much in an official police capacity and in most parts was fairly brief. Only when I started building church community in South Africa, did I really start to engage with the many practical realities of crossing economic, class, and social divisions. Differences in wealth, education, class and social background bring a whole number of challenges to the racial and cultural pot. It's to such issues that I'd like to devote the remainder of this chapter. My intention, as with previous chapters, is not to try and examine every situation likely to be encountered. Rather to highlight important principles and commonly encountered problems that can assist all of us, whether rich or poor, in our cross socio-economic endeavours.

Lessons from the seven

Acts chapter 6 gives a fascinating account of a diverse local church that was building across the cultural and economic divides of society. There were both rich and poor in the church and the leaders were facing a number of problems that needed sorting out. Luke records;

'Now in these days when the disciples were increasing in number, a complaint by the Hellenists arose against the Hebrews because their widows were being neglected in the daily distribution. And the twelve summoned the full number of the disciples and said, 'It is not right that we should give up preaching the word of God to serve tables. Therefore, brothers, pick out from among you seven men of good repute, full of the Spirit and of wisdom, whom we will appoint to this duty'.' (Acts 6: 1-3)

A number of pertinent lessons can be gleaned:

1 Holy Spirit wisdom

Perhaps the most important point to emphasise at the start of our exploring the practicalities of crossing socio-economic divides is our need of God's Holy Spirit and his wisdom. Responding to poverty and differences in financial wealth is a Holy Spirit ministry. There are no quick and easy solutions to be copied and repeated wherever we may go. Disputes were occurring in the Jerusalem church between different widows. The poor were being helped, but seemingly human factors were coming into play and certain widows, either intentionally or unintentionally, were being overlooked. In choosing leaders to handle the situation and oversee the ongoing ministry with the poor, the apostles were adamant that this required people of good reputation, full of the Holy Spirit and wisdom. Dealing with differences in wealth, education and class requires Holy Spirit anointing. Wisdom is required to know when to give and when not to give, how to handle jealousies, anger and misunderstandings, as well as how to create an atmosphere of mutual love, understanding and respect. Where there are poor and uneducated there will be problems. Where there are rich and educated there will be problems. Where there are poor and rich, educated and uneducated together there will potentially be even more problems. We all, whether rich or poor, can learn from books like this, but must be willing to get on our knees and seek God. We have a wonderful counselor who is more than able to direct us through every situation we may face.

In our local churches we should expect and believe God to give us people who, like the seven, have a special gifting and anointing in this area. The seven were not professionals called to handle the poor in their midst, thus releasing the rest of the congregation from any cross-economic involvement. Rather, they were men full of the Holy Spirit, recognised to have an anointing that could build up the church, as well as equip and release others in crossing economic divides. As disputes and misunderstandings were encountered they could be called upon to give wisdom and insight.

At Khanyisa we have several men and women whom I would regard as being especially gifted in this way. They are people I will turn to when I encounter yet another situation I have never come across before. They advise leaders when they encounter problems, act as peacemakers if fights break out and give correction and instruction to church members if they are making potential (and on most occasions unintentional) faux pars. We advise church members that if difficulties arise in their relationships due to the dynamics of people being of different cultures, wealth and education backgrounds, there are leaders in the church they can approach for wisdom and advice.

2 Attitudes

Disparities in wealth, education and class will inevitably expose a number of rotten attitudes and emotions:

Jealousies – Here in the book of Acts jealousy was rampant. The Greek-speaking people complained because their widows were not being helped as much as the Hebrew widows. They were jealous and it was ugly. Such jealousy is a common reaction among the poor towards other poor who are seen to be helped. At Khanyisa we have seen such jealousies in many different ways resulting in a whole number of unforeseen consequences. Some of our wealthier members have, on occasions, given furniture, food, clothing or money to one of their friends in the church. Such is to be expected when there is genuine relationship involved. This has at times caused problems when others have seen this resulting in malicious rumours and gossip. Giving is not the issue but wisdom is required in the way people choose to give and share of their possessions (practical advice on this will be given at the end of this chapter).

Another common form of jealousy in a diverse community context is jealousy by the poor towards the rich. As poor members with little, gaze at the lives of those with much – those with houses, jobs, cars and money to spare, jealousy will inevitably arise. This, of course, is something we can all struggle with. I can become jealous of pastors with rich congregations, large salaries and who drive a better car than I do. It needs to be recognised for what it is, honestly spoken about and humbly repented of. Wealthier people may become embarrassed to let others see what they have and reluctant to invite poorer church members to their homes. They, in turn, can become defensive feeling the need to justify every purchase or acquisition they make. Lisa and I found ourselves doing this recently when a friend asked us to look after her leather arm-chair. A church member later jokingly commented, 'Oh, now we see where our tithes are going.' We immediately felt the need to explain that it was not ours and was temporarily on loan! Poorer congregants similarly, may be reluctant to allow wealthier church members in their homes, embarrassed by what they have and not wishing to be ashamed.

Jealousy is inevitable when dealing with fallen humanity and diverse people of varying socio-economic backgrounds. It must not, however, be pandered to. It should not prevent us from the Biblical mandate to give and share our possessions with one another or pressurise us to treat everyone in the same way. [276] Neither should it deter us from opening our homes to one another. Rather, its reality should provoke us to seek Holy Spirit wisdom and guidance in the way we give, how we help one another and how we practice hospitality together.

Snobbery – I grew up in what was considered to be a middle-class village within the North-East of England. A relative of mine once made a major faux par while talking to friends from a neighbouring town – an area considered by some to be more working-class. Without thinking, he exclaimed, 'Oh, I could never live there – it's so common'. Understandably my friends from that community were suitably put out! When we traverse socio-economic boundaries snobbery will generally raise its ugly head. When Lisa and I got married nearly 300 people attended the reception afterwards. Money was tight so we'd asked everyone to bring their favourite dishes to share at the buffet. The food was plentiful, so we gladly encouraged our poorer friends to take the leftovers home for their families and children. This caused major offense to some of our wealthier friends who saw this to be vulgar and common, unsuitable behaviour for a wedding.

Disapproving snobbish attitudes serve only to judge, belittle, pull others down and make us think more highly of ourselves than we ought. Those of us prone to it need to humble ourselves and dare to go about things in ways that wouldn't necessary be our first choice.

Presumptions – Another area of offense in crossing economic boundaries is that of presumption. The widows in Acts 6, for example, could have presumed it was their right to be helped and receive food because of the fact that they were poor with no means of income or support. Being poor does not grant an automatic right to receive help and support. The apostle Paul, in his first letter to Timothy advised him to distinguish between widows and those who were truly widows. [277] Those who had families or children to support them were encouraged first to go there for support before presuming on the church. In fact, several criteria were identified as to who would be helped and who would not. Factors such as age, godliness and reputation all came into play. Not everyone was treated the same.

Wealthier people can at times feel presumed upon by poorer people. For example, in going somewhere together a situation may arise where money has to be spent such as paying to go into a car park or having a cup of coffee. The wealthier party may feel presumed upon to pay for the bill – though nothing is said. Someone offering a lift in their car may feel frustrated because no offer of money towards petrol is given. It is assumed they are wealthy and therefore have money for the petrol. Though this is true in some cases, many poorer people can feel very uncomfortable about such situations (by the fact that they are not in a position to help). They feel powerless and so the easiest solution is to say nothing and avoid any potential awkwardness. Similarly, poorer people can feel presumed upon by the wealthy – presumed to be always wanting something and not capable of doing anything themselves. Wealthy people can indirectly patronise poorer people seeing them as children, uneducated or unable to make decisions. They may feel the right to speak on the poorer person's behalf as if somehow they do not have opinions of their own. Though this may be true for some, for many this is not the case and can leave people feeling angry and humiliated.

As with all presumptions, if such thoughts go unspoken they invariably lead to wrong conclusions, which if not dealt with immediately, will reinforce divisions, prejudices and separation. At some point, therefore, healthy and appropriate communication is essential between all parties involved. Honest communication of struggles, feelings and perceptions is necessary along with a willingness to hear the other person's perceptions (whether accurate or not) and humbly ask forgiveness if need be. This can be done between individuals as situations arise, though it is helpful for leadership to be proactive and create safe contexts where these issues can be highlighted (even anonymously if need be).

3 Beware of the power of the tongue

James lets us know that the tongue, though small in size, can cause a lot of trouble. Just as it only takes a small flame to set a forest ablaze, so too can an uncontrolled tongue cause problems in our cross-economic endeavours. [278] Such was the case in Acts where uncontrolled tongues in the form of complaints and grumblings, demanded that the apostles address the situation. The potential for misunderstanding among people of different socio-economic backgrounds is great. It is essential, therefore, to be aware of how we communicate and say things to one another. This is not to make us self-conscious about every word we speak. Rather to have a mature awareness of how miscalculated words and promises can cause a lot of damage. Let me highlight three examples:

Hasty promises – Don't make an offer to give something unless you know you can deliver on your promise. Many people in their emotional response to the needs of others make hasty promises that they are unable to keep. One lady, while visiting at Khanyisa, heard someone say that they didn't have a bed. She immediately expressed that she had a spare bed at home that the person could have. A few weeks later, however, we still hadn't heard from the lady and there was no sign of the bed. This promise made in haste caused a lot of unnecessary pain and disappointment, and could so easily have been avoided had she first checked before saying anything. Better that we say we are unable to help and then later change our minds, than to make a hasty commitment that we are unable to keep.

Lies – Lisa and I were once caught out in a lie. While driving one day we pulled up at a set of traffic lights and a beggar came asking for money. Without thinking we humbly apologised to the man and told him that we didn't have our wallets with us and therefore couldn't help him. Immediately our daughter Katey spoke out saying, 'Yes you do daddy, there's the purse in mummy's handbag.' Our faces turned red, embarrassed to have been caught out and ashamed by what we had done. We hastily scrambled for a few coins in the ash-tray of the car, gave them to the man and then sped away as fast as we could as soon as the lights turned green.

When faced with people asking something of us, we can be tempted to lie. Conversely, some people may be tempted to lie in order to try and get something from others. Either way it is wrong. Only with honesty can true friendships be forged and trust developed.

Careless words – A lady was visiting with me in the townships one day and saw a child wearing shoes that were too small for her feet. She immediately chastised the mother of the girl, telling her that she could do irreparable damage to her daughter's feet and that she must get her a larger pair of shoes as soon as possible. The mother, I could see, was frightened by these remarks and embarrassed to admit that she had no money for shoes. I had to advise the lady visiting with me not to be so careless with her words. She had been well intending in her remarks, but insensitive and ignorant to the realities of the situation in which the mother and child were living. I then later returned to the family with some money for new shoes, as well as to apologise for what had been said. On another occasion, a well-meaning gentleman was asked to speak at a funeral about a young boy who had died. He stood up and told everyone how poor the boy was. He had on occasions given the boy some sweets only to see him take them home to share with his siblings. A relative of the child was terribly offended by his remarks and stood up to speak, emphasising that they were not a poor family and had always looked after the child well.

Such unintentional mistakes and offense will inevitably happen as different backgrounds come into contact with one another. It's helpful to be mindful of what we say, learning to not always speak the first thought that comes into our head. Let's desire always to treat others with dignity and be sensitive to their situations. Should we make mistakes, let's be willing to recognise where we have caused offense and humbly apologise if need be.

Lessons from the Good Samaritan

Jesus said in Luke chapter ten;

'…A man was going down from Jerusalem to Jericho, and he fell among robbers, who stripped him and beat him and departed, leaving him half dead. Now by chance a priest was going down that road, and when he saw him he passed by on the other side. So likewise a Levite, when he came to the place and saw him, passed by on the other side. But a Samaritan, as he journeyed, came to where he was, and when he saw him, he had compassion. He went to him and bound up his wounds, pouring on oil and wine. Then he set him on his own animal and brought him to an inn and took care of him. And the next day he took out two denarii and gave them to the innkeeper, saying, 'Take care of him, and whatever more you spend, I will repay you when I come back'.' (Luke 10:30-35)

The story of the Good Samaritan is a provoking parable and helpfully highlights the importance of crossing cultural boundaries. It also raises a number of pertinent issues relevant to the complexities of crossing socio-economic divides:

1 Denial and avoidance

Coming face to face with poverty and its associated consequences (such as violent crime) can be something that, like the priest and the Levite, we would rather avoid and turn a blind eye to. Invariably the easiest solution is rather to deny its existence or avoid any contact altogether. Church community should of course challenge this, but even in contexts where rich and poor are in close proximity, avoidance is still the easier option. The same could be said of the poor avoiding the rich.

Certain wealthier people may avoid contact with the poor because the impact of poverty and the suffering of others can be unpleasant to see. Some, in fact, may be shocked and disgusted by it. To see someone sick and dying in the latter stages of AIDS can be a horrifying and upsetting experience. Few would admit to such carnal reactions, but they are real feelings and emotions none the less. One lady attended Khanyisa for a short time, but in the end had to leave the church because she was terrified that she might catch TB, something that several of our church members were suffering with. The terrible and devastating effects of poverty were too much for her to cope with.

This in turn is not a tendency confined solely to the rich and middle-class. Those from poorer backgrounds can be as equally intimidated to cross the apparent chasmic divides to meet with those from wealthier backgrounds. A young man in our church told me one day that he sometimes avoided events with White people. His reasoning was not that he didn't like White people, but to avoid the embarrassment of not having money or being able to pay his way.

Such responses, though understandable, should be recognised and dealt with accordingly. Some people may require prayer and counselling. Contexts need to be created that allow people to talk through their struggles without fear of judgment and rejection. We should further trust the Holy Spirit to transform and change our hearts so we can truly love our neighbours as ourselves. The Good Samaritan was willing to stop and go over to where the injured man was. He is the example that we are to copy and each of us, whether rich or poor, should be willing to do the same.

2 Motivations

The Good Samaritan was moved with compassion by what he saw. It was this response that motivated him to stop and help the man and get involved in his life. Not all of us can admit to such honourable motivations for crossing the economic divides. A whole number of factors can influence rich and poor alike as they seek to interact with one another. Let me highlight two:

Guilt – This, as we examined in chapter eight, is an emotion that can motivate people to cross cultural boundaries. The same is true for crossing economic divides. In South Africa with its history of apartheid, and other contexts around the world where the poor have been exploited, guilt has influenced many wealthier people in their desire to help the poor. Guilt, however, only motivates as long as people feel guilty and invariably does not sustain for the long-haul. Such impure motivations will be quickly discerned by those being helped and can leave them feeling patronised, angry and used.

Getting from others – Poorer people, on the other hand, may be motivated to reach out to the wealthy to see what they can get from them by way of money, food or jobs. They can exploit the feelings of guilt felt by others, using tactics such as manipulation, lying, pestering and false story telling. On occasions at Khanyisa we have had church members going from one person to the next asking for food or taxi fares. In the end several people, not knowing what others are doing, have all given. Such actions can leave wealthier people feeling used and manipulated.

In its extreme, the motive to 'get from others' can be seen in the form of theft. A young man in our worship team testifies that he originally came to Khanyisa to steal hats. Fortunately, the Holy Spirit convicted him within a few weeks of being with us; he repented of his ways and became a Christian. He is now an active member of the church. It's important to remember, however, that though this may be true for some people, many others do not employ such tactics and we must not fall into the trap of putting everyone in the same category.

Rotten motivation will inevitably be exposed by all when crossing socio-economic divides. This is par for the course and will have to be dealt with on our knees before God. We in turn should not allow bad experiences to hinder us from giving time to loving and knowing our neighbours. In the story of the feeding of the five thousand, for example, people were happy to follow Jesus as long as they were getting something (ie food). The moment Jesus revealed some of the cost of discipleship many turned back and no longer walked with him. [279] Jesus, however, was not perturbed and did not allow this to hinder him from reaching out to the poor.

3 Risk

The Samaritan took a risk walking in an area where robbers operated. Genuine friendships across economic-boundaries will mean visiting one another where we live. This could potentially mean going to a part of town we have never been to before. Many White South Africans have never visited the townships within their localities. Fear invariably is what keeps them away. If true reconciliation and friendships are to occur, fears will have to be overcome and risks taken. Poorer Black South Africans similarly, can be reluctant to enter the wealthier suburbs of their cities, not for fear of being attacked, but rather for judgement by prying neighbours of being robbers and thieves. One young leader at Khanyisa moved from Guguletu to the suburb of Rondebosch to be close to the school where he teaches. He expressed his frustration to me one day because he was regularly stopped by police and security vans. As a Black man, people assumed he was up to no good.

Going to unfamiliar geographical areas can be a challenging experience for people of all backgrounds whether rich or poor. Such is the risk we should all be willing to make as we seek to love our neighbour as ourselves. Genuine love for our neighbour will take us to where our neighbour is; from inner-city to suburbia, from townships to golf estates, from rural to urban, from villages to council-estates and from our home country abroad.

4 Time and resources

Three things will be vehemently tested when developing relationships across economic divides – attitudes towards time, possessions and money.

Time – The Good Samaritan invested his time in building relationships across economic divides. Although the Samaritan was on his way somewhere, he willingly stopped to take care of the injured man and attend to his wounds. This delayed him in his journey. He then took the man to an inn and delayed his journey further by staying the night with him!

Ultimately, success in cross-economic friendships will be determined by the amount of time we give to such relationships. Time is arguably our most precious resource, yet it is the one so few of us are willing to share. We live in a modern world that places high demands upon our time – time for family, for work, for sport, for hobbies, for holiday, and of course, for church. The Good Samaritan gave of his time to someone whom he hardly knew and who was of a different culture and socio-economic background to himself. This more than likely was inconvenient to him and delayed him from his other plans. Yet he willingly did so in his efforts to extend neighbourly love. We too, whether rich or poor, have to do the same.

It is relatively easy to help someone out, give money or share of one's possessions. It's another thing altogether, however, to give time to get to know someone. This doesn't happen overnight. Overcoming misunderstandings and confusion will require time to sit and chat through the issues. We may even have to give extra time travelling distances to meet with one another, especially if we live in different geographical and economic areas. This has been our experience at Khanyisa where, due to the historical impact of apartheid, church members live in very geographically separated areas. Poorer church members will travel on trains and taxis to visit friends in suburbs. Wealthier church members will also go out of their way to collect friends from the townships, bring them to their houses in the suburbs and then take them home again later. Such action requires foresight and intentionality in developing relationships – something that is only possible when there is a willingness to share one's time.

Possessions – The Good Samaritan shared his oil, wine and donkey in helping the man. Cross-economic relationships will challenge both rich and poor in their attitudes towards their possessions. Some of our wealthier people at Khanyisa have been especially challenged in the area of transport and sharing of their vehicles. Some have been provoked positively and others negatively. Jonathan Reed, a fellow elder at Khanyisa, has no need for a large vehicle, yet has continually and deliberately chosen to buy a large people-carrying vehicle to assist others in the church. Every Sunday he faithfully collects a young man called Vuyo, who is confined to a wheel chair due to a stray bullet that went into his spine. Another lady on two occasions, when replacing her motor car for a newer vehicle, has generously given away her old vehicles (that were still in very good condition) to poorer friends within the church. Others, have at times, however, confessed their reluctance to go to their mid week cell group – not because they don't like the group but because they feel burdened having to give people lifts home afterwards. Poorer members have also confessed their embarrassment having wealthier people in their homes. They may feel ashamed of what they have, humiliated by their broken and damaged furniture or by not being able to offer milk in their tea.

Such reactions whether positive or negative are real and genuine responses that have to be humbly acknowledged and dealt with along the way. There are no easy solutions other than honest and loving communication and mutual commitment to loving one another. Yet sharing what we have, whether little or plenty, is a biblical requirement for all of us as we learn to love our neighbour as ourselves.

Money – The Good Samaritan gave the inn keeper money to look after the man and allow him to remain there until he was fully recovered. He was even willing to give more money had the situation demanded.

Giving and generosity are biblical principles relevant to all Christians, whether rich or poor. Sadly, such willingness by the Good Samaritan to share of his money is not always a characteristic readily manifest in the church. Bringing people together from different socio-economic backgrounds has the potential to bring out the best and the worst in all of us. On frequent occasions at Khanyisa, I have been humbled when someone, whom I know has nothing, has given me money to buy sweets for my children. On other occasions I've had to solve disputes where one church member has been pestered by another church member for money, resulting in tension in their relationship.

For many Christians the easiest way to handle giving is to do so from a distance. It can be easier to give into a charity or put money into a special church offering rather than get too close to someone of a different socio-economic background. The giving of the Good Samaritan was up-close and personal. He got involved with the person he was helping. Both distance giving and up-close and personal giving are required in the church. The way in which we give is very important. We must never underestimate the sub-conscious power we have in our hands when we hold the purse-strings and are in a position to be able to give. Similarly, we must never underestimate the frustration and powerlessness felt by those who have no money and are on the receiving end of being helped. Such dynamics can adversely affect cross-economic relationships in two key ways:

Indebtedness – Giving and generosity, normally innocent expressions of thoughtfulness, can be turned into a form of indebtedness whereby those who receive eventually find themselves feeling obligated to the one who gives. A generous person can indirectly rob someone of their dignity and leave them feeling beholden to them. Eventually this awareness can turn to bitterness surfacing as anger and resentment. This, of course can be unintentional on behalf of the giver, but it is a dynamic to be aware of none the less.

Others in their generosity may be in danger of subconsciously expecting something in return. It's interesting to note, for example, that Abram in Genesis 14 refused to take any of the possessions offered to him by the king of Sodom. He said, 'I have raised my hand to the Lord, God most High, Creator of heaven and earth, and have taken an oath that I will accept nothing belonging to you, not even a thread or the thong of a sandal, so that you will never be able to say, 'I made Abram rich' (Genesis 14:17-23). Perhaps Abram had a sense that the king of Sodom would want something in return? Perhaps Abram didn't want to take anything from the king because he didn't want to feel indebted or obligated to him in any way afterwards? [280]

Those on the receiving end of generosity need to learn to receive well and be under no compulsion to be beholden to the benefactor. All giving should be done in a manner that gives dignity to the person receiving. Our motives in giving, therefore, should be humbly examined to make sure we don't subconsciously desire some form of indebtedness in return. It may be helpful at times to give anonymously, through a third party or even the church so that such indebtedness may be avoided.

Ownership and control – Within the local church and mission context, a source of cross-cultural and cross-economic conflict, is the notion that ownership of resources gives one the automatic right to have power over managing those resources. In other words, a donor gives and wants to control how the beneficiary utilises it. A church, for example in the West, donating money towards a church project in a developing world context, may feel a strong sense of ownership and need to lay down stringent guidelines as to how the money is utilised. Similar dynamics can occur with individual giving and the donor expecting to have some say in how the person handles the money given to them. Though few churches or individuals would intentionally seek malicious and blatant control over others, it is within the nature of us all, when we have the power, to believe that our way is right. We have a lack of trust and confidence in others seeing them as having less knowledge, less power, less insight and less authority, and as such feel an overwhelming need to tell them what is best. Inevitably when such conditions prevail, anger, resentment and eventual rebellion will occur.

Commitment

The last point that I'd like to emphasise is how the Good Samaritan was committed in his relationship to the robbed man. Not only did he leave money to take care of the man, but promised to come back and see how he was doing. He didn't leave him on the roadside, walk away and then expect the inn keeper to look after him. He was committed to an on-going relationship with the man and planned to come back and continue what was started.

This possibly is the biggest key to building successful relationships across socio-economic boundaries – commitment to one another through trials, difficulties, hurts and misunderstandings. None of the difficulties mentioned above are insurmountable. With a commitment to one another and a genuine desire to love our neighbour as ourselves, all can be overcome. Poverty is a massive problem that would readily isolate and separate people from one another, but the vision of the Kingdom of God, as D Hughes says, 'is equal to it. It provides as adequate end for all human effort because it is ultimately rooted in a heavenly future. It sustains effort now because the king has promised to be with his disciples in the heart of the conflict. Because the king is endowed with indestructible life we can be sure that even if we lose our own life in his service that our self-sacrificing service will not be in vain.'[281] Let's commit to crossing the cultural and socio-economic divisions of our world with the knowledge that King of Kings is with us in all our efforts.

Practical advice on giving

- We are all to give – whether rich or poor. Give generously and share what you have. Give from a distance ie into offerings. Give up-close and personal out of knowledge, relationship and awareness of individual circumstances. When it is your friend who is struggling, how can you not help?

- Ask for Holy Spirit wisdom to know when and how to give (and when not to give). It may be wise at times to give anonymously or through a third party to avoid jealousies and any sense of indebtedness.

- Don't bow to manipulation and pressure to give. Don't give out of guilt. When you give, give in faith and because you want to. Remember, God loves a cheerful giver.[282] Don't be fearful of being manipulated. It is okay to say no but it's also okay to give even if you are being manipulated. God is gracious and generous to us all. Don't give according to what a person deserves – none of us deserve anything.

- If you find that money is becoming an issue in your relationship with someone you will need to talk to them about it. If you are unsure how to go about this ask your leaders for help and advice.

- Don't lie and don't make promises you can't keep. Keep your word.

- It's helpful for local church leaders to have basic principles or guidelines in place in response to dealing with different situations in the church. Be open to being led by the Holy Spirit. Sometimes you will give to one in a certain way and to another in a different way depending on the situation and what you feel God is saying.

- Give with love – remember, 'If I give away all I have… But have not love, I gain nothing'. [283] Give in a way that imparts dignity to the person receiving.

- Leaders must give training and teaching on giving as well as the practicalities of cross-cultural and cross-economic relationships. Commonly experienced problems brought out into the light can lift hidden burdens off the shoulders of our congregants. Be aware many people are ashamed to talk about the things they think and feel inside their heads.

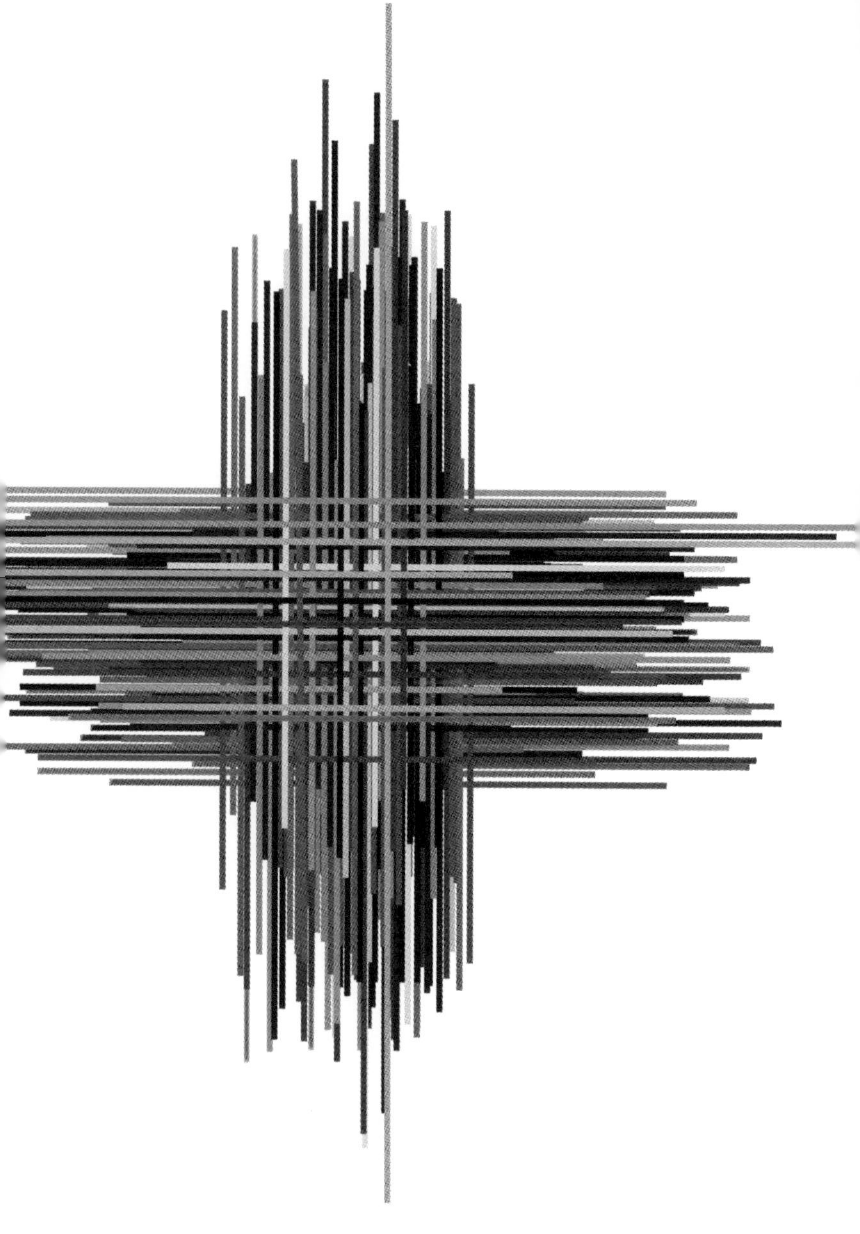

13 Overcoming giants

By Lisa Measures

> 'Our goal is that each child has a real part to play in life.
> They are not drifting aimlessly through life. They were born
> for a purpose – it's even good to build that sense of destiny
> into young children. They are going to make a difference in
> their world. Of course their real destiny can only be fulfilled
> in knowing Jesus and living to please him.'
> (David and Liz Holden)

I will never forget the day when Nigel returned from the
SACLA[284] conference he had attended in Pretoria. With a
mixture of great excitement and trepidation he told me that he
felt God had spoken to him and we needed some time to talk.
I had no idea what he was going to say but had a sense that it
was going to be life changing.

'Lisa, I feel God is asking us to move into the township
community for a year and I would love us to pray about it,' he
said to me while having a meal out together one night. So, in
this lovely restaurant, sitting across the table from the man
I love and respect, I responded with a very positive and
genuine 'of course'! When I rose the next morning to our stable
and familiar life and got our children Ben (4) and Katey (almost
2) ready for play school, the impact of what Nigel had said hit
me like a ton of bricks. What could I have been thinking? How
could we move into the townships with two young children?
Nigel would often be out at night for meetings, leaving me
alone with the kids. What would my family say? Would it be safe
for us living as Whities in the townships? What if my children
were killed? I would never be able to forgive myself if anything
happened to them.

Send the fish

So many things were racing through my mind that I just wanted to run! Run away from Nigel and run away from God's voice. I found myself in crisis as everything that had brought stability and security to my life seemed to be under threat. I clearly recall walking around the park up the road crying my heart out to God wondering why he had chosen this time of our lives to ask us to do this. It would have been so much easier if it had just been Nigel and I. Why now, why us?

One of the things that shocked me the most was that I found myself questioning my faith in God. All those wonderful scriptures that we easily quote came flooding into my mind as I wrestled with God. Did I truly believe that we have a God who speaks to us, a God who is in control and has plans for our lives – plans to prosper us and not to harm us? I was reminded of Jonah, who ran away when the Lord asked him to go to Nineveh, but all I could think of in my anguish and stupidity was, 'send the fish'! Surely that would be easier than the turmoil I was facing now? Yet in my heart I knew that all I wanted to do was to please God and serve him with my life.

It was at this point that I remembered a book that had impacted my life tremendously, and led me to be involved in the townships in the first place. 'Chasing the Dragon,' is a testimony about the courageous life of Jackie Pullinger, who as a young woman went to live in the Walled City of Hong Kong. This was an unbelievably poor community that had been ravaged by drugs and prostitution, but she went there because God asked her to. When I first read the book I said to God that I wanted to live my life like her and do God's will. I was reminded of this and knew that I couldn't run away from my fears. I had to face them with Nigel and rely on the love and grace of God. So that day I asked God for courage and a word that he would protect and watch over my children. The process began.

Lion attack

About a week later I had a nightmare in which I was being attacked by a lion. I literally woke up in a sweat with my heart racing. In my dream the lion attacked me and I went through a terrifying ordeal, but when it was over I walked away alive and as I looked at my body there wasn't a mark on my skin anywhere. The dream ended there.

The strange thing about it was although I was not spared the attack, I was left unharmed. The dream had disturbed me and I needed to talk and pray with someone who was not my husband. I immediately thought of my friend Peggy Lande, who lived in Beaufort West four hundred kilometres away. I needed to spend some time praying with her to help process this decision we had to make. So with Nigel's blessing I left for Beaufort West a week later with another friend Pauline to go and seek the Lord. As we left Cape Town I was feeling well and excited about seeing Peggy, but along the way I developed a raging temperature. By the time we arrived there I was 'as sick as a dog'. I spent most of the weekend in bed. It was real spiritual warfare, but I was determined not to be robbed of going to church with Peggy on Sunday morning, and I dragged myself out of bed to get there.

The promise

Peggy attended an Afrikaans-speaking church and that particular Sunday they had a visiting preacher. He preached (in Afrikaans) a message from Psalm 91 about the amazing promises of God's love and protection. I was gripped when he read verses 13 and 14;

'You will tread upon the lion and the cobra, you will trample the great lion and the serpent.' Because he loves me says the Lord I will rescue him, I will protect him because he acknowledges my name' (Psalm 91:13-14)

As the truth of that scripture washed over me, I remembered my dream of the lion and suddenly laughter and joy began to bubble up from within the very core of my being. God had given me the promise that I had asked for! He had spoken to me in a dream and then brought me all the way to Beaufort West to spend a weekend living in a township with my dear friend. There he took me to a church to hear a man preach in another language about never having to fear if we are in the will of God because he will be with us. What an amazing God we serve! What lengths he was prepared to go to, to give me the promise and the peace that I needed to respond to his calling. I was willing to move. Needless to say I went home from church that day full of the joy of the Lord and completely healed physically.

The strangest thing about all of this is that we never did move into the townships. For what seemed like months we tried to find somewhere to live. At first we looked for a house to rent, but when that option didn't open up we thought maybe we should try and buy. We prepared our families, we prayed, we looked at houses and had several friends in the community looking out for a place for us to stay, but the doors did not open. Now three years later we find ourselves living in the leafy suburb of Pinelands, which at times has left me wondering, 'What was that all about'? All that worry and anxiety, not to mention the process I went through. Some have asked, 'Was it just God testing your willingness, a little like Abraham was tested with Isaac?' I must confess that I don't know exactly why God put us through this testing, but I do know one thing for sure, it highlighted to me how our willingness to obey the call of God on our lives can be challenged when we have children.

Children and mission

One of the greatest life-changing events that we will experience is having children. It seems that over night we discover things about ourselves that we never knew – some bad and some good. The first thing that I think any parent is confronted with when their baby is placed in their arms for the first time, is the overwhelming sense of responsibility for this little life that has been entrusted to them. Yet this soon turns to an amazing love and a realisation how we will do anything for them. On many occasions, as I've looked at my sleeping children, my heart has burst with love for them and all I can think of is how I would lay my life down to protect them and see that they come to no harm. It is amazing to me how through my relationship with my children I have come to understand and connect with the father heart of God in a much deeper way.

My friends Linda Martindale, Debbie and Steve Thomas and their three daughters Emily, Ruby and Rosa, were visiting once at the Cape Nature Reserve; an area renowned for its beautiful scenery and diverse wildlife. While Linda was driving, Emily had fallen asleep on the back seat, so they decided to stop the car and get some fresh air while they waited for Emily to wake up. They parked at a popular tourist stop and left Emily sleeping in the back of the car with the front window open as they all stood talking nearby. Suddenly, from nowhere a large male baboon came and climbed through the open window and sat in the driver's seat. Debbie moved like lightening! She frantically wrestled with the locked back door as Linda nervously hunted for her keys to release the catch remotely. Debbie then fearlessly climbed into the back of the car, stared the baboon out, who at that stage was peering over the front seats into the rear, and then calmly picked up Emily into her arms and lifted her out of the vehicle. Parents will do anything to protect their kids!

The reality is at times, this love and protective desire that we have for our children, has the potential to hinder us from mission. It can cause us to change direction in pursuing the call that God has put on our lives (and for our kids). We might have a vision and calling from God that somehow we feel has to be put on hold now that children have come into our lives. Why is this? It is not necessarily because God has spoken to us, but for a whole load of other seemingly valid reasons, such as:

Protecting our kids – I often counsel people that nothing we do or go through in this life is ever a waste when it comes to God's plans and purposes for us. We know that he works all things together for the good of those who love him. [285] God will use life's experiences to grow our faith and shape the people we become. We need to reach a point as parents where we let God be God in our children's lives, for he has an amazing plan for them. There may be things that they will go through in life, such as; challenges in friendships, failing at something, or things that call them to persevere instead of giving up. The tendency can be to want to rescue them and protect them. But, perhaps all God requires of us is to trust him and walk alongside them through the challenges and offer love and support because some of these things they go through are preparing them for the future and the things God has in store for them.

I don't think there is a single parent who would not agree that raising children in our generation is no easy task! But, it can become even more of a challenge when we respond to God's call to mission, to cross cultural and economic divides, or be part of a diverse local church. We may be tempted to protect our children from dangerous places or different types of people who may not necessarily be a good influence. When Nigel and I had our children we were already leading Khanyisa church in a township of Cape Town called Gugulethu. Anyone who knows the history of our country will know that it was not one of the easiest or safest places to be as a White South African at the time, especially with a young family. But, this is where God had called us to build church and what I have discovered along our own journey is the value and depth that it has added to our children's life as well as our own. We could have chosen to go to a safer area or a church in a better part of town, yet as someone once said, 'the safest place to be is in the will of God'.

God never intended the arrival of children to cause an obstacle in the calling that he places on parents. Children form an important part of that calling, as after all it is God that gives life and he is the one who 'knits us together' in our mother's wombs [286] and has predestined us to do 'good works' that he prepared before hand for us to do. [287] We are chosen by God to be the parents of our children. I am not saying that God may not use the arrival of children to encourage a change. Life changes beyond recognition when we have kids and things do not necessarily continue as they did before. Having children does not mean we lay aside obeying God and using our gifting for the next twenty years until they have left home.

Wanting the best for our kids – Another potential hindrance to mission and responding to God's call upon our lives (and for our kids) can be wanting to ensure the best for our children. Sometimes this is because we want them to have the things that we never had as children such as toys, holidays or a good education. We might be driven to see that our children get these things and not think to ask God what he would like for them. I was cutting hair of a client of mine one day when she told me how her husband was strategising to move house into a good area so that their two boys could get into the best school in Cape Town. The school close to where they lived at the time was more mixed and did not have such a good reputation, but it was still a good school. It was not wrong of them to want to put their children in the best school, but I wondered whether God might have had plans for them in the nearby school mixing with different types of children? Sometimes in wanting the best for our children we may miss out or change the calling that God has for us and our children.

One couple that we know from Chertsey in England were faced with a very difficult situation when it came to the school that their daughter had to attend in the area where they lived. The school was quite rough and drew children from many different backgrounds. In their case they had little choice in the matter, as the government required the children to sit an 'eleven-plus' entrance exam, on which they were then allocated a school place according to test results. Needless to say the couple were concerned about the school but trusted that God was in control and had a plan in this. They were so right! After school their daughter studied and qualified as a physiotherapist, and then went on to do a voluntary youth year at Kings Church in Bedford. Here she worked amongst the poor in the city and had no problem fitting in and relating to the people she came into contact with. Her experience and 'training' received at the rough school helped her to mix and relate with people from many different backgrounds. Her schooling may not have seemed like an ideal first choice, but God was to use this in his plans and purposes for her life. Sometimes we may not understand at the time why God opens certain doors and not others, but one thing we can be certain of is that he knows the future and is always in control.

Children and struggle

2 Corinthians 7 v 9 & 10 says, '…For you became sorrowful as God intended and so were not harmed in any way by us. Godly sorrow brings repentance that leads to salvation and leaves no regret…' (NIV)

The worldly thinking of our generation says to us that we must pursue happiness at all costs and if we are not happy then there must be something wrong with what we are doing. When we read scriptures like the one above the word encourages us that God allows some struggles and sadness in our lives to drive us deeper into his arms – back to the reason we live and do the things we do and back to our great salvation that is in Christ Jesus. In other words there is a sadness and sorrow that comes from God that we must embrace. What we need to ask for here is heavenly discernment to know the difference. In these times some of us may think that we are not at peace and struggling because we are under spiritual attack, or in need of deliverance or simply not in the place that God wants us to be. But with revelation from God we may discover that we are in exactly the place that God wants us to be and he is just working out his purposes in our lives and getting our hearts in the right place.

Why should things be any different for our children? We know that the same Spirit that is at work in our lives is also at work in our children's lives. By this we must conclude that our children will also go through times of testing where they may struggle and find that they are not totally comfortable.

Children and diversity

Children can struggle with diversity in the same way that adults do. Whether with relationships at school, within the community where they live, a mission context or within diverse multi-cultural church, children can struggle to relate with other children who are different to themselves. For a parent the temptation can be to rescue them from this sorrow as opposed to help them overcome.

One couple that we know, following a sense of call from God, moved with their family from England to South Africa. On their arrival they decided to join a church located in a poorer community of Cape Town. They had four children of varying ages and, as far as I know, this was their first experience of mixing with people of a different culture, language and socio-economic background to themselves. At first the transition for them went very well, but as their children grew in age the oldest of the four began to complain about attending church, and was clearly struggling with the diversity. Naturally the parents became very concerned and were deeply worried that if they continued to insist that their children attend their church, they might lose them where their faith was concerned. This was a difficult place for them to be in as parents. After consideration, they responded by allowing the children to attend another local church close to where they lived and close to where their school friends were. The parents still continued to attend the church in the townships. This, of course, was not an ideal situation and it wasn't long before the parents left as well to attend the same church as their children.

There are no right and wrong answers here as it is always important to act according to one's faith. But, it does raise the question of when do we rescue our children and respond to their perceived needs and when do we help our children to push through those pain barriers in God and trust him with their future? How can we best disciple our children and help them? What do parents do, who know that they are where God wants them to be as a family, but see that their children are struggling? How can we envision our children to celebrate diversity; give them a heart for the nations and help them to relate with different types of people? How can we, together with our children, pursue meaningful relationships across cultural and socio-economic divides?

Raising children for the nations

I would like to share some of the things that we have learnt through our own journey with our children. In doing this I'd like to highlight some of the issues children might face (including the challenges and the joys), as well as looking at how we can equip them to wrestle with those challenges in a godly way. By doing this we'll hopefully be able to help them push through the challenges and run the race that God has set out for them in this life. The way that we may handle a teenage child and a younger child may be different in approach, but the principles that we mention here are applicable for both.

1 Vision

We need to envision our children for the nations. We know that the Bible teaches in Proverbs 29: 18 that without vision we perish. This is true for our children as well. We want our children to grow up passionate for the things of God and passionate for the church. But we also know that there are many other very exciting things that the world has to offer that will always be waging war for their attention.

Vision is about the bigger picture and the future, but children are generally not quite as worried or preoccupied about the future as we are. Have you ever given a young child some sweets and told them to keep half for later in the week, or spoken to your teenager about saving for that much-wanted new gadget or game? I will bet you that the response received has been pretty much our experience; 'Are you mad – we want it now – who cares about next week?' So knowing this fact about children, how do we go about envisioning our children for what we are doing?

Envision them to love God – In their book, 'Raising Children – A Parents Privilege,' David and Liz Holden say that;

'Our goal is that each child has a real part to play in life. They are not drifting aimlessly through life. They were born for a purpose – it's even good to build that sense of destiny into young children. They are going to make a difference in their world. Of course their real destiny can only be fulfilled in knowing Jesus and living to please him.' (David & Liz Holden 1995:36) [288]

Vision for our lives comes from God and in all that we do we must train our children to know God and find him in every circumstance. Some of the best ways of doing this is by sharing your faith with them, praying with them and telling them stories about your journey. Children absolutely love stories! Before we had children Nigel and I did a three-day hike at a place called Augrabies. It was one of our all-time favourite holidays and we have often shared stories about it with our children. Through sharing this happy memory with them it has stirred up a passion and a vision in them to revisit this place as a family. Not even the thought of walking for three days has dulled their enthusiasm to do it. They have caught something of our passion for the place and want to experience it for themselves. In the same way we must intentionally share our faith and our experiences in God with our children to enable them to develop a vision for their lives in God.

Envision them to love different people – If we want to raise
our children to love the nations, we must talk to them about
the nations and let them know about God's love for people.
Share with them God's heart for different peoples of all types
and backgrounds. Instil in them the importance and privilege
of being able to mix with and learn from other types of people.
We must talk to them about skin colour and the wickedness of
mankind, but then tell them of God's heart and purposes found
in Jesus. We must converse with our children about racism
and challenge worldly stereotypes and presumptions. Talk to
them about the nations using atlases and maps of the world, as
well as encouraging them to pray for the nations and different
people that they know. The book of Jonah is a good book to
use to teach our children as it communicates something of
God's heart for all types of people, including the ones that
we might not necessarily like. We can also read books to our
children that demonstrate multi-cultural values as well as the
lives of people of different backgrounds. [289]

Envision them through the challenges – If we hear our
children say racist remarks we must not panic, but unpack
what they have said and attempt to bring light to the situation.
If our children struggle to understand other children because
of language differences, let's encourage them to attempt to
learn those languages, as well as help them think about how
the other child might feel not being able to understand them.
Besides cultural differences, language differences and skin
colour differences, my children mix with a lot of children at
church who are from a much poorer background. Some of the
kids may have torn clothes; they may not smell clean or their
may have open sores because of sickness. At times they have
struggled and said comments like, 'we don't want to go to
church'. We have had to sit down and listen to them, hear their
thoughts and feelings, but also try to envision them through
the difficulties.

2 **Lead by example**

One of the most powerful influences on our children's lives is our example. Without even being aware of it they are watching our responses, the values we embrace, and absorbing conversations we are having with others. They don't miss a beat. We need to set a good example and model the way for them.

I recall one occasion when we were about to go to Kenya to spend some time with friends of ours. To obtain visas we all had to have a yellow fever injection, so off we went with Ben and Katey (who were aged five and three at the time), to the clinic for our shots. The nurse who was going to administer the injection insisted on telling them exactly what she was about to do while filling the syringe right in front of their eyes. I remember thinking that this may not have been the wisest thing to do. At that point I glanced over at Ben who was looking considerably paler than normal and had a look of absolute terror on his face. I thought that it would probably be best to get his over and done with first, but as the nurse approached him he backed into a corner and said, 'I think I'll come back tomorrow'.

To ease the tension I came up with the brilliant idea of me going first in order to show him that it wasn't going to hurt. A big mistake! When he saw the needle sink into my arm he made a run for the door as fast as he could! I dived after him and rugby tackled him to the floor while screaming for the nurse to get the needle and 'just do it'! Meanwhile, as all this was happening, Katey quietly and surreptitiously slipped out the door unnoticed. This was one of those occasions where this principle of modelling and setting the example was not as successful as I had hoped it would be.

Jesus was passionate about the principle of leading by example. He followed his Father's example and only did what he saw his Father doing. [290] He hated hypocrisy and on many occasions spoke out forcefully against people who were professing one thing and doing something else. Nobody, regardless of age, likes hypocrisy and in many of our cultures we have sayings that endorse this sentiment, such as; 'actions speak louder than words', or 'practice what you preach'.

The way we approach life as parents, the way we treat people and the way we respond in certain situations will all have a direct impact on our children's behaviour. I once attended a workshop on raising children, in which the speaker said something that really impacted me. She said that she was always so blessed by the reception she received from the children of a friend whenever she visited. This surprised her because, even though she loved the children, she never really felt that she had ever done anything special to warrant the affection she received. She realised one day that the children responded well to her because they knew that their parents loved her very much. The way their mom responded to her had a direct impact on the way her children responded to her.

Leading by example is a biblical principle that will bring stability and security to our children. This is especially important considering that we live in a world where many of our leaders and so called role models live lives of compromise; and where they say one thing and do another. It is unlikely that our children will embrace diversity and respect and value people from all different walks of life if they do not see that we are wholeheartedly doing it ourselves. We must model the way.

3 Encourage cross-cultural friendship

If you were to ask a child or even a teenager to list the most important things in their lives, I can guarantee that one of them would be friends. In most cases friendship would probably be high up on their list. Naturally speaking the people that we develop friendships with the fastest are those that we come into contact with on a daily basis; people at work, children at school, parents we meet outside the school gate, the churches we are a part of, and neighbours in our communities. In most countries where there are suburban communities, they tend to be populated by people from similar backgrounds such as the same faith, the same race or a similar socio-economic status.

If we live in an area that mainly consists of people similar to ourselves we will have to be intentional about helping our children to reach out and build relationships with other children elsewhere – perhaps in different parts of town. It starts, of course, where we are living right now (our Jerusalem), and with the people who are on our doorstep. Due to globalisation the population of most countries is made up of many different people groups from different parts of the world. I am always amazed when I have visited big cities like London. You can spend the whole day in London and hardly hear a word of English spoken.

If our children are going to cultivate friendships with children from other communities we are going to have to get involved as parents. We will need to be willing to offer lifts and open up our homes and invest time getting to know their friends parents. When the friendship is across the socio-economic divide we need to work at overcoming our embarrassment about the things we have or don't have and the place we live compared to others. The funny thing about this is that it works both ways. Over the years I have had friends who come from a poorer background saying that they feel embarrassed to ask me over because they don't have much. Don't allow discomfort to rob you of these amazing relationships.

4 Don't be intimidated by giants

Depending on the country where you live entering someone else's world could mean facing some giants – things that seem so big that they can never be overcome. Some of the giants people face are things like safety, health issues, poverty, commonality and language. These giants can take on a whole new size when it involves your children as well. But, can I say, don't be intimidated by those giants because even in biblical times there were not many of them left standing when it came to faith and the people of God. None of these giants are insurmountable when you look at them through the eyes of faith with the full conviction that this is the heart of God, and that every tribe tongue and nation must be united in him not only in heaven but here on the earth. In all these things we need to pray and ask for the wisdom of God and be open to change and challenge. Don't allow fear to immobilise you as that is always the scheme of the devil, but 'Trust in the Lord with all your heart and lean not on your own understanding'.[291] God will lead you and guide you and make his plans known to you, for you and your children.

Conclusion

Any parent having read this may be left feeling that all this sounds like more hard work. Yet I want to assure you from my own experience, when you pursue this way of life it almost becomes part of your DNA and part of who you are. Anything less seems disappointing. I am a White South African and went through the whole of my childhood living under the apartheid regime. I grew up believing that it was normal and necessary to live separately from the Black people of my country. In 1993 God led me into the townships of Cape Town and began a very painful and wonderful transforming work in my life. I was broken when I saw the evil that had been done and was still being done. Since then I have never left being involved cross-culturally and have had the privilege of building amazing friendships. Through the process of establishing relationships with people different to me and with time I slowly realised how I had been robbed – robbed of the richness and the freedom that comes with diversity. I never want to lose this and my prayer is that I will always have the courage and the faith to lead my children into this freedom. This is my prayer for you too!

14 As it is in heaven

> '…Let your manner of life be worthy of the gospel of Christ,
> so that whether I come and see you or am absent, I may hear
> of you that you are standing firm in one spirit, with one mind
> striving side by side for the faith of the gospel.'
> (Philippians 1:27)
>
> 'The Church today can derive its sense of intention, direction,
> and mission directly from what Scripture tells us about the
> future intentions of God. Remarkably, God invites us, his
> children, to join with him in working for his intentions now. He
> calls us to work for righteousness, justice, peace, reconciliation,
> wholeness and love. That is the mission of the church today…
> to seek first his kingdom.' (Tom Sine) [292]

Diversity, reconciliation, mission, nations, crossing cultural
divides, crossing economic divides and church unity are all on
God's agenda for his church, but the practical outworking of all
this is done our knees. As I stated at the start of the book, the
journey is not easy, and one where we'll more than likely take a
few knocks along the way. Only recently one Xhosa gentlemen
said to me as we chatted at the newly built Spur restaurant
in Guguletu; 'Some of your young men have deserted their
culture and are trying to be like White people.' I could feel
my heart sinking. This was but one of a whole number of
complaints he raised with me about how we were failing as
a cross-cultural church. Once again it felt like I was taking a
few punches and it was hard not to take it personally. Once
again I was confronted with yet more unforeseen challenges
that had arisen from building church community with people
of different races, cultures and economic backgrounds. Once
again I had to choose to remain on the long path of listening

to people's struggles and discerning God's will in the matter. Was this really a cross-cultural issue or one of differences in expectation between old and young? What theological issues were at stake? Were the issues genuine and thus demanding immediate attention, or were they misguided perceptions and misinterpretations of what was going on? Once again I had to muster energy to fight off depression, put wrong emotional responses to one side and lay hold of faith in the situation.

Never give up

The temptation, of course, is to give up. Why bother? Yet my exhortation in this book has been a resounding NO! Never give up and a resounding YES! to:

- Push the boundaries of worldly thinking and go further than we have gone before in crossing the cultural and economic divides of our societies and love people who are different to ourselves.

- Persevere and push through the pain barriers and obstacles to cross-cultural and cross-economic relationships. They really are possible and the blessings outweigh the difficulties.

- Intentionally seek to build and demonstrate loving local church communities that cross not only racial boundaries but economic boundaries as well. We must remember the poor.

- Glorify God in the nations by intentionally building and demonstrating diverse cross-cultural and cross-economic church communities that reveal something of God's intentions for the future here on earth now – his Kingdom come!

We can all love those who are the same as us, but Christ's call is to go one step further and love even our 'enemies' whoever they may be. Jesus' Sermon on the Mount is a foundation course teaching that we are all to take hold of, just as his command to make disciples of all nations is a commission we are all to respond to. This, as we have seen, is impossible to do without traversing the cultural, racial and economic divides that separate people. Mission forces us to cross these divides and in so doing we glorify God. He is magnified in the nations through united and diverse people visibly demonstrating what it means to be one new man in Christ. Homogenous church communities may display one-fold the glory of God, but multi-cultural church communities display so much more – the manifold wisdom of God.[293] Unity in diversity is not an option for the church – it is essential and needs to be intentionally sought after and laid hold of. Tim Sine says;

'The Church today can derive its sense of intention, direction, and mission directly from what Scripture tells us about the future intentions of God. Remarkably, God invites us, his children, to join with him in working for his intentions now. He calls us to work for righteousness, justice, peace, reconciliation, wholeness and love. That is the mission of the church today… to seek first his kingdom.' (Tim Sine: 1994)[294]

What does God intend for the future that we are to work for now? A new Jerusalem; a city on a hill; God's church; a multitude of believers that no one can count made up of people from every nation, from all tribes and languages; all standing around the throne of God and before the Lamb declaring God's praises for eternity. In heaven there will be no separation and barrier between rich and poor, young and old, educated and uneducated, working-class and middle-class or Black and White. It will be one united and diverse community centred on Jesus. The prophet Isaiah depicted Gods' intentions when he communicated a vision of an unusually diverse, but united community – lions, lambs, wolfs, bears, goats, calves, leopards and children, all lying down together in unity and harmony. This was the fruit and evidence of the Kingdom inaugurated by the 'stump-Messiah' Jesus – a startling signal to the nations revealing the knowledge, intentions, will and power of God. So much so, that diverse peoples of all nations would be attracted to know this amazing Saviour – that 'of him shall the nations enquire'![295] Such is my exhortation in this book – to lay hold of God's kingdom and give a taste of heaven for all to savour.

Citizens of heaven

The apostle Paul put it this way in his letter to the church in Philippi when he said,

'…Let your manner of life be worthy of the gospel of Christ, so that whether I come and see you or am absent, I may hear of you that you are standing firm in one spirit, with one mind striving side by side for the faith of the gospel.' (Philippians 1:27)

I'd like to give three final encouragements to us from Philippians as we bring this book to a conclusion:

1 Live as citizens of heaven

My first encouragement and exhortation is for us all to live a life worthy of the gospel of Jesus Christ by living as citizens of heaven with one another here on earth.

To fully grasp the meaning of Paul's words above, the context of the church in Philippi should not be missed. Situated in the heart of Macedonia and named after its founder Philip of Macedon, father of Alexander the Great, Philippi historically was a proud centre of Greek culture, power and Hellenistic influence. The expansion of the Roman Empire, however, had changed all this when Rome invaded the city, seeking to exploit its strategic location and make use of its nearby mineral resources such as gold and silver. Consequently, Philippi was declared to be a colony of Rome – a Roman 'island' in the midst of a Greek 'sea'. Roman culture, architecture, language, customs, clothes and law were encouraged and promoted above all other cultures. Roman war veterans were invited to move and settle in Philippi, and were given land and houses as rewards for all their service to the Empire. It was a place where Roman citizens were held in high honour.

Cultural 'hot-spot' – Inevitably, tensions were rife. Some of the Greeks went with the flow, readily adapting to the Roman ways and doing all they could to fit in, even buying their

Roman citizenship to gain a higher status in society. Others, however, resented such betrayal. They were proud of their Greek heritage and language, and did all they could to hold on to their cultural identity. There was no love lost between them and Rome. It was to this Greek/Roman cultural hot spot that the Lord called the apostle Paul to 'come and help,' and start the church in Philippi. His first convert was a wealthy trader of fine purple cloth – a lady by the name of Lydia whom he'd met down by the river. Of Greek heritage from the city of Thyatira, she had already converted to Judaism and was a God-fearer, but when Paul met her and shared about Jesus she converted to follow Christ. Soon after a slave girl (at the opposite end of the financial spectrum) became a Christian and was set free from a demonic stronghold of fortune telling, something her owners were not too happy about. Consequently Paul and his companions were beaten and then thrown into jail. As always, God turned the situation for good when the jailer, who had been guarding Paul and Silas, also became a believer along with his entire household.[296]

A diverse church – This therefore, was a diverse church community with many different types of people forming the initial Philippian congregation – rich and poor, male and female, sophisticated and unsophisticated, slave and free, Greek and Roman, all united together under the leadership of a Hebrew intellectual man called Paul.[297] More than likely as the church grew there would have been soldiers added into the church along with a whole number of other Greeks (such as Euodia and Syntyche), Romans (such as Clement) and Hebrews.[298] Though Lydia came from a wealthy household, all evidence seems to suggest that many who formed this early church came from poorer backgrounds. Paul, for example, in his first letter to the Corinthians boasts about, '…the grace of God that has been given among the churches of Macedonia, for in severe test of affliction, their abundance of joy and their extreme poverty have overflowed a wealth of generosity on their part' (2 Corinthians 8:1-2). Thus, the church in Philippi was on the front-edge of crossing cultural and economic divides.

Striving together side by side – Paul's exhortation to this diverse community was for them to live a life worthy of the gospel of Jesus Christ. Aware of the importance of citizenship within the prevailing culture (especially Roman citizenship), Paul played upon this by calling them to live and act by a higher citizenship – as citizens of heaven. He especially called for them to display their heavenly citizenship by being united together in mind, heart and purpose. Where in worldly culture there would have been fighting and antagonism between Greek and Roman citizens, (with one culture seeing itself as superior and above the other); they were not to behave in that way. Instead, they were to strive and work hard at being united, standing side by side together because the faith of the gospel was at stake. Being united in heart, mind and purpose, would demonstrate the reconciling power of the gospel and truly show that they were citizens of heaven. They would reveal something of their heavenly kingdom that they represented and in so doing bring glory to their Lord and King – Jesus!

In 2009 a number of xenophobic attacks occurred throughout South Africa towards many Black African refugees living in the country. Somalis had their shops burned down, Zimbabweans were attacked on trains, and many other foreign nationals lived in fear for their lives. Guguletu was not as badly affected as some communities, but gangs of youngsters none the less sought to cause trouble. In Tambo Village this was not the case. Tambo residents worked with local police to assist refugees before any trouble started, and initiated neighbourhood-watch patrols to prevent gangs entering the community and reaping havoc. No refugee living in Tambo was harmed during that time. Christians and non-Christians stood side by side together for the sake of the poor and oppressed. This was a wonderful sign of the Kingdom of God, and evidence to some small degree, of people's cross-cultural perspectives having been changed and shaped by the mind of Christ. If God can do that in this community – he can do it in yours too!

May all of us in God's church take courage and dare to act as citizens of heaven; to live a life worthy of the gospel of Jesus Christ; to strive to break down the cultural and economic dividing walls of our societies, to work side by side together to demonstrate something of heaven on earth now, for the sake of the gospel and to glorify our heavenly King in the nations.

2 Healthy multi-cultural churches and friendships really are possible

'I thank my God in all my remembrance of you, always in every prayer of mine for you all making my prayer with joy, because of your partnership in the gospel from the first day until now.'
(Philippians 1:3-5)

My second encouragement is for us to know that building relationships and church communities across cultural and economic divides really can work!

Though this community was so obviously diverse, bringing together people from many different backgrounds, and though there were genuine relational difficulties in the church – real, genuine, loving and lasting friendships were formed. Paul was a Hebrew, yet the words that he uses to describe his relationship with the Greek and Roman believers are deep, intimate and personal:

- 'For God is my witness, how I *yearn for you* with the affection of Christ' (Phil 1:8)

- 'Because I *hold you* in my heart' (Phil 1:7)

- 'I *thank my God* in all my remembrance of you, always in every prayer of mine for you are all making my prayer *with joy*' (Phil 1:3-4)

There was genuine love and friendship across cultural and economic divides. These were not forced relationships where people had to pretend to get on with one another. They got to the place where they genuinely liked one another and had real friendships that worked both ways. The Philippians brought joy to Paul's life, and he also brought joy to theirs. It wasn't just Paul loving them, but they too cared deeply about him – so much so they were eager to help and support Paul by sending him financial gifts. They cared for his wellbeing and his welfare which is why Paul could say of them, 'No church entered into partnership with me in giving and receiving, except you only. Even in Thessalonica you sent me help for my needs once and again'. [299] They were partners in the gospel that had withstood the test of time, and despite their differences had found themselves equally caught up in the purposes of God together.

This should give us courage and hope. We should take courage from the Philippian example – that it really is possible to have genuine cross-cultural and cross-economic friendships. Differences need not keep us apart. No matter how different we are, no matter what cultural background we come from, no matter what level of education we may have, no matter what language we speak or how much money we may have – it really is possible to have cross-cultural church community that works. No problem or difficulty that we come across is insurmountable compared to the power of the gospel of Jesus Christ.

This is mine and Lisa's testimony, along with many others in my own church and beyond. We've seen, tasted, enjoyed and experienced just a little of heaven on earth – that loving, reconciled, meaningful cross-cultural friendships can happen with people from very different worlds, cultures, races, languages and backgrounds. Despite the struggles we have faced (which I've attempted to be as honest about as possible), we have pushed through and seen the fruit of at all as well. We are not perfect and still have a long way to go, but my hope is that as you've read this book, you too will be encouraged to do the same – if it can happen for us in South Africa, it can happen for you wherever you may be in the world.

3 Christ is with us for the task

'And I am sure of this, that he who began a good work in you will bring it to completion at the day of Jesus Christ' (Philippians 1:6)

My third and final encouragement is for us to know that God is with us in our efforts to cross cultural and economic divides.

Paul was not naïve to the potential difficulties of cultural and economic diversity, and was well aware of issues going on in the Philippian church. Things such as differences in thinking and opinions, lack of love, discord, rivalry, conceit, pride, superiority and selfishness were all happening behind the scenes. Yet Paul was not intimidated or frightened off by such realities. They did not drive him to discouragement, or to negative thoughts over cross-cultural church, or to make him want to give-up on cross-cultural relationships. He did not say 'This is never going to work – you are all too different. Let's give up and just meet with those who are like us. It'll be much easier that way'. Problems, difficulties and discomfort did not deter Paul from the vision set before him. He was confident, in fact, that he who had begun a good work in them would bring it to completion. [300] He was sure that this cross-cultural thing was a good work, that God was with them, that he would help them overcome any difficulties, and that he would finish what he had started.

Christ is with us for the task ahead and his power is available to do even the impossible. I'm reminded of something I saw when I first came to South Africa in 1994. The elections were over and it was officially the New South Africa' The Tambo Square residents that I've mentioned in this book were still in the process of negotiating for housing, and race tensions were still high. The land they'd been allocated to build on had historically been

Coloured land, located within the so-called Coloured area of Manenberg. As such, several Coloured people decided to move and squat on the Tambo land as a sign of their new freedom and liberation, as well as protesting against Black people moving onto their land. As you might imagine the Tambo residents were in uproar over this and marched from Guguletu to Manenberg ready for war. Fearful as to what might happen, Angela Kemm, Lydia Mhlanga (see chapter seven) and I went to the land to pray for peace. It seemed like an impossible situation when we saw the two angry mobs approach one another, each with their guns, knives and sticks visibly displayed. We prayed fervently as we stood between the two groups, appealing for peace and praying loudly for God's help in the situation. We were stunned, none-the-less, when God miraculously intervened. Before our eyes this screaming, angry and violent group of people became silent – they turned to one another, spoke amicably, laughed together and even shared sandwiches with one another. We were 'gob smacked'! The situation did not make sense and the only explanation we could come up with was that God had sent his angels to intervene!

This event impacted my life in a profound way. Firstly, because I saw the difference Christians can make when they dare to follow Jesus and bring his kingdom on earth as it is in heaven. And secondly, because I witnessed first hand the power of God at work to reconcile hostile and hating people – that he is able to do the impossible! We must not forget that we have a God who is more than able to do over and above all that we can ask or imagine. [301] He is with us for the journey ahead.

Let's Follow Christ's example

As I finish writing, race tensions have risen once more in South Africa, following the murder of Eugene Terrablanche who was brutally killed on the Easter Saturday of 2010. Fear, mistrust, hostility and uncertainty are once again rising in the hearts of different people towards one another. Peacemakers and hope-givers are required to demonstrate that diverse races really can be reconciled and united together as one. In South Africa, now more than ever, the church needs to show the way. The same is no less true in others parts of the world. Jesus is our example to follow. He is the one we are to emulate. He traversed the biggest cultural and economic divides of all time – that of God and man. We are invited and compelled to do the same – to intentionally cross and overcome the cultural and economic divides that separate the people and nations of our societies, and so demonstrate God's kingdom on earth as it is in heaven. As we do so a signal will go forth – a sign indicating that God is at work; a visible demonstration that God is alive, and a revealing of the knowledge of God so that; '..at the name of Jesus every knee should bow, in heaven and on earth and under the earth, and every tongue confess that Jesus Christ is Lord, to the glory of God the Father' (Philippians 2: 10). The invitation has gone out – will you be part of the people of God who say YES?

Questions for discussion

My experience of this topic is that it provokes discussion. As such I've included a number of questions that can be used both for individual reflection and for group discussion. Ten questions have been given for each chapter geared around the particular theme or emphasis of that chapter. These themes can be summarised as follows:

- People's journeys and experiences cross-culturally
- The vision of diverse community in Isaiah chapter 11 (The Stump)
- Exploring God's heart for the nations of the world
- Crossing racial and cultural boundaries – is 'cross-cultural' for everyone?
- Crossing socio-economic boundaries – How are we to 'remember' the poor?
- Diverse church community – shocking the world.
- Should every church be cross-cultural? What about homogeny?
- Are deep and meaningful cross-cultural friendships really possible?
- How practically do we enter someone else's world?
- Building multi-cultural churches
- Culture and worldviews
- Racism, prejudices and stereotypes
- Handling differences in wealth
- Children and the nations
- Living as citizens of heaven – summing up the main encouragements of the book

Introduction

Theme: People's journeys and experiences cross-culturally

Choose some of the questions for discussion:

1 What has been your journey relating with people of different cultures or socio-economic backgrounds to yourself? Has it been easy or difficult?

2 What has been your journey as a church in crossing the cultural and economic divides of your particular town or city?

3 What have you enjoyed about your cross-cultural experiences and what have you struggled with? How have you responded to those struggles?

4 How has God used the struggles in your life to change you or help grow you in Him?

5 'Culture shock, culture shock, culture shock'. What is culture shock? In what ways have you encountered culture shock?

6 The biggest challenge to the church today is comfortable Christianity? Discuss!

7 What do you think of struggle? Where does a theology of 'struggle' fit into church in the 21st century?

8 What practical or theological questions do you have around crossing cultural and economic divides?

9 'Many are not willing to embrace human diversity because it forces us to change, disrupts our cozy patterns and engages us in a world where our deficiencies are exposed'. Discuss

10 'Yet for all the less than appealing features of cultural and ethnic variety, important insights about God and his world go undiscovered if we avoid creative engagement with human diversity'. Discuss!

Chapter 1

Theme: The vision of diverse community in Isaiah chapter 11 (The Stump)

Choose some of the questions for discussion:

1 Have you ever ignored a word from God (perhaps a sermon or prophetic word) because you found the message uncomfortable or not to your liking? How have you responded since?

2 Have you ever overlooked people on the basis of their appearance or background? Have you ever been overlooked by others? How did it make you feel?

3 How did Jesus become a 'stump' on our behalf? (Read Isaiah 53:2-3).

4 'So incredible and 'stump-like' was the coming of the Lord Jesus Christ that many people overlooked Him, despised Him, rejected Him and did not esteem Him'. Is it still possible to overlook and 'miss' Jesus today? How and why?

5 What makes successful ministry? Isaiah followed God's word even though people did not respond. How do you think he felt? What kept him going? Do you think you could do what Isaiah did?

6 What examples can you think of where God has used people who are 'the least of the least' (stumps) in the eyes of the world?

7 What do you think the vision of diverse community in Isaiah 11:6-10 means for the church today?

8 'The coming of Jesus ministry is so powerful it can transform nature itself. New life in Jesus will reveal itself through the radical transformation of relationships. Where relationships were once hostile and full of animosity they will be transformed to that of love and friendship'. Discuss where this has happened in your life or that of your local church.

9 'Loving diverse church community will act as a signal to the nations of the knowledge of God'. Discuss!

10 Do some people get overlooked or ignored in your church? Why?

Chapter 2

Theme: Diversity and God's heart for the nations of the world

Choose some of the questions for discussion:

1 'There is something beautiful in diversity that can't be found to the same extent in homogeny' Discuss! What different types of diversity can you think of? What are the blessings of diversity?

2 'There is something beautiful in diversity that glorifies God'. Discuss! How and why does diversity glorify God? Why does human diversity glorify God?

3 'Diversity is indeed beautiful, but it can be a messy business'. Discuss! What are some of the potential difficulties of diversity? Why can human diversity be a messy business?

4 What 'mess' of diversity have you encountered in your church or local community?

5 'From the first few verses of Genesis to the end of Revelation, God's heart and passion for diversity seems to ooze through the very pores of the Bible'. Discuss! What is the evidence for this in the Bible?

6 'One book of the Bible that communicates something of God's passion for the nations around us is the book of Jonah'. What is God's heart for the different nations of the world? How is this seen in the book of Jonah?

7 'Some people are happy to cross borders and go to the nations in other parts of the world, but are reluctant to cross railway lines or motorways to the numerous nations on their own doorsteps'. Discuss! Is this true and if so why do you think this may be the case?

8 'There are more nations than we realise and we can be 'blind' to the diversity of peoples around us'. Discuss!

9 In what way has your life been enriched by the diversity of people God has put on the face of the earth?

10 'God authored human diversity. This fact calls all of us to deal with cultural diversity, see it as good and honour it as the handiwork of the wise and sovereign creator'. What do you see that is good about the 'handiwork' of God? In what ways have you honoured the 'handiwork' of God? Have you in any way dishonoured the 'handiwork' of God or not seen it as good?

Chapter 3

Theme: Crossing racial and cultural boundaries – is 'cross-cultural' for everyone?

Choose some of the questions for discussion:

1 Who do you know who is good at mixing and relating with people of different cultures and backgrounds? What is it about them that you admire? Is there anything about them that intimidates you?

2 'As long as there is time, and as long as there are nations to reach Jesus' demand to go and make disciples is valid'. This is relevant to all Christians of all ages of all countries and all backgrounds. Discuss!

3 Jesus encouraged His disciples to lift up their eyes and see the fields in front of them that were ripe for harvest. How and why can our eyes be blinkered to different types of people right in front of us? Are there any ways you need to lift up your eyes to see those around you?

4 What can you do where you are now to get to know people from different cultural, class and economic backgrounds?

5 What has stopped you interacting and mixing with people of different cultural and racial backgrounds? What excuses can people give so as 'not' to relate cross-culturally?

6 Some people say that, 'It takes a certain type of person to do the cross-cultural thing'. Discuss!

7 Some people say that being 'Cross-cultural is a gifting from God that not everyone has'. Discuss!

8 It has been argued that 'God calls some people to one homogenous grouping', therefore 'doing the cross-cultural thing is not for everyone'. Discuss!

9 'Any burden we may have for specific nations, sociological groups or peoples of this earth that does not spread and reach out to other nations as well, is no true prophetic burden from the Lord'. Discuss!

10 What can be done in your church to envision people more about God's heart for different nations of the world? What can you do in your church to encourage and help people to mix with others who are different to themselves?

Chapter 4

Theme: Crossing socio-economic boundaries – How are we to 'remember' the poor?

Choose some of the questions for discussion:

1 What relationships do you have with people from different wealth and class backgrounds to yourself?

2 What do you find difficult about such relationships?

3 What has blessed and encouraged you about those relationships?

4 'It's only logical that if we are to go the nations of the world, not only will we encounter people who are different to us in culture, language and traditions, but also in 'class,' education, wealth and socio-economic status.' Discuss!

5 'Remembering the poor is a 're-building' the wall issue. It is crucial for the church today and central to all of God's purposes for the nations'. Discuss!

6 'God seems to especially love the poor'. Discuss

7 'If you have come to help me you are wasting you time, but if you have come to work out your liberation together with mine, let us work together' (Aboriginal woman). Discuss! What are different motives for rich wanting to be with the poor or the poor wanting to be with the rich (both good and bad)?

8 'It is a dangerous and slippery path to go down when church leaders target certain peoples, sociological groupings or education types in preference to others'. Discuss!

9 'The poor are more than a ministry'. Discuss! How are you as a church seeking to reach the poor of your communities?

10 To what extent are you seeing the poor saved and added into your church? Is genuine fellowship happening with people across the economic divides? To what extent are both poor and rich being caught up in ministry together in the life of the church?

Chapter 5

Theme: Diverse church community

Choose some of the questions for discussion:

1 'Church is community. This is the underlying great assumption of the New Testament'. Discuss! What have been the greatest blessings to you being part of church community?

2 To what extent do people ask questions of you about your relationship with God because of the way you live your life? What makes radical, question-raising church?

3 'Factors of race, class, sex and national identity shape and define the lives of Christians just like everybody else. No one expects anything different from Christians. The predictability of the Christian lifestyle, or, more to the point, the loss of a distinctively Christian lifestyle, has severely damaged our proclamation of the gospel. We have lost that visible style of life that was evident in the early Christian communities and that gave their evangelism its compelling power and authority'. Discuss!

4 'Christians in the early church were charged for having no appreciation of social class and not making distinctions in rank, outward appearance, wealth, education, age or sex'. Discuss the evidence for this in the church today.

5 'The church is God's new humanity on display for all to see'. Discuss!

6 'Unity in the church needs to be intentionally sought, visibly seen and intentionally maintained'. Discuss!

7 'Throughout the New Testament one does not get a sense of homogonous neatness with like and like meeting together. Rather the overwhelming sense is one of beautiful, but slightly messy diversity'. What evidence is there for diversity of different cultures, nations and social backgrounds in the early New Testament churches?

8 To what extent is your church community visibly displaying 'one new man in Christ'?

9 To what extent are problems of disunity in your church related to people being from different cultural and economic backgrounds? What are you doing to maintain unity in the church?

10 What evidence is there in your church for people loving others who are different to them, of loving not only as well as the world around them, but better than the world?

Chapter 6

Theme: Should every church be cross-cultural? What about homogeny?

Choose some of the questions for discussion:

1 How has God used people from different backgrounds to impact and change your life?

2 Do you find it easier to stick to your own kind – why?

3 How homogenous are the churches in your particular village, town or city?

4 'People like to become Christians without having to cross racial, linguistic, or class barriers'. Discuss!

5 'Homogeny weakens Christian discipleship'. Discuss!

6 'The new humanity is not a trend or when a church is known for attracting one particular kind of demographic, like people of this particular age and education level, or that particular social class or personality type. There's obviously nothing wrong with the powerful bonds that are shared when you meet up with your own tribe and hear things in a language that you understand, and cultural references that you are familiar with. But when sameness takes over, when everybody shares the same story, when there is no listening to other perspectives, no stretching and expanding and opening up – that's when the new humanity is in trouble'. Discuss!

7 'Homogeny denies the reconciling nature of the gospel of Jesus Christ.' Discuss!

8 To what extent does your church reflect the multi-cultural pattern of how people are relating outside the church?

9 To what extent has homogenous teaching influenced the way you are building church community?

10 'There has been considerable debate in recent years whether a local church could or should ever be culturally homogenous. A consultation on this issue concluded that no church should ever acquiesce in such a condition… Every homogenous unit church must take active steps to broaden its fellowship in order to demonstrate visibly the unity and variety of Christ's church'. Discuss! What steps can you do in your particular context to broaden fellowship?

Chapter 7

Theme: Are deep and meaningful cross-cultural friendships really possible?

Choose some of the questions for discussion:

1   To what extent do you have intimate 'deep and meaningful' friendships with people from different cultural backgrounds to yourself? What has helped those friendships to develop?

2   To what extent are your cross-cultural relationships with people of similar 'class' or education level?

3   Where have you benefited from casual encounters with people from other cultures? How has your life been enriched?

4   Who is 'sharpening' you? Are you mainly sharpened by people similar in culture, thinking, background and class status to yourself?

5   Is it really possible to have 'deep and intimate' relationships across cultural and socio-economic divides?

6   'It is unrealistic to expect the kind of intimacy and understanding in those relationships that one might reasonably seek and enjoy in relationships within one's culture of origin'. Discuss!

7   'It is difficult, if not impossible, to build a core community that meets the deepest needs for intimacy and understanding of people with radically different backgrounds and seeking to do so almost always results in painful divisions and burnout'. Discuss!

8   'The goal is authentic interrelation – not integration – so that it's OK to maintain predominantly white and predominantly black institutions, churches and communities, so long as all of them relate meaningfully and authentically with one another'. Discuss!

9   'Becoming faithful friends is an adventure into personal vulnerability. It is not always easy. However when we are with someone who accepts us as we are, listens attentively to what we share and is committed to mutual interaction, courage is given for the first steps in the life-sharing experience.' Discuss!

10 'The unity of the Spirit that is achieved when diverse peoples of different backgrounds become Christians should not be underestimated. It should come as no surprise to know that the author of diversity is more than able to assist in the development of intimate and close cross-cultural friendships.' Discuss!

Chapter 8

Theme: How practically do we enter someone else's world?

Choose some of the questions for discussion:

1 'Building cross-cultural relationships is about being willing to enter, however briefly, the world of someone different to oneself'. Discuss! How far do we go with this?

2 'It may be difficult to teach a person to respect another unless we can help people to see things from the other's point of view'. Discuss! How have you attempted to enter into other people's worlds and 'see as they see'?

3 'The greatest example of breaking down the dividing walls that separate us, entering other people's worlds and interacting with those different to ourselves, is Christ Himself.' Discuss! How did Jesus enter our world and see as we see?

4 'Jesus was intentional about crossing cultural and economic divides. In the church today we must do the same'. Discuss! How intentional have you been? How can you become more intentional?

5 'Entering the worlds of others forces us to get out of our comfort zones'. Discuss! How willing have you been to get out of your comfort zones and associate with people of different cultures?

6 How willing have you been to make mistakes, listen and learn from others and go to places where previously you never would have gone?

7 'Those who 'stay with their own' and don't choose to embark on the adventure of building cross-cultural friendships are missing out.' Discuss!

8 'The way Jesus chose to enter our world was important. His attitude was one of pure humility with no sense of superiority or patronising attitude towards those He was relating with'. Discuss! What are wrong motives for wanting to be cross-cultural and mix with different kinds of people?

9 What excuses can we give that would stop us from entering the world's of others?

10 'Let's have some fun together'. Discuss the fun that can be had in relating to people of different cultures and backgrounds. What funny experiences have you had?

Chapter 9

Theme: Building multi-cultural churches

Choose some of the questions for discussion:

1 'Increasingly the subject of multi-cultural churches is entering the radar screens of topical conversation, comment and consideration'. Discuss! Why do you think this is the case?

2 What has been your experience of multi-cultural church community?

3 'There is a minefield of thinking about cross-cultural church'. Discuss the differences in models presented in chapter 9. Does your church fit into one of the models of cross-cultural church? Why do you think there is so much diverse thinking and practice in this area?

4 'Cross-cultural churches are local communities of believers that are intentional in their efforts to embrace diverse types of people across racial, cultural and economic divides; are committed to racial reconciliation and demonstrating genuine loving community that magnifies the oneness of believers in Christ and brings glory to God in the nations' Discuss what makes a cross-cultural church truly cross-cultural!

5 Many multi-cultural churches adopt homogenous practices in the way they build community. How much homogenous thinking has influenced the way your local church builds cross-culturally?

6 'A church can be multi-cultural in terms of different people present, but not truly cross-cultural in terms of heart attitudes with one another'. Discuss!

7 'The goal of cross-cultural church is not for the minority cultures to 'assimilate' and adopt the majority culture.' Discuss!

8 Does the use of translation mean that sermons have to be simple? What are the advantages and disadvantages of translation?

9 Is it possible to learn to worship God in a language that is not one's mother tongue? How can you encourage worship in different languages in your own church congregation?

10 How theologically convinced are you that cross-cultural church is on God's agenda? Discuss practical things that can be done in church community to encourage genuine interaction and relationship among diverse people.

Chapter 10

Theme: Culture and worldviews

Choose some of the questions for discussion:

1 How has your cultural and economic background shaped the way you think?

2 'We are all shaped into thinking that our way of doing something is 'normal' and 'right'. Discuss!

3 We need to recognise that we all have a culture and worldview. What is worldview? Discuss the culture test highlighted in chapter 10.

4 'In relation to the gospel some of our cultural thinking and practices are positive and directly in line with Christian values, some are negative and in need of transformation, while others are relatively neutral and can be embraced without any qualms by Christians'. What aspects of your culture do you think glorify God?

5 What aspects of your culture are neutral?

6 What thinking and practices in your culture go against the gospel? Are they still part of your life? Are you willing to change?

7 How do we discern which parts of our culture and traditions need to be 'leaked' and which parts to hold onto?

8 Have you ever encountered cultural conflict? What did you do about it?

9 What aspects of culture commonly spring to mind when we think of cultural differences? Discuss some of the visible aspects of culture outlined in chapter 10.

10 What hidden aspects of culture are we less aware of that can take us by surprise if we are not aware? Discuss some of the hidden aspects of culture highlighted in chapter 10.

Chapter 11
Theme: Racism, prejudices and stereotypes
Choose some of the questions for discussion:

1 How do you classify yourself racially? (ie Black, White, Coloured, Negro, Mixed Race etc). Where do you get your identity from?

2 What expectations do other people place upon you because of your racial background?

3 'We are all tinged by racism'. Discuss?

4 How do we recognise racism in ourselves, others and in our churches?

5 What assumptions, stereotypes and prejudices crop up in your life? What assumption, stereotypes and prejudices have you encountered in the church?

6 'We need to be colour conscious and not colour blind'. Discuss

7 'The issue of racial prejudice and snubbing and suspicion and mistreatment is not a social issue; it is a blood-of-Jesus issue'. Discuss!

8 'We need to break the silence on racism'. Discuss! Why is racism such a hard thing to talk about?

9 'Confronting the barriers of race, class, culture and gender was perhaps major social drama of the New Testament church. Overcoming those division was seen as a primary test of spiritual authenticity. If the churches would reclaim the call to spiritual warfare, this time against the principality of racism, how might the battle against racism be transformed?' Discuss! How should the church be giving herself to tackling this principality of racism?

10 What are the advantages and disadvantages of creating forums to discuss racism in our churches?

Chapter 12
Theme: Handling differences in wealth
Choose some of the questions for discussion:

1 How much have you shared of your money or possessions in the last month with other people.

2 What do you find difficult about mixing with people from different economic or social backgrounds to yourself? What difficulties have you encountered in your church community because of differences in wealth and money between people? How do we handle such differences?

3 What presumptions do people make about you on the basis of your wealth or lack of wealth? How does it make you feel? What presumptions do you make about others?

4 How do differences in wealth affect the dynamics of relationships?

5 'Disparities in wealth, education and class will inevitably expose a number of rotten attitudes and emotions.' Discuss!

6 'We are all to give whether rich or poor'. Discuss!

7 'Responding to poverty and differences in financial wealth is a Holy Spirit ministry'. Discuss!

8 'In the early church rich and poor were forced together into church community and loving fellowship occurred across such divides. The same needs to happen in the church today'. Discuss!

9 'Three things will vehemently be tested when developing relationships across economic divides – attitudes towards time, possessions and money'. Discuss!

10 The way we give is important just as is the way we receive. Discuss what are good and helpful ways of giving and receiving.

Chapter 13

Theme: Children and the nations

Choose some of the questions for discussion:

1 In what contexts are your children encountering and mixing with other children of different cultural and economic backgrounds?

2 'The love and protective desire that we have for our children has the potential to hinder us from mission. It can cause us to change direction in pursuing the call that God has put on our lives (and for our kids).' Discuss!

3 Wanting the 'best' for our kids also has the potential to hinder us from mission and responding to God's call upon our lives (and for our kids).' Discuss!

4 In what ways has concern for your child's welfare influenced decisions you have made about who your children mix with?

5 'Children can struggle with diversity in the same way that adults do'. Discuss! What struggles have your children encountered? What can you do to help?

6 'It's a fine line between knowing when to rescue our children from problems or helping them to overcome and persevere through the difficulties.' Discuss

7 How do we envision our children to love God first and foremost?

8 'We need to envision our children for the nations, to love different people and to work through the associated challenges'. Discuss! How can we do this?

9 'The way we approach life as parents, the way we treat people and the way we respond in certain situations will all have a direct impact on our children's behaviour'. Discuss!

10 'If our children are going to cultivate friendships with children from other communities we are going to have to get involved as parents'. Discuss! What can you do as parents to help you children build healthy cross-cultural relationships?

Chapter 14

Theme: Living as citizens of heaven – summing up the main encouragements of the book

Choose some of the questions for discussion:

1 'We must push the boundaries of worldly thinking and go further than we have gone before in crossing the cultural and economic divides of our societies and love people who are different to ourselves.' Discuss!

2 'We must glorify God in the nations by intentionally building and demonstrating diverse cross-cultural and cross-economic church communities that reveal something of God's intentions for the future here on earth now – His Kingdom come!' Discuss!

3 'We are to live a life worthy of the gospel of Jesus Christ by living as citizens of heaven with one another here on earth'. Discuss!

4 'Healthy multi-cultural churches and friendships really are possible'. Discuss!

5 'God is with us in our efforts to cross cultural and economic divides'. Discuss!

6 'Jesus is our example to follow. He is the one we are to emulate. He traversed the biggest cultural and economic divides of all time – that of God and man. We are invited and compelled to do the same.' Discuss!

7 What cultural, racial and economic tensions are you facing in your particular town and country at this moment in time? What can you do about them?

8 What evidence have you seen of God's miraculous intervention and reconciling power in the area of race relations? Where do you need to ask God for His miraculous intervention, knowing that He can do more than all you can ask or imagine?

9 What evidence have you seen of Christians making a difference in their communities? What difference can you make?

10 The invitation has gone out – will you be part of the people of God who say YES?

End notes

Introduction

[1] Because 'race' categories are artificial, but are used for descriptive purposes, each time a racial categorisation is used, it has a capital letter.

[2] G Cook: 1992; (Edit DM Smith); 'The Apartheid City and Beyond – Urbanisation and social change in South Africa'; Routledge, p126.

[3] The Vineyard church was under the leadership of Graham Ingram at the time. However, a few years later the church changed its name to Jubilee Community Church under the leadership of Simon Pettit in 2000. At this stage the church also became part of Newfrontiers an international family of churches under the apostolic leadership of Terry Virgo.

[4] This amount later became R17 million rand.

[5] At Khanyisa you often hear talk about 'Old Tambo' meaning the shack community where the original Tambo residents came from. 'New Tambo' or Tambo Village means the community that developed when eventually the residents left their shacks to build new houses on the land (Tambo Village) that had been allocated. This community now consists of many other people beyond the 'old Tambo' residents, including people from Guguletu and Manenberg.

[6] I'll share more of Lydia and Angela's story in chapter 7 as we discuss whether it is possible to have 'deep and meaningful' friendships with someone of a different culture and economic background.

[7] An Afrikaans word for a criminal.

[8] Quoted in Sojourners study guide: 2000; 'Crossing the racial divide' p68.

[9] Duane Elmer: 1993; 'Cross Cultural Conflict – Building relationships for effective ministry'; IVP, p23.

Chapter 1 Life from a Stump

[10] 2 Chronicles 26:15

[11] Isaiah 6:3

[12] Isaiah 6:8

[13] Isaiah 6:13

14 EH Petersen: 2007; ' The Jesus Way – a Conversation in Following Jesus'; Hodder and Stoughton, p139

15 Cf Isaiah 6:13

16 Ibid Petersen: 2007:141

17 Isaiah 6:9

18 Isaiah 53:2-3

19 Matthew 25:42,43

20 Cf Isaiah 11:2

21 Cf Isaiah 11:3-5

22 Cf 1 Samuel 16:7

23 JA Motyer: 1993; ' The prophecy of Isaiah'; IVP, p124.

24 Cf Isaiah 11:9-10

25 Cf Isaiah 11:6-8

26 Cf Isaiah 11:7

27 Cf Isaiah 11:6

28 Galatians 3:28

Chapter 2 **Glorious diversity**

29 John Stott: 2006; 'Issues Facing Christians Today'; 4th edition; Zondervan, p288.

30 J Piper: 1993; 'Let the Nations be Glad – The Supremacy of God in Missions'; IVP, P212.

31 Rob Bell & Dan Golden: 2008;' Jesus Wants to Save Christians'; Zondervan, p154-155.

32 Cf Genesis 1:31

33 D Elmer: 1993; 'Cross Cultural Conflict – Building Relationships for Effective Ministry'; IVP, p24.

34 Cf Genesis 1:27

35 Acts 17:26

36 D Devenish: 2005; 'What on Earth is the Church For?'; Authentic Media, p22.

37 Cf Genesis 11:4

38 Cf Romans 1:24; see writings of AW Pink: 1922; 'Gleanings in Genesis'; Moody Press, p135. See also M. Eaton: 1997; 'Preaching Through the Bible - Genesis 1-11'; Sovereign World, p152.

[39] See D Hughes: 1998; 'God of the poor'; OM Publishing, p221.

[40] Cf James 2, Hebrews 11

[41] John 1:47

[42] Cf Jonah 1, 2

[43] Jonah 1:7-16

[44] Cf Jonah 3:8

[45] Cf Jonah 1:4

[46] Cf Jonah 4:8

[47] Cf Jonah 4:6

[48] Cf Jonah 4:9

[49] Cf Jonah 4:3

[50] Cf Jonah 4:1-2

[51] Compare Jonah 1:6 to Mark 4:38

[52] Cf Psalm 103:8

[53] Cf Matthew 12:41

[54] Jonah 4:11

[55] Cited in Piper 1993:189

[56] See J Piper: 2004; 'Brothers We Are Not Professionals'; Mentor, p191.

[57] Genesis 12:3

[58] R Winter: 1981; 'The New Macedonia: A revolutionary New Era in Missions Begins'; in Ralph Winter and Steven Hawthorne, eds.,' Perspectives on World Christian Movement'; Pasadena; William Carey Library, p302.

[59] See Jeff Peires: 1981; 'The House of Phalo – A History of the Xhosa People in the Days of their Independence'; Jonathan Ball Publishers, p3.

[60] See M Ramphele: 2002; 'Steering by the Stars – Being Young in South Africa'; Tafelberg, p18-19.

[61] Ibid: D Elmer 1993:24

[62] J Hosier: 2002; 'The Lamb, the Beast and the Devil – Making sense of the Book of Revelation'; Monarch Books, p76.

[63] Cf Revelation 21:24-26

[64] B Milne: 2002 'The message of Heaven and Hell', BST; IVP, p32.

[65] Ibid: Elmer 1993:23

Chapter 3 **Lift up your eyes**

[66] Matthew 28:19-20

[67] Cf Matthew 24:14

[68] John Piper: 2006; 'What Jesus Demands From the World'; Christian Art Publishers, p366.

[69] Cf John 4:7-42

[70] John 4:35

[71] Cf Acts 2:8-12

[72] Cf Luke 9:51-56

[73] Cf 1Corinthians 12:1-6

[74] Cf Romans 12:6

[75] Cf 2 Timothy 4:5

[76] Cf 1 Corinthians 14:1,39

[77] Cf Colossians 3:16

[78] John 20:21

[79] Cf 1 Corinthains 14:29

[80] Cf Jeremiah 17:9

[81] Psalm 51:10

[82] Cf Galatians 3:1

[83] Cf 1 Corinthians 12:4-6

[84] Cf Acts 10:15

[85] Cf Acts 10:17

[86] Cf Acts 10:28

[87] Cf Acts 10:34

[88] Cf Acts 12:17

[89] See comments by Michael Eaton: 1999; 'Preaching Through the Bible – 1 Peter'; Sovereign World, p14.

[90] Cf Acts 17:17, 19:10

[91] Cf Acts 18:6

[92] Cf Galatians 2:11-13

Chapter 4 **Freedom together**

[93] This community no longer exists as the residents now have housing in Tambo Village (though the Palm Tree after which it was named is still visible for all to see)

[94] Die dam is an Afrikaans word for a well.

[95] Here are some scriptures pertaining to the poor:

Widows and orphans - 'This is pure and undefiled religion in the sight of God our Father, to visit orphans and widows in their distress.' (Jas 1:27) , See also Dt 10:18

Aliens - 'Show you love for the alien for you were aliens in the land of Egypt' Dt 10:19,

'Provide the poor wanderer with shelter' (Is 58)

Hungry, thirsty, stranger, naked, sick, in prison -
Mt 25:35-36 'For I was hungry and you gave me something to eat, I was thirsty and you gave me drink, I was a stranger and you invited me in, naked and you clothed me, I was sick and you visited me, I was in prison and you came to me.'

Heb 13:3 'remember those in prison as if you were their fellow prisoners and those who are mistreated as if you yourselves were suffering'

Oppressed, exploited and mistreated - Jas 5:4 'Behold the pay of the labourers who mowed your fields and which has been withheld by you cries out against you and the outcry of those who did the harvesting has reached the ears of the Lord of the Sabbath.'

Is 58:1 'Is this not the fast which I choose, to loosen the bonds of wickedness, to undo the bans of the yoke, and the let the oppressed go free and break every yoke?'

Lonely - Ps 68:6 'God makes a home for the lonely, he leads out the prisoners into prosperity'

Note John Stott categorizes three groups of poor from the 200 or so references to the poor in the Old Testament;

The economic poor – These are people who lack the bare necessities of life – food, clothing, shelter.

The oppressed poor – Those who are socially or politically oppressed, the powerless victims of injustice

The humble poor – those that acknowledge their helplessness and look to God for their salvation
(see Psalm 34:6)

[96] Quote cited in J. Wimber:1994; 'The Gospel to the Poor'; Oasis Bible Study notes; Frontier Publishing.

[97] This list came from a workshop amongst Cape Town church elders grappling with some of the complex challenges associated with poverty.

[98] Cf Nehemiah 5:3

[99] Cf Nehemiah 5:7

[100] Cf Nehemiah 5:8

[101] Cf Nehemiah 5:9

[102] Cf Mark 10:21

[103] Cf Psalm 103:8

[104] Deuteronomy 10:17-18

[105] Cf Psalm 146:7-9

[106] Isaiah 61:3

[107] Cf Luke 4:18,19

[108] Cf Acts 4:13

[109] John 20:21

[110] David Devenish: 2005; 'Demolishing strongholds'; Word Publishing, p28.

[111] Cf Nehemiah 4:6

[112] Cf Nehemiah 6:6

[113] Cf Galatians 2:10

[114] Cf Galatians 2:10

[115] Luke 4:18

[116] Gordon Mcdonald – source unknown

[117] Cf James 1:27

[118] See James 2:14-17

[119] Newfrontiers Magazine Jan- March 2009: Volume3, Issue 10: Page15

[120] RJ Sider: 1999: Chapter 8; 'Good news and good works – A theology for the whole gospel'

[121] Cited in Sojourners 2000; 'Crossing the racial divide – A study guide', p66.

[122] **How did Jesus remember the poor?**

He identified with the poor and was born poor – 'For your sake he became poor' 2 Co 8:9

He gave the gospel, brought salvation, grace, mercy and forgiveness of sins (Luke 4:18 – the Spirit of the Sovereign Lord is upon me to preach good news to the poor, Mark 1:5 forgiveness of sins to the paralytic)

He had compassion (Luke 7:13 – the widow who lost her only son, Mark 1:41 – the leper)

Brought the poor onto his leadership team (Mt 4:18 – choosing of 12 fishermen Peter and Andrew). Discipled the poor. Luke 6:20 'Turning his gaze on his disciples he began to say, Blessed are you who are poor for yours is the kingdom of God'

Spent time with the poor and overlooked – see most of the gospels (eg Luke 18:16,17 – children)

Preached on helping the poor (Luke 3:11 'Let the man who has two tunics share with him who has none')

Gave advice to the poor (Mt 6:25-34 advice re trusting God for needs)

Gave honour to the poor in OT who were used by God
(Luke 4:24-27 – a non Jewish widow and non Jewish leper)

Jesus was baptised by the poor (John Baptist – Luke 7:25 what did you expect to see – someone in fine clothing?)

Touched the poor and allowed the poor to touch him
(eg Mt 8 the healing of the leper)

Ate with the poor (Luke 15:2 'this man receives sinners and eats with them', Mt 9:11-12, Mt 26:6)

Developed genuine friendships with poor (Peter, Simon the leper)

Gave honour and respect to the poor (John Baptist Mt 11:7-12, Widows mite Mk 12:41-44,)

Gave dignity to poor (eg Bleeding woman who had spent all she had on doctors till she had nothing left Mt 9:18)

Supported restitution to poor (Zaccheus Luke 19)

Fed the poor (Luke 9:12 feeding of 5000)

Spoke to the rich regarding the poor (Rich ruler Mt 19:21)

Healed the poor (blind Bartimaeus begging Luke 18:35)

Attacked those exploiting the poor (Mt 21 money changers in temple, Mt 23:14 Woe to you who 'devour widows houses… neglect justice and mercy...'

Prayed for the poor and asked the poor to pray with him
(Mk 14:32 Gethsemane, John 17)

Gave authority, gifting, commission and purpose (Mt 10:1 authority over unclean spirits, Luke 10:1 sent out 72, Mt 28 :19 – go and make disciples)

Jesus died with the poor (Luke 23:39 – next to thieves on the cross)

How did the apostles and early church remember the poor?

Apostolic burden – Gal 2:10 'All they asked was that we should continue to remember the poor the very thing I was eager to do'

Preached the gospel. Shared their possessions – individually and corporately (Acts 2:44)

Took up offerings (Acts 11)

There was a seriousness and severity about this
(Acts 5 – Ananias and Sapphira)

Changed mind shift from being receivers to givers. Established a paradigm that is different to the world – working for rewards in Heaven – focused the church on another Kingdom.

Didn't just help the poor – treated the whole person- tied up in salvation.

Appointed teams of leaders full of the Holy Spirit to help serve the poor (Acts 6). Apostles were involved.

Encouraged the gifts of Helps, Mercy. Healings (Ro12, 1Co 12)

Preached the gospel to the poor

Preached and taught church re poor and response to the poor (James 1:27 'This is pure and undefiled religion in the sight of God to visit orphans and widows in distress')

Inter church response – The churches cared for one another - Acts 11:29 'the disciples each according to his ability decided to provide help for brothers living in Judea – this they did sending their gift to the elders by Barnabas and Saul'

Sacrificial giving (Macedonians In 2 Corinthians 8)

Poor empowered and released in ministry – (1 Tim 5 widows helped other widows. Philemon 10,11, Colossians 4:9 Onesimus the runaway slave faithful and useful in the church)

Poor mightily used - Acts 4:13 'Now as they observed the confidence of Peter and John and understood that they were uneducated and untrained men they were marvelling and began to recognise that they had been with Jesus'

Relationships/friendships developed across the socio-economic barriers – Jas 2:15 'if a brother or sister is without clothing or food'

The poor went to the world

Remembering the poor is a Holy Spirit ministry (Acts 6)

The church made mistakes

Fed the widows and brought order

We see in the early church that the gospel was indeed good news to the poor:

The poor were helped

The poor received salvation and the forgiveness of sins – connected to God

The poor received a new way of living, loving and relating by being added into the church. The motherless received mothers and the fatherless received fathers

The poor received acceptance with God and with others

The poor received grace, mercy and healing

The poor received material support

The poor received a caring body in which if one part of the body suffered the other parts of the body felt it and did something about it.

The poor received purpose, commissioning and anointing from God

The poor received gifting

The poor were raised up in leadership – at all levels

The poor were used to advance God's Kingdom – trophy's of God's grace to shame the wise

Those who were forgotten and overlooked were truly Remembered!

[123] Cf Philemon 16

[124] Some of the practicalities of crossing socio-economic barriers will be covered in chapter 12.

[125] Cf 2 Corinthians 8:2

[126] Cf 1 Corinthians 12:13

[127] Cf 1 Samuel 16:7

[128] EH Petersen: 2007 ; 'The Jesus Way – a Conversation in Following Jesus'; Hodder and Stoughton, p239.

Chapter 5 **The church in all it's glory**

[129] Adrian Plass: 1987; 'The sacred diary of Adrian Plass'; Fount, p14.

[130] Cf Ephesians 5:25

[131] Cf Mt 16:18

[132] 'Ululate' is an African expression of praise made by rapid movements of a persons tongue.

[133] Jim Wallis: 2006; 'The call to conversion – Christianity's radical manifesto'; Monarch Books; p116.

[134] Cf 1 Thessalonians 3:12

[135] Cf 1 Thessalonians 5:11

[136] Cf 1 Corinthians 12:20

[137] Cf Galatians 6:2

[138] Cf Ephesians 4:32, Colossians 3:13, Matthew 28:19

[139] See Gordon Fee: 1996; 'Paul, the Spirit and the People of God'; Hendrickson Publishers Inc, Hodder and Stoughton, p66.

[140] Trevor Hudson: 1995; 'Signposts to Spirituality – Towards a Closer Walk with God.'

[141] Cf Matthew 5:13

[142] Cf Matthew 5:14

[143] Cf 2 Corinthians 5:15

[144] Cf Ephesians 4, Romans 12

[145] Cf 2 Corinthians 5:20

[146] Cf 1 Peter 2:9-12

[147] Cf Ephesians 6, Joshua 5:14

[148] 1 Peter 3:15

[149] Ibid Wallis: 2006; p112

[150] Cf Isaiah 11: 9-12. See also chapter 6 where this vision of diverse community is explored in more detail.

[151] See Matthew 5:22

[152] Ibid: Wallis:2006;21-22

[153] Michael Greene: 1970: p120 quoted in Wallis 2006:17

[154] Cited in Rob Warner: 1998; 'The Sermon on the Mount'; Kingsway, p86.

[155] Ibid: Wallis 2006:15

[156] Aristides Apology 15 cited in Wallis 1986:15-16

[157] Cf Isaiah 11:6

[158] The word Gentile was a term referring to any peoples who were not Jews. Hence Gentiles could refer to a whole number of different nations and people groups e.g. Romans and Greeks

[159] Cf Ephesians 1:10 and Ephesians 2:11-22

[160] Some would argue that the 'in him' of Ephesians 1:10 refers to the visible universe and not men and women. I have argued with the likes of Michael Eaton that 'God's plan is to bring his world back together again in unity by putting it under Christ'. This includes hostile men and women. See Michael Eaton: 2002; 'Preaching through the Bible – Ephesians'; Sovereign World, p39.

[161] Cf Ephesians 2:11-12. See also the writings of Michael Eaton 2002:40-42

[162] See R Bell and D Golden: 2008; 'Jesus Wants to Save Christians'; Zondervan, p153.

[163] Ephesians 2:14-15

[164] Cf Ephesians 1:13-14

[165] Cf Ephesians 2:16, 4:4

[166] Italics mine

[167] Ibid Wallis:2006;118

[168] Ibid: R Bell and D Golden: 2008;154

[169] Cf John 17:1

[170] John 17:11

[171] Duane Elmer: 1993 'Cross Cultural Conflict – Building Relationships for Effective Ministry'; IVP, p26

[172] Cf Ephesians 2:16

[173] See John Stott: 1979; 'The Message of Ephesians'; BST; IVP, p154.

[174] Cf Acts 18:24, 19:1-10; Ephesians 5:22, 6:1, 6:5

[175] Cf Ephesians 4:25-31; 5:1-33

[176] Cf Ephesians 5:18-6:9

[177] Cf 1 Corinthians 1:10

[178] Cf Galatians 3:5-16

[179] Cf Philippians 1:27

[180] Cf Romans 14:13, 19-20

[181] Cf Acts 18:8,10

[182] Cf Acts 18:8, 1 Corinthians 1:26

[183] See David Prior: 1993; 'The message of 1 Corinthians'; BST, IVP, P19.

[184] Cf 1 Corinthians 12:1-7

[185] See Michael Eaton: 2000; 'Preaching through the Bible – 1 Corinthians 10-16'; Sovereign World, p56.

Chapter 6 Daring to go further

[186] John Stott: 2006; 'Issues Facing Christians Today 4th edition'; Zondervan, p290.

[187] J Wallis: 2006; 'The Call to Conversion – Christianity's Radical Manifesto'; Monarch Books, p119.

[188] Khanyisa is a church that was 'planted' out of a larger church called Jubilee. Approximately 50 adults and 30 children (who had been attending Jubilee) left the Jubilee congregation to form the nucleus of the new church plant.

[189] J Daniel Hays: 2003; 'Every People and Nation, A Biblical Theology of Race'; (Leicester: IVP), p205 cited in J Stott: 2006; 'Issues Facing Christians Today, 4th edition'; Zondervan, p290.

[190] See D McGraven; Wagner C Peter: 1970; 'Understanding Church Growth'.

[191] See D McGraven; Wagner C. Peter: 1970; 'Understanding Church Growth'.

[192] See comments made by Maylon College, Queensland Baptist College of Ministries; Homogenous Church versus heterogeneous Church; www.maylon.edu.au

[193] We'll examine this in more detail in chapter 9 where we will explore some of the diverse models of multi-cultural churches being practiced.

[194] See Tim Chester: 2006 – timchester.worpress.com/2006/12/08/the homogenous unit principle

[195] Rob Bell & Don Golden: 2008; 'Jesus Wants to Save Christians'; Zondervan; p156.

[196] Jean Vanier 2001:45; 'Community and Growth'

[197] G Fee: 1996; 'Paul, the Spirit and the People of God'; Hendrickson Publishers Inc; Hodder and Stoughton, p70.

[198] Cf Colossians 1:15-20

[199] J Wallis: 2006; 'The Call to Conversion – Christianity's radical manifesto'; Monarch Books, p119.

[200] See Tim Chester: 2006 – timchester.worpress.com/2006/12/08/the homogenous unit principle

[201] McGraven, D; Wagner C Peter (1970) cited in Tim Chester 'The Homogenous unit principle'; timchester.worpress.com/2006/12/08/the homogenous unit principle.

[202] Ibid: Tim Chester: 2006

[203] John Stott: 2006; 'Issues facing Christians today 4th edition'; Zondervan, p290.

[204] John Stott: 2006; 'Issues facing Christians today 4th edition'; Zondervan, p290.

[205] J Piper: 1993; 'Let the nations be glad – the supremacy of God in missions'; IVP, p213.

Chapter 7 Becoming faithful friends

[206] Trevor Hudson: 1995; 'Signposts to Spirituality – Towards a Closer Walk with God'.

[207] Non payment of rent was a form of protest to the policies of the apartheid government and was part of a whole number of domestic strategies carried out to destablise the apartheid regime.

[208] A 'Sjambok' is a traditional African stick like whip.

[209] Being part of the 'Struggle' was a term used to describe people actively resistant to apartheid and the united quest by people of all backgrounds for freedom and liberation from the oppressive political system

[210] The marshals were security members for the African National Congress to protect officials during political raleighs and marches.

[211] See the introductory chapter to the book.

[212] See Sojourners www.sojo.net

[213] Ryan Roderick Beiler: 10-03-2008 quoted from God's Politics blog. sojo.net/2008/10/03bart-compolos-tough-questions-on-cross-cultural-com.

[214] Trevor Hudson: 1995: 'Signposts to Spirituality – Towards a Closer Walk with God.'

[215] John Stott: 2006; 'Issues Facing Christians Today – 4th edition: Zondervan, p289.

Chapter 8 Seeing as others see

[216] Jean Vanier: 1996; 'Letter to My Brothers and Sisters in l'Arche – Introduction', p14.

[217] Acts 16:3

[218] Cf John 1:14

[219] Taken from notes made by Simon Pettit on sharing the gospel cross culturally – original source of this quote is unknown.

[220] Cf Isaiah 61:1-3

[221] Luke 7:36-50

[222] See Philip Yancey's book 'What's so Amazing about grace?'

[223] We'll examine this further in chapter 10.

[224] Cf Revelation 2:7, 11, 17, 26; 3:5, 12, 21

[225] Hebrews 4:15 (NASB)

[226] We'll examine this in more detail in chapter 10.

[227] Cf Luke 10:30-3/

[228] We'll examine this in more detail in chapter 11.

[229] Philippians 2:6

[230] John 3:16

Chapter 9 Building together

[231] Dr Gilbert Bilezikian cited in B Hybels: 2002; Courageous Leadership'; Struik Christian Books; p12.

[232] Ken Davis: 2003; 'Multicultural Church Planting Models'; The Journal of Ministry and Theology; Spring 2003, p114.

[233] Owen Hylton: 2009; 'Crossing the Divide; A Call to Embrace Diversity'; IVP: p15-16.

[234] Ibid 2009:17

[235] Such models would be common within countries like the United States, South African and the United Kingdom.

[236] I've made my definition based and adapted from definitions by Ken Davis and Dr Peart cited in Davis: 2003; 'Multicultural Church Planting Models'; The Journal of ministry and theology; Spring 2003, p 115.

[237] Ibid 2009: 118

[238] John 5:19-210, 30 (NIV)

[239] John 17:6-7 (NIV)

[240] The use of camps for strengthening cross-cultural friendships has been a great tool and something that we have repeated on several occasions over the years.

241 Dr Gilbert Bilezikian cited in B Hybels: 2002; Courageous Leadership';
Struik Christian Books; p12.

Chapter 10 **Cultural tapestry!**

242 Karris: 1985; p70 cited in Jerome H Neyrey (ed): 1991; 'The
Social World of Luke – Acts: Models of Interpretation'; Peabody,
Massachusets: Hendrikson Publishers, p361.

243 John Stott – source unknown

244 Taken from Colin Lago; 'Race, Culture and Counseling'.

245 D Elmer: 1993; 'Cross Cultural Conflict – Building Relationships for
Effective Ministry'; IVP, p50.

246 Ibid 1993: 52

247 Elmer argues this point very well – Ibid 1993: 43-44.

248 Elmer, for example, identifies several more indirect methods of
conflict resolution displayed throughout Scripture (see chapters 5, 6,
7 and 8 in Elmer 1993:65-134 eg

Mediation and the use of a mediator

Storytelling and proverbs

The one down position and vulnerability

Inaction, misdirection, silence and indefinite persons

249 Adapted from 'Foreign to Familiar' by Sarah Lanier published by
McDougal.

250 Ibid 1993: 11-16

251 It should be noted that things like births, marriages and funerals,
for example, are not always simple cultural issues; they can also be
points where there may be very real strongholds that need to be
broken and repented of.

252 Ibid 1993: 14

Chapter 11 **Breaking the silence**

253 Jim Wallis: 2000; 'Crossing the racial divide'; Sojourners, p24.

254 See chapter 2 – Glorious Diversity.

255 See the introductory chapter for more of this story.

256 The English would call this a pick-up-truck.

257 Rick Joyner: Overcoming Racism.

258 The Times and Telegraph are two main British newspapers. The Sun
is a British tabloid newspaper.

[259] The Stephen Lawrence Enquiry report p20, par 6.4 cited in John Stott: 2006; 'Issues facing Christians today'; 4th edit; Zondervan, p270

[260] Ibid 2006: 270

[261] Rick Joyner: 'Overcoming Racism'.

[262] The Rwanda genocide, for example, would be an example of Black on Black racism, used as a counter argument in this case.

[263] Owen Hylton: 2009; 'Crossing the Divide'; IVP, p63.

[264] John Piper: 2003; 'Brothers We Are Not Professionals'; Mentor, p197.

[265] BD Tatum: 1993; 'Why are all the Black Kids Sitting Together in the Cafeteria?' Basic Books; p193.

[266] Ibid Tatum 1993:200

[267] CW du Toit – Confession and Repentance.

[268] These comments have come from a variety of contexts including inter church racism work shops or honest discussions within my own church. Some have also come from amongst leaders within Newfrontiers discussing some of the dynamics of our working and interaction together as a family of churches.

[269] Including a variety of Black Africans from within South and Southern Africa, Coloured people and Indian People.

[270] Including Europeans as well as various English and Afrikaans speaking South Africans.

[271] Source unknown

[272] Cf Luke 20:46

[273] Ibid Tatum 1993: 205

Chapter 12 **Go and do likewise**

[274] Peter H Davids: 1994; Chapter 2 of 'Who is My Neighbour – Economics as if Values Matter'; study guide; Sojourners, p 47.

[275] D Hughes: 1998; 'God of the Poor;' OM Publishing, p25.

[276] The apostle Paul in 1 Timothy 5 highlights another local church response to the needs of poor widows in their midst. They had developed a list of guidelines and criteria for helping the poor in which a strong emphasis was placed on the character of the person to be helped. Factors like jealousy and gossip could in fact cause someone not be helped if they did not get their hearts right with God and with others. See 1 Timothy 5: 3-10.

[277] Cf 1 Timothy 5:3

[278] Cf James 3:5

[279]Cf John 6:66

[280]See D Elmer: 1993; 'Cross Cultural Conflict – Building Relationships for Effective Ministry; IVP, Page 94-95 for further comments on this.

[281]D Hughes: 1998; 'God of the Poor;' OM Publishing, p25.

[282]Cf 2 Corinthians 9:7

[283]1 Corinthians 13:3

Chapter 13 Overcoming giants

[284]South African Christian Leadership Assembly

[285]Cf Romans 8: 28

[286]Cf Psalm 139

[287]Cf Ephesians 2:10

[288]David & Liz Holden: 1995; 'Raising Children – a parents privilege'; Kingsway, p36.

[289]Beverly Tatum in her book, 'Why are all the Black Kids Sitting together in the Cafeteria?' (Basic Books: 1997) gives a helpful list of suggested multi-cultural books for children and adolescents. Page 214-220

[290]Cf John 5:19

[291]Proverbs 3:5

Chapter 14 As it is in heaven

[292]Tom Sine cited in J. Wimber: 1994; 'The Gospel to the Poor'; Oasis Bible Notes for In-Depth Study, Word Books, p21.

[293]Cf Ephesians 3:10

[294]Ibid Tim Sine: 1994

[295]Cf Isaiah 11:10

[296]See Acts 16: 6-40 for a full account of this story

[297]See comments by G Fee; 1999; 'Philippians', IVP New Testament Commentary Series, IVP; p 24-26.

[298]Cf Philippians 4:2-3

[299]Cf Philippians 4:15-16

[300]Cf Philippians 1:6

[301]Cf Ephesians 3:20